NOTES FROM A
SMALL MILITARY

Major-General Chapman joined the British Army in September 1980 after sponsorship at Lancaster University. He joined 2nd Battalion, The Parachute Regiment (2 PARA) and fought in the Falklands campaign, including the Battle of Goose Green. He stayed with 2 PARA until May 1985, which included his first Northern Ireland (NI) tour in South Armagh. He was an instructor on the Platoon Commander's Division before returning to 2 PARA as Adjutant. In 1989–90 he served on exchange with the Canadian Airborne Regiment prior to attending UK Staff College at Camberley in 1991.

On graduation, he became Chief of Staff 5 Airborne Brigade. In 1994, he returned to 2 PARA as a company commander for an 18-month operational tour in Belfast, prior to becoming 2IC 1 PARA. He was promoted lieutenant-colonel in March 1996. He served on the directing staff at both the Staff College and the UK Joint Services Command and Staff College. In July 1998, he became SO1 Operations in NI and went on to command 2 PARA from August 1999–December 2001. His tour as CO included a NI reinforcement tour and the weapons-collection mission (OP BESSEMER) in Macedonia.

He was promoted colonel in December 2001 and appointed Colonel Military Operations 2 in the Ministry of Defence (MoD), dealing with counter-terrorism. As a brigadier, he commanded 19 Mechanised Brigade from 2003–5, prior to becoming the last Chief of Staff in NI (his fifth NI tour). In this role, he planned the conclusion of the 38-year OP BANNER (the UK NI operation). He was Head of Counter-Terrorism and UK Operations in the MoD from 2007–10. His final tour before retiring from the Army was as senior adviser to US Central Command in Florida.

MAJOR-GENERAL CHIP CHAPMAN CB

NOTES FROM A SMALL MILITARY

I COMMANDED AND FOUGHT WITH 2 PARA AT THE BATTLE OF GOOSE GREEN. I WAS HEAD OF COUNTER TERRORISM FOR THE MoD. THIS IS MY STORY.

JOHN BLAKE

Published by John Blake Publishing Ltd,
3 Bramber Court, 2 Bramber Road,
London W14 9PB, England

www.johnblakebooks.com

www.facebook.com/johnblakebooks 🖪
twitter.com/jblakebooks 🅴

First published in hardback in 2013
This edition published in paperback in 2015

ISBN: 978-1-78219-910-6

British Library Cataloguing-in-Publication Data:
a catalogue record for this book is available from the British Library.

Design by www.envydesign.co.uk

Printed in Great Britain by CPI Group (UK) Ltd

1 3 5 7 9 10 8 6 4 2

Papers used by John Blake Publishing are natural, recyclable products made from
wood grown in sustainable forests. The manufacturing processes conform to the
environmental regulations of the country of origin.

Every attempt has been made to contact the relevant copyright-holders,
but some were unobtainable. We would be grateful if the appropriate people
could contact us.

To Geinor, who has followed the flag
with unstinting good humour, fortitude,
devotion and love.

ACKNOWLEDGEMENTS

I have served with so many people. All have, in one manner or another, contributed to this book. The greatest privilege is to be given command of paratroopers. I was lucky to command (among others) the best soldiers possible in 6 Platoon, B Company 2 PARA; the Medium Machine Gun Platoon of 2 PARA; D Company 2 PARA; 3 Commando of The Canadian Airborne Regiment – and the greatest privilege of all – commanding 2 PARA. All have shaped who I am and what I believe. Far too many have now ridden off to the Valkyries, either through death in combat or through the curse of cancer, or because they could not cope with what life threw at them after their military service. In particular, RSM Jack Lemmon, who was a legend, 'Louis' Lewis, and the recent sad addition of Hank Hood to their number. They have all 'gone to Hell to regroup' as the Toms would say.

Those looking for a unified theory of the military within this book will not find it. There are contradictions. This is deliberate, because it is a story of people and how they react. And of how I reacted at various times in my career. I had a fourfold intention in writing this book: to make you laugh, to make you cry, to inform you and, occasionally, to make you think.

I give special thanks to those who were platoon commanders with me in the Falklands: John Shaw, Guy Wallis and Mark Coe of A Company; Geoff Weighell and Ernie Hocking of B Company, and Shaun Webster, Jacko Page, and Chris Waddington of D Company. And to Jim Barry, who did not come back.

There have been those from whom I have picked up traits, habits or even 'education' during my career; those who I truly admired. These include John Crosland, Phil Neame, David Chaundler, Adrian Freer, David Benest, 'Cedric', Tim Granville-Chapman, Nick Parker and Graeme Lamb. One of these told me always to rebel against 'gnomes'. He will know who he is. There are some gnomes within the following pages. Gnomes need to be slayed. More recently, I thank General Jim Mattis of US Central Command – the finest warrior leader I have encountered. I wish him a happy retirement after all he has contributed to the USA.

My professional thoughts have been influenced by various military thinkers. On the 25th anniversary of the Falklands campaign, I included Field Marshal Slim and T E Lawrence in my list of six favourite military books for *The Times* Books section (Saturday 21 April 2007.) I also admire Field Marshal Wavell and Liddell Hart greatly. You will see this during the book.

I thank Peter Russell, that great photographer friend of the Airborne, for his permission to use a number of his magnificent P Company and parachuting pictures (www.peterrussellphotography.com).

The army is going through a time of change. While it was in the hands of General Peter Wall, as Chief of the General Staff, it had pragmatic sense. Nick Carter, as his successor, will continue this: a fine officer of sound intellect and an old sparring partner of mine at Staff College. I hope my personal endorsement of these two fine officers has not ruined their future!

Finally, I give special thanks to Rosie and Tom Chapman who were disruptively dragged around the world when they were growing up, living in far too many places for their own good. They have been the most brilliant kids: they also served!

CONTENTS

PREFACE

'Please understand there is no depression in this house and we are not interested in possibilities of defeat: they do not exist.'
– Victoria R I (and the maxim on the desk of General James Mattis, Commander US Central Command, Tampa, 2010 – 2013)

Everything written here is false. If it were true, you would think it false. Galileo discovered by observation that the world was round and revolved around the Sun. Until his discovery, and beyond, many people believed the world to be flat. That was false but it was not a lie. So, everything here is true – otherwise it would be a lie. I will leave you to make up your own mind on that account.

Miss D V House wrote on my school report, aged 11: 'Chapman has discovered much from books, films, talks and general observation. He assimilates the knowledge before presenting it in his very own way, conscientiously and in a clean attractive style.' I hope you might in part agree. Some names have been changed to protect the living and the dead, those guilty and those who were innocent. Whoever they were, they have given me a rich tapestry of experiences.

The great British prime minister, Lord Palmerston, was once told by a foreign national that, 'If I were not a Frenchman, I should wish to be an Englishman.' Palmerston replied, 'If I were not an Englishman, I should wish to be an Englishman.' It has been a privilege to serve in two great institutions: the British army at the macro level, and the one that is even stronger than the British army at a lower level: the Parachute Regiment, an exemplar of the best of the regimental system and cohesion between men in adversity.

The wonderful collection of characters represented in the pages that follow are largely from the annals of airborne forces. To paraphrase Palmerston, if I were not in the British army, I should have wished to be in the British army. And if I were not a paratrooper, I should have wished to be a paratrooper. In my meanderings around the globe and throughout the world of defence, I have had the privilege of not needing to wish on either account.

CHAPTER 1

LIONS LED BY DONKEYS

I joined the army in 1980 on a three-year Short Service Commission and managed to extend it for 30 more years. It was an army 229,700-strong, including the Territorial Army (TA), and still full of historic names and nuances. The TA was more widely known among regular soldiers at the time as 'Stupid TA Bastards' or STABs. Now that the army is an Equal Opportunities Employer such language is no longer used: the TA now has an equal opportunity to be killed in Afghanistan alongside regular colleagues.

The TA reciprocated in their dislike of regular soldiers, who were known by them as 'Arrogant Regular Army Bastards' or ARABs. The Territorial Army is to change its name for the first time in more than 100 years to become the Army Reserve (AR) and we already have the first two letters of a new acronym for the regular army to use. Orwell was probably right that although all animals are equal, some are more equal than others; not that we were animals. The army's two component parts, the Regular and the TA, each thought the others were bastards, and so collectively the army was made up a bunch of bastards – but an increasingly professional bunch of bastards.

We had Hussars and Lancers (including 'vulgar fractions' with regiments such as the 16/5th Lancers), and KINGS and QUEENS. A notice board in Gibraltar once told me to be warned as '4 QUEENS were exercising' which seemed a more appropriate sign for a gay bar in the Vauxhall district of London, more particularly the famous Royal Vauxhall Tavern (or RVT), rather than as a military unit going about its tactical business.

Lest you think that there is anything untoward and prejudiced in my picture of the RVT, let me say that I lived in Vauxhall for three years. I walked to work, and on my way to the Ministry of Defence my route took me past the RVT, and then via either the Queen Ann Pub (reputedly the oldest strip joint in London), or the Headquarters of MI6 (or to give its official name, the Secret Intelligence Service). In my career, I only ever visited one of these three locations. It should be obvious which of these three it was, but let me say that both the RVT and the Queen Ann have security on a par with trying to get in to Sir Terry Farrell's architecturally interesting Embankment Headquarters of the SIS. For the sake of both the Bond franchise and reasons of national security, I assume that MI6 have a refined business continuity plan, for the SIS Headquarters was blown to pieces in *Skyfall*.

It was a male and testosterone-dominated army, *very* different from the *very* professional inclusive army of today. There would have been no noted contradiction between the *Soldier News* front-page headline of 12 December 1980 that

proclaimed 'GIRLS TO GET GUNS' following the announcement in the House of Commons by Francis Pym, the Secretary
of State for Defence, with that newspaper's 'Soldier Bird' colour
photo portrait of a Miss Lyn McCarthy. Soldier Bird really was
the title of the pin-up page. Although, as this was Christmas,
the 1981 calendar included an added untitled double-spread
bonus of another lady without pyjamas a few pages later. Miss
McCarthy was currently appearing in *Wot! No Pyjamas?* at the
Whitehall Theatre. I can confirm that she was not wearing any
pyjamas. I do not believe you will see this theatrical *tour de
force* from the artistic stable of the noted Soho impresario,
Paul Raymond, revived any time soon. Nor did we know much
about the role of women in the army. One exam howler on this
subject included the statement: 'Women were used extensively
during the Second World War; some were even shipped over
to France.'

I came from a family with little military background. There
were no famous generals or soldiers in our lineage. If I had
featured in the TV series *Who Do You Think You Are?* the
bland answer of generations of Cornish agricultural labourers
would not have been too far from the truth – and that was the
successful side of the family.

Like most British families, we had suffered from death in the
First World War: a great-uncle had been killed at the Battle of
Loos as a young private in the 8th (Service) Battalion of the
Devons, but that was about the limit of the family military
prowess. Great-Uncle Albert Stone was one of the 1,105,553[1]
British military casualties in the 20th century, when a military
death occurred at an average of one every 48 minutes.

The Second World War passed us by, bar the death of my

3

grandmother who was killed in a Luftwaffe raid on Plymouth during the night of 22/23 April 1941 as she harboured in a communal air raid shelter that took a direct hit: the worst single civilian tragedy of the war in Plymouth. She was also a part of an increasing trend in the 20th century and beyond – that the brutality of war now reached civilians in a way that it had not in previous centuries. More civilians would die with each war (particularly in non-state conflicts such as civil wars) and the consequences of war would touch far more people, and in a wider arc, as the century unfolded. My father was an orphan at the age of five.

The catalyst for my application to join the army had been no more profound than watching the BBC current affairs programme *Panorama* about Sandhurst. I thought all the assault courses and running around looked like quite good fun: I could do that. Going to Sandhurst might at least solidify my future apolitical leanings. At university, one flirted with everything. I even flirted with anarchy: I attended an anarchist meeting. The assembled anarchists waited outside a locked room. They could not gain entry. The hall porter came along and inquired as to who was in charge.

'No one, we're anarchists,' came the reply.

'Well, someone has to say they are in charge and sign the book,' the hall porter grumpily replied.

Suitably miffed, and in contravention of the universal principles of anarchy, an individual fulfilled the leadership burden and duly signed. For the next two hours, our nascent anarchists discussed how to arrange the chairs in a non-hierarchical fashion. My flirtation with anarchy was over. Not that this was serious. Student politics were absurd. At a student University General Meeting, the International Socialists

4

proposed a motion to send a coach to attend an annual protest march against Bloody Sunday in Northern Ireland. I put an amendment to their motion to quash it. Thankfully for us all, the entire apathy of the student body meant that all came to naught, for the meeting was not quorate.

My Sandhurst training course was entitled Post-University Course Number 9, shortened to POSUC 9. This was accommodated in and run out of Victory College. Every officer cadet in the college was a university graduate and all were deemed to be already semi-competent, due to their service at a University Officer Training Corps (Liverpool OTC in my case). We were only to complete 17 weeks training at Sandhurst before we graduated. Our former OTC service meant that we were seemingly competent in the art of being able to dress ourselves and to strip and assemble a self-loading rifle (SLR). On completing the course I won a prize of sorts, being presented with the 'Show Clean' book by Colour Sergeant Scott of the Welsh Guards. If there was any dirt or crease out of line, this was recorded in the book every morning. It was this book that was paraded at 2200 hours, the misdemeanour was read out and it was checked whether the error had been corrected. My copy of the book was inscribed that it had been given to me for my inability to 'appear neat, clean and tidy in any form of dress whatsoever'. A 'show clean' would be determined at the morning ritual of being inspected and being found wanting. In particular I could not bull (army parlance for polish vigorously) shoes to the correct standard of shininess. I still cannot. I still have those shoes, and they are still not very clean. Fluff was particularly offensive. Our mission at Sandhurst was not to destroy the enemy or hold a particular piece of ground: it was to rid the world of its offensive fluff.

We bounced off the walls with multiple 'changing parades'. There was a different form of dress for different lessons at different parts of the day. The horror of being incorrectly dressed, or not having pristine clothing, worried more than the most junior. On 6 February 2011 – during my time as Senior British Military Advisor, HQ United States Central Command, Tampa – I was watching an evening screening at an American cinema of *The King's Speech* in which Colin Firth gives his fine Oscar-winning representation of George VI. The audience seemed a curious assortment. The cinema was full of only two types of people – women and gay couples. I was the only heterosexual male member of the audience. I now know this to be because it was the same evening as Super Bowl XLV. This event, won in 2011 by the Green Bay Packers, attracts the largest television viewing figure of the American calendar. I can safely tell you which demographic is not watching the Super Bowl, if that would be of help to future advertising agencies.

The King's Speech led to a number of requests to the British team working in Florida, via the British Consulate in Miami, for information on what the medal ribbons worn by George VI represented. Ever willing to do our bit for British foreign policy, the team duly complied. One of our young naval officers knew an academic at the Britannia Royal Naval College at Dartmouth who was an expert on the subject. In fact, the naval uniform of King George VI was kept on display in a glass cabinet at the college. This was a saving grace on the occasion that Field Marshal the Viscount Montgomery of Alamein KG (Knight of the Garter – the senior chivalric order of the UK) came to take a pass-off parade at Britannia. One detail was missing. His uniform was without the star of the Knight of the Garter. The professional head of the Armed Forces – the Chief of the Imperial General Staff – was incorrectly dressed. Or he would have been if his aides had not broken in to the cabinet containing the naval uniform of George VI, unpicked the Order of the Garter and quickly attached it to Monty's jacket. He was now once again a KG. In former days, being incorrectly dressed would have been a treasonable offence.

Monty would have recognised elements of our dress from his own service in the trenches. This was the late 20th century, yet we still wore puttees around our ankles: pieces of flannelette cloth that would have been familiar to those who fought in the Boer War. These neatly complemented our Directly Moulded Sole (DMS) short combat boots, which were comfortable but made of compressed cardboard. These had only been introduced in 1958 so were a comparatively new addition to our fighting prowess. The compressed cardboard construction had an obvious flaw: when it rained they soaked up water like a sponge. A *Daily Express Magazine* article a couple of years later on 'the boot that nearly lost us the Falklands War' was not wholly inaccurate. Every other army in the world was wearing combat high boots.

My brief sojourn at Sandhurst was not the shortest course available. That was reserved for professional officers (a curious paradigm in that it might have contrasted with the notion that the remainder of us were *unprofessional* officers). Professional officers were those who had already completed training for a profession before joining the army. There were men of the cloth, doctors, nurses, lawyers and veterinary surgeons: they only did four weeks training. This really was only enough time to get to grips with the correct end of a rifle barrel and the right way to put on their pieces of flannelette. This course was fondly known as the 'Vicars and Tarts' course.

In the days of the Cold War, we often mused why doctors joined the army when they would be dealing only with blisters and venereal disease. As my career progressed, army doctors would indeed earn their pay dealing with the trauma of the battlefields they would subsequently confront with alarming regularity. But that was to be in the future. In the interim, it remained their lot to dole out condoms when a battalion exercised overseas. They were always conveniently positioned at the Guard Room as the soldiers exited an overseas camp to sample the local delights.

Soldiers have always been up for some 'horizontal refreshment'. Field Marshal Montgomery (when a mere major general) nearly ended his career prematurely with an edict that condoms – and recognised brothels – should be used to prevent VD during the Phoney War with Germany of 1939. The complaints from the assembled chaplains of Monty's so-called obscene language went right to the top of the army and Viscount Alanbrooke (who we will meet later) came to his rescue. Monty later reflected that his written order had caused VD to cease, although given the strictures of medical-in-confidence abided to by the medical fraternity I reckon Montgomery was in boastful territory on that one. Monty returned to the VD charge later in the war, chastising the New Zealander, General Freyberg (a VC winner from the First World War) about the health of the Second New Zealand Expeditionary Force. Freyberg is reputed to have replied, 'If they can't f***, they can't fight.' Not much has changed.

I leave the army as it seeks to implement 'Army 2020'. This does not mean that the army will be left with only 2,020 soldiers. There are still seven years left to bring the figure down to 82,000 regulars and increase (if they find the funding) the TA to 30,000. The army has been reducing in size ever since the Korean War in 1952. At least the modern soldier no longer wears puttees.

The height of my incompetence at Sandhurst came on the one day when I was actually well turned out with good shoes, and no fluff. But *the system* was not to be outdone – this was not enough: it was raining and 8 o'clock in the morning. I was told to present myself at the 10pm 'show clean' parade and 'show good weather'. Thankfully, I did not have to show sunny weather, as a raw December evening would have presented me with insurmountable problems.

Show clean parades were always preceded in the early evening by cleaning parades. This communal activity occurred for about two hours when the officer cadets collectively bulled their shoes, or buffed their Sam Browne leather belts. It meant there was no time for studying tactics manuals – a slight flaw when, within a year, I would be off to fight in the Falklands campaign. Sandhurst, as the instructors will tell you, is not an academy for tactics – it uses infantry tactics as a basis to teach or refine leadership.

Upon graduating from Sandhurst, young officers would go to their arm or branch of service, such as the artillery or infantry, for their special-to-arm training. For the infantry, this is the Platoon Commanders Battle Course (PCBC). I did rather well on that course, as did six of the seven Parachute Regiment officers who attended with me, as by 1983 – having already completed three years of service – the six had *already* fought a war. In the 1980s and 1990s, officers on Short Service

9

Commissions did not do their special-to-arm training until they were shown to be serious about the army, and had an intention to convert to a longer commission. Only full-career officers were deemed to have a need to be competent. The army has now changed this. Due to duty of care considerations, it is deemed imprudent for you to be killed when you don't know what you are doing.

We caught up and recovered from our perpetual tiredness by sleeping through the central lectures on battles, warfare and the history of warfare that were held in the Churchill Hall. There are very few officer cadets in the history of the Sandhurst Academy with a complete set of notes from any given military history lecture. This was a shame, as I might have learnt at an early age about those things that perplex later in one's career. For instance, that concepts such as fear, honour and interest as related to us by Thucydides (in his classic book on the Peloponnesian War that should be required reading for all future military students) remain as relevant today as they were in the ancient world when seeking to understand why wars are fought. And that 'tactics without strategy is the noise before defeat', according to the ancient Chinese military general, Sun Tzu. All that would have to wait. The current instructors at Sandhurst, who sit in on lectures at the Churchill Hall, inform me that to overcome the problem of fatigue and prevent sleeping among officer cadets, a simple solution has been devised. The heating is turned down or off: the shivering assembled students can do no other than stay awake.

I was to join the Parachute Regiment. I had already been selected while at university. Each regiment of the British army looks for differing qualities in its officers. The Parachute

Regiment, a regiment that believes its place to be in the 'van of battle', looks for a warrior leader (or at least I did when I went back to sit on boards to select officer cadets of the required quality), with intellect, who can triumph in adversity. A cavalry colleague of mine once told me that having sat on various selection boards, he believed that he had now got his system down to a fine art and actually only needed to ask one succinct question: 'With whom does your mother hunt?'

Each regiment has its own flavour and particular social and cultural register given the subtle differences to which I have alluded. One is not better than the other – they are merely different. I know this to be true, for I had the temerity as a staff college student to do my research paper on 'The Social and Educational Origins of the British Officer Corps in the Age of Meritocracy', and to have my paper marked by a furious Guards lieutenant colonel. My top tip for youngsters wanting to join as an officer is: if you want to be a general do not join the Pioneer Corps. If you do want to be a general, joining the infantry, cavalry, artillery or engineers improves your prospects immeasurably.

The most meritocratic organisation in the British army is the Parachute Regiment. This is a proven fact. My own studies showed that 50 per cent of Parachute Regiment officers were from public schools and 50 per cent from grammar/ comprehensive schools. We have everything from Old Etonians (one of the four officer cadets joining the regiment in my intake was indeed from 'Slough Grammar', the sobriquet for Eton schoolboys) to those who went to (the generic) 'Workington Comprehensive'. There was no hidden agenda in my interest in this subject; for me, it was a follow-on from a 'War and Society' course I had completed at Lancaster

University (and where I first theoretically met the Prussian military theorist, Clausewitz) under the wonderful Professor John Gooch. This was back in the days when, in the university student lavatories, there would invariably be graffiti above a toilet roll holder of hard wax paper that told us: 'Sociology degree – please take one'. With the passage of time, and changes in society (very close to what 'War and Society' was about – we no longer purchase our commissions), I gather that the modern equivalent is 'Media Studies Degree: please take one'. Does anyone do sociology these days?

Napoleon once said, 'Space I can recover, time, never'. So it was for us at Sandhurst. My space was in Room 101 (George Orwell would have been proud), a tiny enclave where dust was the enemy of the righteous and bad hospital corners on blanket ends incurred the wrath of the colour sergeant. To conserve time, and never having perfected the art of hospital corners (a fact to which my wife can testify), I spent too many nights sleeping on the floor in an army issue sleeping bag. I am glad to say that we have now progressed to the point where the duvet is now an acceptable sleeping accessory and that the modern generations of officer cadets do not know how lucky they are. Duvets are a real sign of progress. A wizened old Parachute Regiment quartermaster, Norman Menzies (inevitably nick-named 'Norman the Store Man'), who had joined the army in the late 1950s, once bemoaned to me that the army had gone soft when they started issuing sleeping bags in the 1960s instead of two blankets as part of the marching order equipment for exercises or operations.

Despite my incompetence, I graduated well. This had as much to do with the fact that I was very fit and very sporty.

Being in the football First XI and one of the Academy's star boxers was always a bonus. You even got to miss some exercises (a double bonus, as there were no show cleans on the hills of Scotland or on the rainy/snowy hills of Brecon). I even got to miss some of the drill parades in the mornings, as I would damage my nose (or rather my opponent would – I was no malingerer) in just about every bout and needed to report sick the morning after my pugilism to be patched up. I think they called this 'duty of care'.

I left Sandhurst consciously incompetent. Fortunately – for the army and defence – I managed to move further to the right on the scale of competence with time and each succeeding job. With our postings system we change jobs roughly every two years, and the cycle begins again – subconsciously incompetent leading to consciously incompetent status and onwards to a state of being consciously competent and then the real nirvana of subconscious competency.

I had the illusion that I was competent when I received my first appraisal report. It told me that I was 'GOOD'. I was rather pleased that I was good. I did not realise, due to inexperience, that this was code for CRAP. Above GOOD stood VERY GOOD and above VERY GOOD was EXCELLENT. This led to the pinnacle, which was OUT-STANDING. I was initially a D-grade officer.

During my RMA Sandhurst course, Ronald Reagan was elected US President, which I marked with a 'permission to break out the live rounds' radio message to higher HQ on a wet November night on Salisbury Plain. This message was a marvel – it showed I had managed to tune the impossibly difficult A41 Larkspur radio and that the batteries worked. The A41 battery resembled four house bricks in size and weight. Radios and batteries are the bane of all those in the infantry. If anyone out there can invent a battery that does not weigh far too much and that holds its power long enough not to require so many house bricks, I promise to buy them their choice of ale. Volunteering to carry five days' worth of batteries on an airborne exercise was never the choice of a sane man.

Fortunately, we were issued with the new Clansman radio system in time for the Falklands War. This worked perfectly, and we were now down to two house bricks. The technological advancement of the last decade means the army now has the Bowman radio system. In its initial trials, its initials were deemed to stand for 'Better Off with Map and Nokia', thus proving that technology never delivers what it says and on time. Field Marshal Rommel once said that his most important weapon system was a radio; he never mentioned the batteries.

Weight is the bane of the infantry. Those who crossed no man's land at the Somme in 1916 were carrying 90 pounds on their backs. Now we have equipment such as Osprey – the ballistic protection system (or body armour for those who like their language brief and simple) and one of the most inaptly named pieces of army equipment. An osprey is fast and agile, seizes its prey in an instant and carries the fish away (the fish is caught and carried so that it is forward facing, both for aerodynamic reasons and so it gets a good view of the world on its final fatal journey). The modern infantry is anything but agile, fast, and aerodynamic. The Osprey body armour weighs 22 pounds.

I thought I had put my description of the curse of weight to bed in my musings when I came upon an article in the August 2011 edition of *Jane's International Defence Review*[2] This is what it said, with my reflections in square brackets:

Burden reduction has been an abiding theme of DCC [Dismounted Close Combat. I preferred the more descriptive former title: FIST (Future Infantry Soldier Technology). But we always made a ham fist of bringing any equipment in which actually reduced the burden] systems since 2008 and will remain so. To date the maximum weight carried by the individual infantryman has been driven down by 9kg to 66kg. [That's 145 pounds in imperial weight[3]] through battery and power management improvements, adoption of lighter radios, polymer magazines, lighter equipment, water scavenging, and 'other measures'. [So why is it still more weight than the first day of the Somme?] The aim is to reduce the maximum to 60kg by the end of Epoch 1 of the DCC capability management plan (which runs from 2010 – 15) to 40kg by the end of Epoch 2 (2016 – 20) and to 30kg by the end of Epoch 3 (2021 – 35).

This is a classic example of how defence 'mystifies and misleads' (a phrase first used about the Confederate general, Stonewall Jackson – acknowledged as one of the few geniuses of the American Civil War). The reader will be quite content with the familiarity of a number of years bracketed together and quite baffled (as am I) by what on earth the meaning of an epoch is that so sets it apart from the years.

Apparently, the insights I have let you into in the preceding section came from Major General Colin White. Now, I have come across Colin White and he is a very sound and competent officer. I remember him mostly for the fact that he had the most outstanding eyebrows of anyone I have met in the British army. You could land a helicopter on them: they protrude like a landing pad, and with such length. They are a marvel of eyebrow technology.

Major General White worked in the Defence Equipment and Support area (DE&S) when he shared his insights at a conference into the weight-carrying burden of the infantry. Given that we are still asked to carry more than the average mule, you might think that Major General White is one of those senior officers who must be a Gilbert and Sullivan caricature: the real life model of a modern major general. He is not. I am being careful here in not equating mules and donkeys in case you think I am one of those 'lions' (our soldiers) 'led by donkeys' (our officers). I am more in favour of Talleyrand's suggestion (from the French Revolution) that he feared one lion leading 100 sheep more than he feared one sheep leading 100 lions. I would like to think that my career has shown a lion leading a pride of lions – an apt description of the pure leadership joy of working with motivated men – which is always the most efficacious outcome.

Major General White's eyebrows and their proximity to helicopter landing pads and his employment in equipment procurement lead me to think of disastrous stories in this field. Helicopters (unlike General White's eyebrows) are fragile machines. God created birds to fly. He did not intend helicopters to invade the space of birds, and that is why the testing of helicopters before they enter service includes their potential to cope with bird strikes. One test apparently involves launching dead chickens from a machine to simulate a bird flying into the windscreen of a helicopter. To show that this is a contemporaneous story, the helicopter in this case was the Merlin – the newest in the aviation inventory of the armed forces. What was not supposed to be in the test was the launching of a *frozen* chicken. It will not surprise you to learn that not only did the chicken penetrate the windscreen, but it also passed completely through the helicopter and exited after having punched its way through the disintegrating tail rotor. I hope I am never in a helicopter that runs in to a frozen chicken while in flight, for there is a sage lesson here that has nothing to do with the recipe for stuffing.

You would never expect two frozen chicken stories in a career, but another appeared during my sojourn in Tampa. This one was even more bizarre. During the Arab Spring of 2011 – 2012, a Yemeni garrison was beleaguered in a town called Zinjibar near the historic former Royal Naval coaling station of Aden. Al Qaeda in the Arabian Peninsula (AQAP) was poised to overrun the garrison. The Americans used global positioning system (GPS)-guided parachutes to drop a number of days of resupply to the garrison in the expectation that a relieving local force from Aden would attack to produce a link-up with Zinjibar. Unfortunately, the relieving brigade sat on its haunches. The Americans became exasperated and after a number of days of Yemeni inactivity decided they would not waste their time resupplying the garrison for a second time. So it was left to a neighbouring friendly country's air force, who were slightly more concerned with the situation than were the Americans, but with less technological know-how and capability to drop (among other commodities) 6,000 pounds of frozen chickens – along with sweet edible dates, because it was Ramadan – and other essentials such as bullets, fuel and water to help relieve the garrison.

Those not acquainted with military matters may have visions of frozen chickens with individual parachutes drifting towards terra firma. I can put your mind, and imagination, to rest on this account: these were palletised. Most of the chickens landed in the hands of the enemy from a spectacular miss-drop, well away from the intended objective.

I came across equipment woes early in my service. A certain Private Arpino of B Company 2 PARA in the Falklands War thought he was carrying the excellent Carl Gustav 84mm Anti-Tank weapon system. This was known more popularly as the 'Charlie Gee', except that the Charlie Gee was not popular, being apparently invented with the specific purpose of being the most difficult man-portable (a very loose use of that term) weapon system ever invented. It had a spongy and slightly elasticised carrying strap that made 33-plus pounds of metal bounce incessantly. It was the least-favoured weapon to be forced to carry on a company run and had to be rotated frequently to preclude it being tossed into the Aldershot Canal in times of peace. But we were now at war, and the Charlie Gee might come in useful against the limited number of Argentinian armoured vehicles scattered around the Falklands.

Arpino carried the Charlie Gee throughout the entire conflict. He had not had the chance to fire it in anger until an opportunity presented itself at the Battle of Wireless Ridge. The sun broke after the night attack, and so had the enemy. Their will to fight had collapsed. From the ridgeline, one could see Argentinian soldiers fleeing the hills surrounding Port Stanley. It was just about the end of the Falklands War. And there in the valley at Moody Brook lay a lone and docile abandoned helicopter. Arpino gave a pleading puppy dog look to the company commander, who needed to do no more than slightly acknowledge and nod his head to signify that Arpino deserved his moment to finally use his weapon system. The Charlie Gee required a loader for its rounds. Here is what happened.

Arpino: 'Load.'

The Loader: 'Load' (repeated by the loader to indicate he had understood and would comply with the instruction from the firer) followed by 'Loaded' when the system was 'bombed up'.

Arpino: 'Firing now'... Click... Pause... 'Misfire'... Click again. 'Misfire, unload.'

The drill was repeated and repeated with nothing happening. The firing pin was replaced... and still nothing happened. Arpino had been carrying a lump of useless metal rather than a functioning weapon system.

But we rarely broke out the live rounds during the era of Reagan and Margaret Thatcher in the way that the USA and UK did in the subsequent decades that followed from the 1990s onwards. Well, the UK might have broken out the live ammunition in the Falklands in 1982, and the Americans in Nicaragua and Grenada in 1983, but these were sideshows in the stable era of the Cold War.

But sideshows can have a dramatic influence on individual lives. It is when ordinary men can do extraordinary things – and some pay with their lives. One of those who died in the Falklands was Corporal Steve Prior. Twenty-eight years later I was asked to attend a 2 PARA Goose Green lunch at Colchester. The guest of honour was a frail Margaret (Baroness) Thatcher. One of the men serving in 2 PARA was the nephew of Steve Prior. He asked to meet me. He was subsequently killed in action in Afghanistan in 2011 at the same age, 27, as his uncle. His wife had given birth only some weeks before.

I had the privilege – and I use that word advisedly – to attend the funeral of Corporal Mark Wright in 2006. It does not matter if the following story is not 100 per cent accurate, for as the famous line in John Ford's film *The Man Who Shot Liberty Valance* tells us, 'When the legend becomes fact, print the legend.' In military circles that is amplified more than most – think Melville and Coghill saving the Colours at Isandlwana in 1879 prior to the defence of Rorke's Drift, best known from the film *Zulu*. We do not know what really happened, but for their troubles, and following a tireless campaign by Mrs Coghill, both were – perhaps slightly extraordinarily – awarded the Victoria Cross 29 years after they were killed.

The Mark Wright story goes something as follows. Corporal Mark Wright had joined the army because he was in awe of his uncle Andy, who was originally in 3 Para. Wright was a Mortar Fire Controller (MFC) on a hillside in Afghanistan when a number of his fellow paratroopers were caught and wounded in a Soviet era minefield. When the personnel were 'hit', Mark Wright left his position and prodded in to rescue the first man. He then rescued the second. He was rescuing the third when, the story goes, a Chinook helicopter hovered above and the downdraft set off a number of 'sympathetic' explosions (a totally inappropriate but technical phrase in the military). Mark Wright was badly wounded. The paratrooper he was rescuing at the time (who had lost a leg) said, 'You're going to be OK; you're going to be OK.'

'I'm not,' Wright replied. 'It's 45 degrees out here and I'm f***ing freezing, I'm dying, but before I die I want you to pass on two messages. First, tell my fiancée Gillian that I love her, and secondly, tell my Uncle Andy that I died a professional soldier.'

It is men like this that I had the privilege to serve with – the good and the bad, but all committed to each other, with an innate sense of 'mate-hood'. Sergeant Barry Norman of 2 PARA (Lieutenant Colonel H Jones' bodyguard in the Falklands) summed this up a few years after the Falklands War when he said of the men in that conflict: 'It was the blokes... It was the section commanders and Toms who went forward and took the enemy positions. They didn't do it for the government; they didn't do it for the Falkland Islanders; they didn't even do it for Maggie Thatcher. They did it for each other.'

The first battle honour for the Parachute Regiment was the Bruneval Raid in France in February 1942. At a time when Britain was on the strategic, operational, and tactical defensive, Churchill demanded an active raiding policy designed to keep the spirit of the offence alive. In February 1982, 2 PARA celebrated the 40th anniversary of that battle with the living veterans. The CO of 2 PARA at the time, H Jones, gave the after-dinner speech pleading that if we, the modern 2 PARA, were ever committed to battle, then he hoped that we could live up to the deeds of those who had come before. He could not have predicted that only four months later, on 28 May 1982, he would be leading a charge at Goose Green that would lead to his own death. Nevertheless, the spirit lived on. He was not merely the CO, he was the custodian of all those great officers and paratroopers who had come before. For the Parachute Regiment, the spirit of our early defining Battle of Arnhem lived and still lives on. In General Eisenhower's letter to the defeated General Urquhart of 1st Airborne Division, dated 8 October 1944, Ike said, 'Your officers and men were magnificent. Pressed from every side, without relief, reinforcement or respite, they inflicted such losses on the Nazis that his infantry dared not close with them. In an unremitting hail of steel from German snipers, machine guns, mortars, rockets, cannon of all calibres and self-propelled and tank artillery, they never flinched, never wavered. They held steadfastly.'

The British army is still like that. About 25 years ago we rediscovered the military philosopher, Clausewitz. What that great Prussian said some two centuries ago is still applicable today, as the British army continues to campaign in trying circumstances, sometimes akin to Arnhem in its current fights in Afghanistan. The steadfastness that Clausewitz spoke of resonates wider. It is summed up in his words, and is as applicable to individuals, units and the wider army. It is this: 'An army that maintains its cohesion under the most murderous fire; that cannot be shaken by imaginary fears and resists well-found ones with all its might; whose physical power like the muscles of an athlete, have been steeled by training in privation and effort; that is mindful of all these duties and qualities by virtue of the single powerful idea of the honour of its arms – such an army is imbued with the true military spirit.'

We still have such an army: whether we will for much longer might lead you to the final chapter. My Sandhurst course was not to equip me with the above qualities – but the Parachute Regiment eventually, and by chance or design, would.

---

[1]From 'A Century of Change: Trends in UK Statistics Since 1900', House of Commons research paper 99/11, dated 21 December 1999.

[2]*Jane's International Defence Review*, Volume 44, August 2011, page 6: 'UK Seeks Coherence for Dismounted Close Combat'.

[3]Equivalent to the weight of a light welterweight boxer for the WBO, super lightweight for the WBA and junior welterweight for the IBF and WBO. Boxing is more confusing than the army. I use light welterweight as it is the weight I boxed at every time an opponent broke my nose. No one has ever gone in to combat carrying a boxer on his back but we continue to want our infantrymen to do so.

CHAPTER 2

JOINING 'THE REG': P COMPANY AND PARACHUTING

There is no point being a member of the Barbie Club if you are a fan of the fantasy game *Warhammer*. The Parachute Regiment is *Warhammer* on steroids. It also believes itself to be – and it is – an elite organisation. Every man in the regiment, officer or soldier, has a bond that is sealed in the privation and shared experience of having had to undergo the same rigorous selection to earn and wear the Red Beret. Part of that is inculcation into the ethos of this particular 'band of brothers'. It is best described by Field Marshal Montgomery's famous quotation, which almost all paratroopers know off by heart:

What manner of men are these who wear the red beret? They are firstly all volunteers and are then toughened by hard physical training. As a result, they have that infectious optimism and that offensive eagerness which comes from physical well-being. They have jumped from the air and by doing so have conquered fear.

Their duty lies in the van of battle; they are proud of that honour and have never failed in any task. They have the highest standards in all things, whether it is skill in battle or smartness in the execution of all peacetime duties.

They have shown themselves to be as tenacious and determined in defence as they are courageous in attack.

They are, in fact, men apart – every man an Emperor.

Before you can become an emperor, you have a period of apprenticeship: a rite of passage. For the Parachute Regiment this is formed by Pre-Parachute Selection (PPS), more commonly known as 'P Company'.

Not all pass, and the denouement after the conclusion of all the selection events is brutal. Each person stands up as an individual and is told simply in one-word terms, 'pass' or 'fail'. There is absolutely nothing in between, and no discussion of the why or wherefore of the decision. I'm not too sure if this 'men apart' band has now been broadened to include 'men and women apart'. It should, so that all genders have the equal right to pass if they are good enough, and fail if they are not good enough. That is and should be the standard: without any social engineering to take account of physiological or other factors, because the last time I looked, the enemies on the battlefield do not place much credence in social engineering. They merely want to kill you.

It is probably bleeding obvious that the first requirement is to be fit. But there is more beyond that: mental determination to carry on when the going gets tough, and for officers to show leadership and not to shun the limelight, merely seeking to 'get through it'.

Cleanliness – both of clothing and body – really was next to godliness. Godliness only involved two things: fitness and determination. We all knew that God was Airborne: it was drummed in to us. Bullets and shrapnel may not take fitness into account, but many soldiers' lives have been saved after they have been wounded because they were fit, and had the mental attitude not to give in.

These were the final days for the young officers on the course when they would have no overt leadership or command responsibility. You only needed to know two mantras and one quotation to sustain you and to help you through:

A thoroughbred horse runs until its heart gives out.

We have it easy compared to the French foreign legion.

No one actually expected us to die because our hearts had given out, but they certainly did expect us not to give up. By the end of the first day, the 51 who started the course had been whittled down to 46. Five were already not godly enough. They had not driven through the 'no pain, no gain' expectation to win the prize of their red beret, or as G B Shaw put it: 'The most intolerable pain is produced by prolonging the keenest pleasure.'[3] We wanted that red beret.

P Company had a ritualistic feel to it. Each day of the two-week 'beat-up' prior to the selection week began the same way with the Army Basic Fitness Test (BFT) along Queens Avenue in Aldershot. The BFT was a squad run for one-and-a-half miles followed by a 'best effort' one-and-a-half miles back. The rule of thumb was that anyone who could not complete the BFT in less than nine minutes, in their Directly Moulded Sole boots and puttees tucked in to their green lightweight army trousers, would struggle to pass. It was cannily accurate.

Each candidate wore their army issue red or white PT vest with their name written across the front. In some cases, this would be the front and back to cope with officers with double-barrelled names such as Lt Stewart Larter-Whitcher or Lt Nick De Tscharner-Vischer. It was probably a good thing that the officer with probably the longest name in the army – Patrick Elrington O'Reilly-Blackwood Davidson-Houston – never attempted P Company, for there would have been a problem finding enough black ink to write it on any shirt. I once went to a meeting where a fellow officer (the current Chief of Defence Staff, General Sir Nick Houghton, when he was commanding 38 Brigade in Northern Ireland) briefed that his oral report would be of greater brevity than PEO'R-BD-H's name. I could almost imagine Patrick Elrington O'Reilly-Blackwood Davidson-Houston having to 'mill' (a form of boxing but without the Queensberry Rules) against Christopher James Piers De Lukacs Lessner De Szeged. I imagined them trading blows, with each blow leading to a letter of their respective names falling from their PT vests until we were left with an exhausted winner and the pronouncement that they had fought a good fight and the winner was declared by the 'last letter standing'.

We would change into our army issue blue shorts and black PT shoes for gym sessions. The equipment issued to the British army has historically come in for a lot of criticism, but I have to commend the cotton blue PT shorts for their ruggedness and longevity. I still wear those shorts 32 years later. They are still working well. They may not have a designer logo on them but they sure are tough wearing. I even wore them in a race in 2012 while in Tampa. The whole-life cost of those shorts is something to behold; they represent real value for money. The same could not be said for our PT shoes. In reality, they were black plimsolls; exactly the same as worn as a young child in junior school. Soldiers really did complete half marathons and suchlike in these plimmys, even into the 1980s. It was no wonder we had so many lower-leg and foot injuries.

The conclusion of each day of P Company led to a ritual: officers would head back to the officers' mess to indulge in a soothing Radox bath in an attempt to get some of the stiffness and pain from their aching limbs. In those days, ice baths were unheard of. In the evenings we drank nothing more at the bar than an orange juice and lemonade. Alcohol was verboten. It was little wonder that an orange juice and lemonade was ordered at the bar by its own official name. You would merely ask for a 'P Company' and the fizzy yellow concoction would appear.

Our administrative requirements as officers were simple. On the 'things to do/things to buy' list during P Company, the daily and weekly requirements were no more complex than:

Wash kit
Buy Vaseline (for nipple rash)
Check kit in drying room
Clean boots and plimsolls
Press kit (lightweight trousers, PT shirts, puttees)
Adjust webbing and rucksack (to save on further applications of Vaseline elsewhere on the body)
Check alarm timing on clock radio
Buy Radox, foot pads, glucose drinks, energy tablets

The set events in Test Week were designed to simulate various portions of an airborne battle. I'm not sure how 'milling' takes its place within the context of an airborne battle. Milling is like boxing, but one is not allowed to box. It is pure fighting. The object is to land as many blows on your opponent for as long as possible over a two-minute period in order to show tenacity, courage and determination. If one is knocked down, there is merely a brief pause while one gets up to start the battering (one way or another) again. I still recall the name of the opponent I fought – Baxter from 9 Parachute Squadron Royal Engineers. I was given as the victor for my bout. Fortunately, I was up against someone of comparable weight, so the bout was evenly matched. If the P Company staff did not like you, or wished you to be taught an early lesson, the weight differentials could be what one might term 'unfair'. Acceptance of this unfairness was expected. After all, if we were to be clever in warfare we wanted and should expect an unfair fight. In most cases, and using the principles of war, this unfairness should be in our favour. As you will see throughout this book, it was often the other way around!

I believe that in the modern era of 'health and safety' and 'duty of care', the current P Company candidates are now allowed to wear head guards during the milling. We were protected only by our blue army shorts and white PT vests. The latter could be problematic, as it could quickly become bloodied. One was expected to turn out in pristine white PT vests *sans* blood for follow-on activities. Buying additional PT vests to lessen the load on the overworked washing machines was a sound policy in lessening the groundhog-day simplicity of the 'things to do' list.

Some people fell quickly by the wayside, not being able to

complete the high bars confidence course successfully. The *piéce de resistance* of this event was the shuffle bars test 30ft above ground. This consisted of shuffling along a couple of parallel scaffolding bars, with the added bonus of being required to delicately raise your feet over the scaffold brace about half way along in order to proceed to the end, then bend over and touch your toes while screaming out your army number. The whole episode was a slight illusion; if you fell off there was a safety net somewhere below. But the illusion worked. There were people whose fear of heights paralysed them. There were people whose fear of heights was overcome by their determination to succeed. Those who were paralysed were instantly given the red card: there was to be no pass or fail for such soldiers or officers. They were, in the words no one ever wants to hear, Returned to Unit or RTU'd. If this was an officer who had been sponsored through Sandhurst by the Parachute Regiment he would now be instantly looking for another regiment to accept him. He was a casualty of peace.

Military marching with heavy weights is part of the Parachute Regiment ethos. They are good at it. Marching in the Paras is known as tabbing, which is supposed to be an elongated acronym for 'tactical advance to battle' (something I did not know for about 10 years). The Royal Marines' equivalent is known as yomping. You will never get anyone from either organisation using the vernacular of the other; that would be akin to a criminal offence. Yomping is like tabbing but much, much slower. The Royal Marines will, in the competitive world of elite forces, tell you that it is the other way around.

Marching (tabbing) is therefore a core part of P Company. Two of the test events were the 10-miler, with a 10lb rifle and

35lb pack, to be completed in one hour and 45 minutes, and a 14-miler on the South Downs Way. Part of the start day ritual would be the weigh-in of all our backpacks (bergens) to ensure that no one could cheat on the weight. The only ones allowed to do that were the instructors: the clipboards they carried weighed more than their packs (but they did do the distances day in and day out, and so the toll on their knees over a two-year posting made this concession understandable). Although the location of P Company has changed over the years (it is now in Catterick, North Yorkshire, since Depot Para in Aldershot closed under earlier defence cuts), the style and pain remains the same. You, dear reader, now have your own chance to experience the 10-miler: there is now an annual 'Paras 10' charity event run in Catterick, Aldershot and Colchester. You can now pay to be put through the agony and hills of Catterick. The concession is that you can do this with or without a bergen – and you get a medal.

The key requirement in all the test marches was to stay with the main group. If you began to fall back, you would always be chasing the error in attempting to catch or keep up with the group. And it would begin to eat at you mentally as you crossed the features seared into our memories: Hungry Hill, Flagstaff Hill, Miles Hill, Seven Sisters (why are large sequences of hills always called sisters or, as in Australia and Cape Town, the 12 apostles?), Concrete Hill and finally, what sounded like the luxury of a valley but was in reality the energy-sucking glue of Long Valley. There were a lot of hills. If you had fallen behind, the worst thing would be to think you had caught up during one of the quick water stops, only for the group to set off again, once more beginning to leave you behind. Being 'off-pace' was weakness and therefore not tolerated.

Two other endurance events on the *plat du jour* of P Company were the Stretcher Race and the Log Race. Both of these are universally hated for the pain they inflict. The Log Race is designed to simulate bringing an artillery gun or large anti-tank weapon into action. This is a good idea, although I cannot think of too many battles – no, change that to 'I cannot think of *any* battle' – where a bunch of men have had to run two miles to bring an artillery piece into action. The Naval Gun Race that used to be so popular at Earls Court in the days of the Royal Tournament was conducted over the length of two football fields and simulated a Boer War naval brigade engagement. Maybe our log race was designed to simulate trying to get the weapons in to Arnhem from the 1944 drop zones, for the distance involved was not dissimilar to this event.

In both the log race and the stretcher race, the most heinous crime was to come off the log or the stretcher. When it was your turn to be part of the carrying party, you were to be fixed to it no matter how painful or tired. To 'jack', the colloquial shortened version of to 'jack something in' (cease doing something), would once again lead to a fail. It showed a lack of determination and guts. The log was a spruce pine about 14ft long. The carrying handles were not designed by Conran, but by the Marquis de Sade. They were no more than thick ropes with a toggle on the end. They bit in to your hands, and with a number of log runners on the left and right, had the ergonomics of a dysfunctional attempt at sculling in an Oxford v Cambridge boat race – but one that you tried to row in once the boat had overturned.

The stretcher race was a similar distance and the stretcher too had been designed by the Marquis. With shortened scaffolding poles of tubular steel and a flat top, it resembled a stretcher but it was made of heavy metal. In the history of medicine there has been no example of a stretcher made of scaffolding poles – but our test was not designed to replicate medicine, more the pain of having teeth pulled without an aesthetic.

The assault course and steeplechase events (muddy deep water to wade through as routine and guaranteed to sap your energy) almost completed the P Company events. The most famous horse-racing steeplechase is the Grand National at Aintree. The average winning time is a touch over nine minutes ('Mr Frisk' holds the course record with 8:47.8 for those about to go to the pub quiz after reading this chapter). Our steeple-chase was scored on points rather than position. You only got six points for 18 minutes and 30 seconds of two miles of soft-going agony, and like Aintree it was two circuits. The preview of running the steeplechase was rather like a jockey doing his own notation at Aintree:

Attack the first water obstacle by going to the left.
Attack the second by going left.
Jump all poles; trying to clamber over them will slow
you down.
Large pole: keep right, watch the second ditch.
Single pole: shallow, watch your ankle on landing.
Run and run until your heart gives out.

The assault course was more like Aintree in relation to its timings. A scoring mark of six points only required you to complete the course in seven minutes and 30 seconds. Considering that most of the soldiers could run a mile in somewhere around six minutes, this was no ordinary assault course. Neither were the instructions. They were far simpler than the steeplechase: '*Always* run and *attack* all obstacles.'

The final 14-mile South Downs march was a picnic after the previous events. My reward came when we were back in base and assembled in a silent room. I was asked to stand and was told, 'Pass'. I was now the official proud owner of a red beret.

There were two interesting cultural bookends either side of P Company. Just prior to the start of P Company, I attended an army football dinner. The speaker was the first England football manager from 1946 to 1962, Sir Walter Winterbottom, who gave an insight into the pressures of being a top class football manager.

At the conclusion of P Company, I travelled to Blackpool to stay with a university friend for the weekend. I had never been on such a depressing train journey. The coaches were for a 'holiday special': two words that did not fit easily together in any trip to Blackpool in the early 1980s. The average age of those on board was about the same as the top speed of the train, with the packed ranks heading to the north to re-live the memories of their youth. Blackpool is as good a reason as you can find for cheap air travel.

I hope the good folk of Blackpool will forgive my memories of the place, but its heyday was rather like the era of the speaker we turned up to see at a country club – the legendary Stan Mortensen. As every soccer-loving fan will know, he scored a hat-trick in the 1953 'Matthews Final' – Blackpool's 4-3 defeat of Bolton Wanderers. I sincerely hope that that, like the modern Blackpool football team, the town is once more enjoying moments in the regenerative sunshine, as they did under that newest of football philosophers, their manager Ian

Holloway. But he has now moved elsewhere, and my memories of Blackpool may cast me in the same treacherous mould as those who turn their backs on their football teams. Football is not, despite the pressures that Winterbottom and Mortensen spoke of (and both served in the Second World War), a matter of life and death. What I would experience in 1982 most certainly was.

With P Company done with, it was time to complete our jumps training at RAF Brize Norton. The sun seemed to shine relentlessly. It was a glorious summer, and the final few weeks that the officers on the course would have with no responsibility before they would be unleashed on their unsuspecting battalions. In many ways, those halcyon summer days put one in mind of the seminal work on the RAF during the Second World War – Richard Hillary's *The Last Enemy*.[4] For some, this notion of a halcyon summer before a storm would become a reality: one of our fellow parachuting students was Captain John Hamilton who had just passed SAS selection and was also completing his jumps training. He was killed in the Falklands War almost a year later.

The on-camp cinema at Brize Norton showed the film *A Bridge Too Far*, and all the soon-to-be-qualified paratroopers would rush to see it. It had been released in 1977 and it was now 1981, so either the film was on a continuous loop, the most successful and longest-running film in history, or recycled with every parachuting course that trooped through the base. I favour my final theory.

It may seem curious that in a parachute course that lasted for four weeks, one was required to complete only eight jumps, with and without equipment, and by day and by night. Military parachuting is something that does require an almost automatic and learnt response, for time in the air in which to correct errors is precious, and the decision-making needs to be swift.

While it is rare these days for people to be killed in military parachuting, the numbers of jumpers in the air at any one time can be vast – all potentially occupying, or attempting to occupy, the same air space. Air space, along with time, is a precious commodity, for an 'air steal' – where someone glides across the top of your canopy – causes your own parachute to deflate and collapse. Should this occur the laws of physics apply, and you have the aerial buoyancy of a stone. Plummeting to earth occurs unless corrective action is taken – and quickly.

The first weeks are conducted in a large hanger in either flight swings, or on rubber mats, learning, relearning and reinforcing what has already been learnt. It is little wonder that the motto of the Parachute Training School is 'Knowledge Dispels Fear'.

Everyone remembers their first jump. It occurs at Weston-on-the Green, near Oxford, overlooking the A40. Four men rise from the ground in a cage with a large barrage balloon inflated above them. This initiation will be the balloon jump. It is eerily quiet as the jumpmaster declares, 'Up 800, four men jumping.'

A winch cranks into gear, and a soft, swaying journey takes place. Sergeant Martin, the parachute jump instructor from the RAF, does a supreme man-management job in the ascending balloon to take our minds off the altitude. The winch stops. We are 800ft above the ground. The balloon blows gently, and the first novice is called to the door.

Me: 'Red On'.

Hands swiftly close on the top of the reserve parachute.

'Go.'

A leap occurs into the air.

'1,000, 2,000, 3,000, CHECK CANOPY.'

You look up in anticipation that above your head is a growing envelope of silk attached by parachute cord to the webbing straps that secure the harness via your 'risers' to your back. The inside of the canopy is a welcome sight. The noise as the chute opens reminds me of the wind billowing through bed linen on a washing line from my childhood days. The absence of a canopy leads to the instant deployment of the reserve chute – rare on a balloon jump. You quickly separate the risers to peer above, beneath, and around to assess that you are in clear air space. You are now a parachutist. You smile with glee, and then keep all body parts tightly together to conduct a safe roll as you come in to the ground. You smile after you collapse your parachute and roll it up. It will be repacked for a future descent. Your smile is now ear-to-ear. You are happy. You are on your way to earning your wings and become part of Airborne Forces. And someone has paid for you to have that smile.

As more descents occur, further complications are added. These include aircraft, equipment, people trying to invade the same air as you, and the night. Additional vocabularies are added. An unclean aircraft exit inevitably leads to a few spins and the authoritatively shouted informative instruction to those around to 'STEER AWAY, I'M IN TWISTS!' This is rightly shouted in capital letters, for until one has managed to kick out of twists, the ability to control any movement of the canopy is severely constrained. Other jumpers must steer away, for you are at that moment a dangerous hazard.

'Twists' also mean you cannot lower your equipment. Military parachuting requires you to carry all that you need with you. The rucksack, which will be carried once on the ground, is attached by a device to the legs. Once in clear air space, you must lower your equipment as quickly as possible; failure to do so will almost inevitably lead to broken legs, as there will be no ability to turn off the limbs for any sort of landing. Watching men fail to lower their equipment due to entanglements with other parachutists (another not-to-be-recommended technique or procedure for landing) or other problems will inevitably lead to screams from those already on the ground to 'LOWER YOUR EQUIPMENT!!' The capital letters will get bigger as the parachutist gets closer to the ground. You assume that reserve parachutes have already been deployed in the first few seconds after an entanglement: entwined parachutes look more like a basket of laundry. They also have the properties of a bag of laundry and not of a parachute. Deployment of the reserve parachute must be a reflex action. It almost inevitably is.

The third jump saw us jumping at the maximum permitted wind speed of 13 knots. The fourth was at night. Sixty exited our plane; three were injured as they attempted to distinguish between the darkness of the night and the darkness of the ground. They all suffered ankle fractures after attempting to do a 'pointy toes' impression of a three-year-old having a first ballet lesson. They had forgotten 'never anticipate the ground; keep your feet and knees tight together'.

Jumps five, six and seven all took place on the same day. They required me to revisit my 'administrative requirements matrix' and specifically to 'check alarm timing on clock radio'. We mustered at four in the morning for increasingly complex jump sequences with both equipment and multiple parachutists in the air from both port and starboard doors of the Hercules aircraft as we practised simultaneous stick exits. On 19 June 1981, I completed my eighth and final qualifying jump. I now had my wings to go with the red beret.

Military parachuting can be dangerous. The most senior non-combat death since the Second World War is Brigadier O'Kane. He died in a parachute malfunction whilst commanding 44 Parachute Brigade (Volunteer). A rather unfortunate exercise name was the ill-fated DYNAMIC IMPACT. This battalion drop by 1 PARA in Sardinia led to around 28 serious casualties with the paratroopers exiting in high winds into a badly reconnoitred drop zone strewn with debris. The most poignant and frequent sound you hear on a DZ, even if it is pitch black, which only serves to amplify the effect, is the scream of 'MEDIC!!' It comes from those who have, in the popular vernacular, 'creamed in' and become casualties who will not walk off the DZ under their own steam. All men want to get out of the plane as quickly as possible, for RAF pilots have to fly at low level. This entails them flying at 200ft to simulate evading radar. The buffeting this provides to the paratroopers inevitably leads to sustained amounts of sickness in the aircraft. Not all of this will land in the blue-and-white sick bags. There is nothing worse than streams of vomit splashing up and down the floor of a buffeted C-130. The smell and colour provides further contagion. Military parachuting in large numbers cannot be described as anything like sports parachuting. It is a relief when they open the jump doors and the men once again get to taste fresh air.

Wind on the ground can be as problematic as wind in the air. The first action on landing is to get rid of one of the capewells – the metal risers on either shoulder – which helps to deflate the canopy. Failure to execute this manoeuvre leads to a wind-assisted drag along the ground at speed, with all the facial and bodily abrasions that follow.

Hard landings can lead to concussion. Once this occurs, the injured party is banned from parachuting for two weeks. On a major exercise, a number of simulated parachute assaults may take place within a couple of weeks. This occurred in February 1982 when 2 PARA were exercising in Thetford. Corporal Taff Evans was concussed in the first jump, and subsequently not allowed to parachute during the remaining exercise jumps. He was confined to the drop zone at Tottington Warren as 'hired ground support help' when an unfortunate paratrooper landed (and was stuck) in a tree. This is not recommended. Corporal Evans raced over to the entangled jumper and shouted to him to jettison his container. The container is the 'wrapping' for all the operational equipment, including the fighting order and weaponry that the men use on the ground. It is the life-blood: of their rations, ammunition, medical stores, clothing, sleeping bag and any ponchos for living in the field protected from the elements. The soldier duly dropped his container, which landed squarely on the head of Corporal Evans. The medics shook their heads in disbelief as they drove the once more unconscious corporal to the hospital for the second time. He never even had the opportunity to cry 'MEDIC!'

Corporal Evans became the 28th casualty of the February 1982 jump. It was one of those jumps where the ground party hides the wind meter under their jackets to make the jump seem within legal limits – or at least that is what we used to tell ourselves on those jumps with large casualty numbers. These figures did not include Private McVey, who did not jump, as he had passed out from extreme air sickness in the

Hercules aircraft after two hours of low-level buffeting over the North Sea.

Concussions and hard landings are all amplified if forced to conduct a back landing. In the menu of landings there are really only six alternatives: a forward left, a forward right, a side left, a side right, a back left and a back right. There is no such thing as an 'ass over elbow straight forward' or 'straight back', as each jumper is required to pull on the risers on one side in order to enable a landing in the best direction, which is determined by the wind. Pulling on the risers, which spills wind from the canopy above, is also the technique to steer away from other jumpers in the crowded airspace.

Jumps involving large streams of Hercules aircraft (affectionately known as Fat Alberts) used to occur regularly on ABEX's (Airborne Exercises). In the 1980s and 1990s there would be nine stretched Hercules which could each drop over 90 troops, with a further six aircraft dropping platforms with heavier equipment such as trucks or light artillery pieces. A typical stream would drop 792 troops in one wave – as long as the DZ was big enough. I was the Chief of Staff of 5 Airborne Brigade when our Staff Officers Handbook, the bible on planning from that era, told me that we had over 60 Hercules in the fleet. With the attrition of the fleet since that time, and the air bridges to Iraq and Afghanistan of the last 10 years, we now only have around one-third of that total.

I was CO of 2 PARA when we assembled nine Hercules aircraft for a large battalion-sized jump back into southern England from an exercise in Scotland. The weather was perfect. It was a bright summer's day with no wind and no cloud cover – ideal parachuting weather. What we did not bank on was the incompetence of the senior staff officer of 16 Air Assault Brigade. Under the latest round of defence cuts in late 1999, 5 Airborne Brigade was disbanded and merged with 24 Airmobile Brigade. The majority of the staff of 24 Airmobile Brigade stayed in place to form 16 Air Assault Brigade. Not many of the staff knew much about parachuting. As it turned out, not many of them even knew how to tell the time.

All operations around the world (and military exercises) are timed against Zulu time so there is a common baseline for all clocks. It was the summer and we were now on British Summer Time, which is Alpha time: one hour forward of Zulu time. The staff had never been taught the 'spring forward, fall back' approach to understanding where the clock should be at the correct time of the year.

We commenced our activity at P minus 40 minutes (P hour is parachuting hour) with checking our equipment, hooking up and getting ready for the jump. But when we approached the DZ we were told we would have to abort: there was live firing on the ground and we would run straight into it. We would be killed by rifle fire should we jump. Our jump window had closed one hour earlier. The staff had used the wrong clock. I was furious. To give the commander of 16 Air Assault Brigade his due, he subsequently came to my office to apologise. This was one of those rare occurrences – normally the protocol is the other way round – as he metaphorically 'placed his feet in my in-tray'. His chief-of-staff who had made the cock-up never did progress very far in the army, but the apologetic commander was a gentleman and became the Chief of the General Staff and Head of the Army as General Sir Peter Wall. I would follow him to war anywhere and at any time (as long as he has staff who can convert the time zone clocks).

You can never have too much information on time zones. In the digital era, I had four clocks on my wall in Tampa, which read from left to right and top to bottom:

| 12:31 | 16:31 | 19:31 | 21:01 |
| TAMPA | ZULU | QATAR | AFGHANISTAN |

Confusion of time zones leads to bizarre anomalies. They forgot to adjust the clocks incrementally on the voyage to the South Atlantic during the Falklands War, so there was a four-hour time jump on our watches in one go while in the same latitude and longitude, producing a sort of 'jet lag by proxy'. Once we had landed in the Falklands, we got up at 11am according to our Zulu time watches (in reality it was 7am local time). We attacked Goose Green at 6am on our watches: 2am in the Falklands. Video conferences may take place at a leisurely 11.00am in London but it is 6am in the USA (the bane of my Monday mornings on my Tampa, USA tour).

Not one of these parachuting problems occurred at Brize Norton. With the jumps course completed and men awarded their wings, the soldiers and officers scurried away to sew their prized new possessions on their sweaters. It was remarkable how many sewed them on the left arm – the wrong arm. They were very much still 'crows': those with no experience and novices.

I now had my beret and my wings. I was about to lead the lions of 6 Platoon, B Company, 2 PARA who already had their berets and wings, and by the end of the Falklands campaign in June 1982, I might even class myself as one of that breed. I would then be a lion in a den of Daniels. I would absolutely know the real meaning behind Talleyrand's saying that he feared one lion leading 100 sheep more than he feared one sheep leading 100 lions. I make no apologies for repeating that from the opening chapter.[5]

---

[3]All of these were written in my diary. Shaw's quote is from *Man and Superman*. We wanted to be the latter.

[4]Richard Hillary was also included as a subject in a chapter in Sebastian Faulks' book *The Fatal Englishman*. The army equivalent of this is probably *Memoirs of an Infantry Officer* by Siegfried Sassoon. My naval colleagues have not come up with a satisfactory answer to their seminal work, although one told me that the seminal RAF book is probably *The Brake Fluid Manager's Handbook*.

[5]I am related by marriage to the famous comedian, the late Ronnie Barker. His sister is my Aunt Eileen who married my mother's brother, Uncle Raymond. I think he would have rather liked my use of the English language in this section.

CHAPTER 3

MEN AT WAR – THE FALKLANDS 1982

On 23 March 1982, the young officers of 2 PARA had an air of excitement about them. They believed they might be going to war. They had arrived on that date in Belize, Central America: the same day as a junior officers' coup d'état in Guatemala. These officers had supported the extreme right in the recent Guatemalan election, and had pledged to recover Belize as part of their historic duty: it was their territory. The coincidence of our arrival with the coup was a sign of destiny. There was eager anticipation for the forthcoming six-month tour in the jungles of Belize. The subalterns headed off to the jungle with instructors from the SAS to ready themselves for the coming conflict.

The first week of instruction concluded with a 48-hour patrolling exercise. In the Privassion jungle camp (which we will encounter again later) news came over the radio that Argentina had invaded the Falklands. We *were* going to war, but we had anticipated the wrong country and the wrong enemy. Our six-month tour of Belize lasted precisely 16 days. On 6 April we were back in Aldershot contemplating Sassoon's words that 'never before had I been so intensely aware of what it meant to be young and healthy in fine weather at the outset of summer' before he headed off to war.[5]

Two days before we departed for Portsmouth, the officers of B Company were in an 'orders' group with Major Crosland. The office phone rang. The caller wanted to speak to Lieutenant Ernie Hocking. It was his girlfriend; an army nurse called Pamela. Suitably embarrassed, Ernie told Pam he could not talk right now and put the phone down. The meeting finished, and Major Crosland inquired what the phone call was about. The reply? 'I'm getting married at six o' clock tonight in the Aldershot Garrison church.'

There followed the worst-dressed wedding in history after a whirlwind romance. I was notified that I was to be the best man. My fine Gieves and Hawkes suits were all boxed up to be placed in storage. I had only an old checked jacket, some corduroy trousers and a pair of the desert boots that were *de rigueur* for Paras in the 1980s in my possession. I did not see Ernie Hocking much in the Falklands. He was commanding his platoon, and I was commanding mine. But on the gorse line at Goose Green, I was pinned down when from nowhere Ernie Hocking appeared next to me. 'What are you doing here, Ernie?' I shouted at him with wide-eyed astonishment.

'I've come to get you out of the shit.'

Smoke grenades exploded as we scurried along, with everyone else, back down a slope to good cover in a valley. At that moment I don't believe Ernie was thinking of his newly won bride. At that moment, he loved me more – and I reciprocated.

The wonderful Field Marshal Slim once said that there are four great commands in the service: a platoon, a battalion, a division and an army. A platoon is one of best commands 'because it is your first command, because you are young, and because, if you are any good, you know the men better than their mothers do and love them as much.' At the age of 23, I was to see what one of those great commands in war was all about.

What Slim did not tell us was that platoons are those that are 'caught in the mangle' – those parts of the army that 'do the grinding' and the 'smacking'. Now smacking is a non-mission verb. Mission verbs in the Falklands would be to attack, to capture, to defeat, and to destroy. These were all doctrinally correct terms. Paratroopers liked such mission verbs, but they liked the vernacular of smacking even more. In the army, the mission is everything. Success in achieving the mission is paramount. Bringing everyone home alive is not. If everyone is brought home alive that is fantastic, but we were realistic enough to know that was not going to happen.

I was still on the wrong side of being consciously competent. My 17 weeks at Sandhurst following my Liverpool University Officer Training Corps *in*competence was now somewhat tempered. I had some time under my belt in the battalion having been in 2 PARA for one year after completing the Pre-Parachute Selection and the jumps course. I had also exercised abroad with my wonderful men of 6 Platoon, B Company 2 PARA in Denmark, Kenya, and on Salisbury Plain (which I still thought in my naiveté was a bar of chocolate).

General Krulak of the United States Marine Corps became a guru in the early part of this century when he talked of the 'three block' war, where you might go to the first block – and be war fighting; go to the second block and you might be peacekeeping; and go to the third block where you might be delivering humanitarian aid. This is the sort of complexity that has plagued those campaigning in Iraq and Afghanistan. The Falklands was a different war. We were going to be involved in nothing other than unadulterated war fighting. This would be immensely different than the future wars of Iraq and Afghanistan where the British army would confront the three U's: the unexpected, uncertainty, and the unimagined. The Falklands was to be a war like the British had not fought since Korea.

There were no complexities on the ground in this war. At Goose Green, having received our orders late, which meant there was a compression in giving orders to subordinates, it almost became a matter of simplicity. We would treat the movement forward from our Start Line (the 'jumping off place' of the First World War) as an advance to contact. Two sections would be forward, one in reserve. Anything that was in the way should be regarded as enemy and dealt with accordingly.

The prize was to get to the settlement before breakfast. Our explicit direction from Major Crosland was that he 'wanted General Menendez's balls on the end of his rifle barrel for breakfast'. It was a metaphor, for Menendez was commanding the Argentinian forces from Port Stanley, but we knew exactly what he meant. The fighting of the night, and the unfortunate passage of the night to daylight, meant we never achieved breakfast in Goose Green until the day following.

The night was our friend. The day – with the limitations it imposed on our movement over ground that on a fine summer's day seems to resemble a billiard table – our enemy. It is remarkable that to look at the battlefield now is to be shocked at how open the landscape is. The most frequent refrain from those who go back and see Goose Green is 'How on earth did we do this?' followed by 'If we had been defending this place, the enemy would have been massacred.' They have a point.

There are four parts to any organisation. For the army there is a technical part where an understanding of the capabilities of your weapon systems (including radios) helps to determine how to use them for maximum effect. There is an organisational part – how one structures itself to best employ these systems. A procedural part – and we were a well-trained unit at every level that could *successfully depart* from a mere drill-type approach and standard operating procedures (SOPs). We were a living, breathing, thinking organisation more akin to free-form jazz and playing off each other than the more usual analogy of a conducted orchestra (the metaphor used by Slim about commanding a division). But the last part of any organisation is the human factor: we were dealing in the lives of men. Too often this is forgotten. Everything would revolve around the lives of these men in the spring and summer of 1982.

The men varied in age, experience and ability. Among the Toms – the universal Parachute Regiment term for the soldiers of the regiment – were real youngsters such as Eddie Carroll, who had only just turned 18 years of age on the voyage to the South Atlantic. At least two of the platoon joined the battalion on 2 April 1982 – the same day the Argentinians invaded. Their struggle would be as much to fit in with their more experienced kinfolk, as it would be to confront the enemy. They worried perhaps more about the former than the latter. Carroll contrasted with others such as the wizened Jim Moodie – currently a private after one of the swings in rank that would see him see-saw from private to lance corporal and back. Both would excel.

My corporals all had some regional or wider hew (for the Paras are nothing if not national and international). Commanding my three sections were Corporal Scouse Margerison, Corporal Brummie Robinson and Corporal Manny Eisermann. The heritage of the first two is self-explanatory. Manfred was more complex. His claim to fame was that his father had fought on the winning side at the famous airborne battle at Arnhem – the German side.

The section commanders were complemented by their lance corporals: Bradford (from Blackpool in reality), Bishop (not aptly named) and Bardsley (from Manchester). Lance Corporal Bardsley would later rescue Corporal Margerison who had been shot and wounded at Goose Green while under heavy fire. For this feat he was awarded one of the few Military Medals in the campaign. He committed suicide in 2014.

The platoon was thus balanced with three sections of eight men, complemented by a platoon headquarters of four. Each section had two general purpose machine guns. The Paras were the only part of the army that adopted this approach, as we enjoyed the additional firepower that it brought to bear, even if it meant that each man carried an additional bandolier of 200 rounds in order to keep the guns supplied with additional ammunition.

We trained hard on the way down, pounding the metal plates of the converted North Sea ferry, the MV *Norland*, which had been commandeered with many others using the acronym of STUFT (Ships Taken Up From Trade). In our Directly Moulded Sole boots, we weaved in and out of walkways and gangways. We ran up and down circuits of ladders to replicate hills, all in order to maintain our fitness levels. Despite this, it was like training in Florida: boats are generally quite flat platforms. We knew everything about the climate and weather of the Falklands and speculated where we would land. We also knew that a North Sea ferry is not the world's safest ship to be on should it be attacked by an Argentinian aircraft or submarine. A scare with a supposed enemy submarine contact did occur off the Ascension Islands, but as we lay in our bunks on this flat-bottomed boat, wearing our helmets and bright red life vests, nothing more than another poor whale met its demise.

In early May, the *General Belgrano* was sunk with great loss of life. The next day, the senior naval officer on MV *Norland* gave a lecture on naval operations. It seemed to instil confidence, for the Royal Navy had the most wonderful computerised weapon systems. Two hours later, HMS *Sheffield* was sunk. We concentrated once more on infantry tactics and men contemplated their own mortality (we rarely like to use the 'death' word).

A notable exception was a young soldier in B Company named Northfield. He was more regularly known as 'Merlin', after the magician. He liked to dabble in the dark arts and favoured tarot card readings. He would have liked the fact that the British Forces Postal Office (BFPO) number for the Falklands Islands was BFPO 666 – the mark of the Devil. On one session in the days before the landings he produced a set of cards and went around the circle of assembled soldiers:

'You're going to die,' he claimed after the first card was turned.

'You're going to get wounded,' he stated after the second card.

'You're going to get wounded,' he reiterated after the third card.

One of the assembled members (Corporal Scouse Margerison)

then put an end to this disturbing and perturbing run of cards. But everyone that Merlin pronounced upon did indeed get killed or wounded. We will never know if this was because they were truly fated, whether they did something they might not otherwise have done as they believed their time was up, or whether some people just have that sense that things will not work out for them – a 'feeling' often described in books. One of our officers said he had better take a good hard look at Portsmouth and the coast as we departed with the band playing 'Don't Cry for Me Argentina'. He 'felt' he would never see them again. He was killed in action.

Merlin did not pick up his tarot cards again on the voyage home and I recently learnt that he never picked them up again. The soldier whose death he had foretold was struck in the neck by an enemy bullet. It was said by the dead soldier's section commander, who had witnessed the tarot reading, that he saw a long jet trail of blood spurt from the wound. He described it as akin to seeing his life leaving him in the moment it took for the ejaculating blood to cease its momentum. The section commander returned to the Falklands for the first time in 2012, and shed a tear at the exact spot that the soldier was killed.

Despite everything, we maintained our sense of humour. On the voyage south, Lieutenant Guy Wallis had received a compilation tape of songs through the mail from his sister. Our favourite was 'Moonshadow' by the artist formerly known as Cat Stevens. We particularly liked the verse that mentions losing your legs and not moaning or begging because you won't have to walk no more.

During the Goose Green battle, one young soldier did lose his leg. As he lay screaming 'I've lost my leg, I've lost my leg!', a

54

comradely but black-humoured soldier corrected him with the line: 'No, you haven't. It's over there...'

We even thought it would be beneficial to take out insurance cover on each other. In the event of our deaths, our fellow officers would be the financial beneficiaries and be able to hold one hell of a wake. 'The system' rejected our novel approach to death in combat.

The majority of soldiers come to an agreement with God. This is based on God not bothering them and the soldiers reciprocating by not bothering Him. But mortality does mean it is worth having an insurance policy, and the church service held for 2 PARA in the bowels of MV *Norland* a few hours before the beach landing was massively well attended. The 2 PARA padre, the Reverend David Cooper, was universally liked and a confidante of the troops. He was a man of practical faith, and was constantly warned that if he persisted in moving up with the advancing troops he would undoubtedly be killed, but saw it as his primary duty to be near those who would be soon departing their mortal life. Mortality and potentially life-ending events have their own predilection for religiosity. War is the severest test of spiritual and bodily strength. In war, character outweighs intellect. Many stand forth on the field of battle that in peace would remain unnoticed. I would see this in action.

But I was to be a platoon commander. When I was in contact in the front line, I was (effectively) to be responsible for British defence policy. I would be the one with the sharpest pencil (pens were not things that really worked, given the vagaries of the weather). To paraphrase Field Marshal Slim, it would be true that 'Army Commanders use a wave of the hand over a map, Corps Commanders will point with three fingers, Divisional Commanders with two, Brigadiers with one, while the junior commanders must go more and more into detail with an increasingly sharp pencil.'[6] My pencil and I were ready for action.

The night of the landing was crisp and clear. The Falklands air was so sweet and clean that you could taste it. You could see all the stars in the heavens. We, however, did not have time to suck in the beauty of the night – we were really scared. Most books on the Falklands War and the landing of 2 PARA (Op Sutton) at Blue Beach 2 detail that the troops did not exit the Landing Craft Utility (LCU), as they did not understand the two Marine words of command 'Troops Out', and only reacted on the parachute jumping command of 'Green On', followed by 'GO!' This is one of those great myths, and another example of 'when the legend becomes fact, print the legend' – as when John Wayne allows James Stewart to take the credit for cleaning up the town by killing Lee Marvin in *The Man Who Shot Liberty Valance*.

The orders for the landing called Op Sutton were for a four-phase operation that concluded with 2 PARA to be established on a reverse slope position on Sussex Mountain, 7.8 kilometres from the beach landing site. The first LCU was to carry A Company, C Company and Battalion Tactical HQ. The second, B Company and Battalion Main HQ, with Support Company on LCU 3 and D Company on LCU 4. All timings were in Zulu (UK) time. The battalion embarked from MV *Norland* between 0315 and 0415z (four hours ahead of local Falklands time) and were due to land at 0630z (which was 0230 in the Falklands). Each LCU was supposed to have a capacity of 200 pax. There were 176 people on LCU 2 and it was full to the gunnels with huge bergens. These contained everything the men would live with – and often without – for the duration of the war.

The orders included the preparatory words of command as follows:

'Prepare to beach' (life jackets off, bergen on, life jackets passed to the rear).

'Down ramp' (shuffle forward into a position ready to disembark).

'Out troops' (disembarkation commences).

In reality, the second LCU became the first to land (the boat I was on with 6 Platoon and the rest of B Company). My diary note was as follows: 'One would like to say that the landing was a glorious storming of the beach. It was nothing of the sort. The ramp was lowered and the executive word of command "Out Troops" was given. No one moved. The reason was that we were some way from the shore and since no one had worked with Marine landing craft before no one was sure how deep the water would be. The LCU Commander reiterated, "Out troops" and followed it with, "You'll just have to get your feet wet."'

And so 2 PARA landed soaking wet and with a monster TAB (Tactical Advance to Battle) ahead under air attack warnings which disrupted the momentum of the march and ruined the feet of a number of Toms. It was one of the hardest physical nights of my army career. A few hundred yards from the landing site we shed some of our enormous weight and dropped off the mortar ammunition 'greenies' (large plastic tubes that contained the bombs). Each man had carried two of these in the side pouches on his bergen. The relief only lasted a few minutes until our feet and thighs once again recognised that they were being asked to endure things that our grandfathers in the First World War would have recognised. It was agony.

We finally reached Sussex Mountain in broad daylight, and

dug in. The Falklands weather proved unrelenting. There were four seasons in every day. The water table was a lot higher than any soldier would have liked. Digging down more than a few feet produced water-filled trenches that again our grandfathers would have recognised. We built up using rocks to provide a sanger-like (temporary fortified position) external appearance. The landing, the water table and the elements were akin to Napoleon marching on Moscow. Although this was late May, in the Falklands it was their winter. One of the members of 6 Platoon – Private Alfred – was evacuated with trench foot after three days on the beachhead, re-joining after the war was over.

General January and General February were to play a part in this war. Fortunately they were to play a bigger part for the Argentinians: wading ashore aside, we were used to such hostile conditions. Every army training area over a 100-year period had been purchased with an eye for barren moors and unpopulated areas. The Falklands War was as much won on the training areas of Sennybridge, Otterburn and the winters of Salisbury Plain, as it was in the Falkland Islands. All these played their part in enabling our troops to endure.

The first week on the Falklands saw us waiting, waiting. It was not without incident. On the first day, 5 Platoon had been ordered to patrol out to find an Argentinian pilot who had bailed out some miles south of our position after being shot down by the SAS, who were conducting a diversionary raid on Goose Green to cover the landings. Lt Ernie Hocking led his men and away they went into the unknown. The tranquil landscape and clear views were punctuated by almighty crashes as artillery shells burst over our heads. The Argentinians were already on to us – or so we thought. They were not. This was our own artillery registering and recording their targets and for whatever reason (the meteorology is a big factor in the accuracy of gunfire) had placed air-bursts right above our position. In one of those flukes of war, the shrapnel from the shelling all landed in the vacated trenches of 5 Platoon. Sometimes, friendly fire is anything but; and you will understand the reason the infantry colloquially name the artillery as 'drop shorts'.

We took part in daily rituals. My platoon headquarters staff comprised three Scots: Sergeant Bill McCulloch, 'Beast' Kirkwood (so called as he was unfairly deemed to be one of NATO's ugliest men), and 'Jock' Skey (one of them, as a minimum, had to have an ethnic nickname). They had been brought up on porridge laced with salt. We ate communally at breakfast from a grenade tin with all our four porridge rations mixed together – the army, perhaps with no hint of irony, had issued us with arctic rations packs for the campaign. It was akin to a daily communion.

We watched and waited. We saw HMS *Antelope* explode into flames with a spectacular fireball as we changed radio shifts at night while maintaining a watching and continuous radio presence. We saw HMS *Antrim* pummelled from Argentinian aircraft in a display of ship-against-aircraft that we could do nothing to influence. We cheered as two aircraft passed overhead, trailing smoke on their way back to Argentina after attacking the fleet lying in San Carlos Water. Both were hit and were not going to make it back: both splashed down some miles further on. We almost danced on the tops of the trenches with men shouting, 'Die, die!' In retrospect, this was aimed at the planes rather than the pilots. We just did not want those planes to return the next day to inflict more wide-angled viewing misery. The morale of the men soared on these 'kills' – each

Tom who had employed his machine gun swore blind that it was *his* fire that had been decisive.

And all the time, with the weather and the harshness of the conditions, we were physically degrading. We were suffering from 'the actualities of war – the effects of tiredness, hunger, fear, lack of sleep, weather, inaccurate information... and so forth' as Field Marshal Wavell put it in his memoir . We degraded in language: Beast could not get his radio to work on one occasion: 'The f***ing f***er's f***ed!' he cursed, not realising that he had used a verb, a noun and an adjective in one sentence. But we never degraded in spirit. The NAAFI hut at Ajax Bay was supposedly bombed. I don't believe it was, but it gave the Quartermaster, Tom Goodwin, the excuse to bring forward free cigarettes and Mars Bars – the stores of a bombed warehouse could be written-off. Days in a trench can be boring and tiresome. I started smoking; they were free and I might be killed in a few days. The least of my worries was the thought of dying of lung cancer. A fellow platoon commander, when pinned down, asked one of his nearby soldiers if he wanted a cigarette:

'I don't smoke, sir.'

They could not move to the left, they could not move to the right. They could not move forward. They could not move back. The answer the platoon commander gave was about right for their predicament of the moment: 'I suggest you start.'

I attended another funeral in 2006 that reminded me of my own smoking adventure in the Falklands. It was another sad occasion. Not only were the family of the deceased soldier in attendance, but what I can only describe as 'a sea of wounded' – and from 'all ranks'. There were private soldiers, corporals, sergeants, colour sergeants and sergeant majors: this was the worst form of battle meritocracy in action. One young platoon commander was drinking a pint of lager and smoking at the wake held at the Garrison Sergeants' Mess in Aldershot. He had suffered the loss of three soldiers, killed during that 2006 Afghanistan tour. I asked him if he had smoked before Afghanistan. He had not. He then told me that one of his soldiers had developed a throaty cough from smoking the very strong local cigarettes. The platoon commander, concerned for his welfare, implored him to stop smoking them or they would be the death of him. The soldier was killed in action the next day: he never got to develop lung cancer, and neither did the prospect worry him. You can see why.

There is nothing lonelier on a battlefield than being a private soldier. This is a strange paradox, for the comradeship between soldiers is almost unique, and is probably the thing that soldiers most miss when they return to civilian life. But on a battlefield they are lonely. Death is random – there is no pattern to it. There are even random deaths after conflict has ceased. One of the saddest was that of Captain Matt Selfridge of 3 PARA who survived the Falklands War only to be killed during his post-tour leave when his parachute failed to open while jumping at a civilian free-fall club.

A further example of the random and 'luck' factor played in to the death of Lt Jim Barry, killed at Goose Green. Jim Barry was a charming young officer who was a great sailor. So much so, that in 1982 he was selected to be part of the UK America's Cup team. He left the battalion in March 1982 to undertake the training for that year's attempt at glory, and his platoon was handed over to a new officer. The Argentinians subsequently invaded, and Jim was recalled to lead his platoon. If the invasion had been a few weeks or months later, he would not have been recalled. Following his death, the officer he had replaced, Jacko Page, again took over his platoon in D Company. He was knocked off his feet with some bruising at the Battle of Wireless Ridge when an ammo pouch on his webbing received a bullet strike. To lose one officer from a platoon would have been bad enough; to lose two would have been tragic. Jacko Page is a great officer who subsequently had a marvellous career achieving the rank of Lieutenant General. Jim Barry is remembered not for his sailing exploits but for the circumstances of his death under what became known as the 'white flag' incident.

Being a junior officer is a lot easier than being a lonely soldier. You have been issued with orders from your superior headquarters, and given them to your subordinates. You have a map. You have an idea of where you are going. You have a radio, and you have some amount of control – even though you might choose to delegate that to the lowest level of initiative in the heat of battle. You are a decision-maker with communications. A young soldier has probably received his orders late, probably in the dark; he will have no map, little idea where he is going, and no radio. He is a follower until he can identify where he can engage the enemy and make a difference. It is amazing how much fortitude soldiers show in such circumstances. It has been said to me that this is still true in Afghanistan, with one further, compounding and terrifying loneliness now added – that we make a young soldier a 'lead' point man with a mine-detecting device. He has the physical terror and the psychological weight of the safety of all those who follow in his footsteps in his every move.

There are three types of soldiers in war: thrivers, stickers, and failures. I think I was one who thrived. I thought my entire platoon were of the same ilk. I thought we had all had a good war. We did – at the time. With hindsight – and General Hindsight is the greatest general in the world – I was wrong. Even today there are men from my platoon who suffer from post-traumatic stress disorder (PTSD) – men who I thought were thrivers but with the passage of time found it difficult to come to terms with what they saw and did. Many of those who have the awful responsibility as lead mine detectors in Afghanistan will, I suspect, follow in their unfortunate psychological footsteps in future years.

The soldiers of 6 Platoon were among the first to come into contact with the enemy at Goose Green. The platoon were the left-forward element of B Company and crossed the 'start line', the modern equivalent of leaving the trenches to go forward in to battle, at 0230 in the morning.

We progressed in the dark when a whispered alert arose from Corporal Margerison:

'Watch out, there's a scarecrow in front.'

This almost seemed plausible, for in the 'ground' section of our orders, telling of the features and significance of the area we would fight across, it was stated that we would be moving over the best agricultural land in the Falklands. I had visions of cabbage fields and the like. This was also a myth.

'Watch out, the scarecrow's moving!' followed shortly after.

This was not Wurzel Gummidge, but an Argentinian soldier standing and moving in the pitch black of the night. He was covered with a poncho in the bitter cold and he was shot. To this day, I do not know what he was doing, or what, if any, threat he presented. We could take no risk on his intent, for this initiated a platoon attack upon a sequence of Argentinian trenches. The attack was successful. We lost no men and came through our baptism of fire unscathed. The movement of the platoon into the attack, and their swift execution through the enemy position with the sky lit periodically by friendly flares, was simply stunning in its efficiency.

From that moment forth, 6 Platoon believed we were invincible and that our will to win was stronger than the enemy's. We could not lose. That attack was, for me, the seminal moment of the war.

Fear is a constant part of battle – and waiting for battle. There is a perpetual knot in the stomach which is akin to permanently watching England's football team take penalties in a World Cup semi-final against Germany: the butterflies of anticipation. On occasions there is even amplified fear. I had three of these.

AMPLIFIED FEAR 1
My platoon (it was not really my platoon – it was all of ours) had been successful in our initial attacks in the darkness and early hours of combat at Goose Green. We were 10ft tall: we were the invincibles. We had established our moral authority – we were not going to lose – but we were mortal. My first so-called sixpence-dustbin rectal palpitation occurred as we skirmished up a hill towards the prominent gorse line at Goose Green. A small puddle to the left of my head suddenly plopped a couple of times as enemy bullets narrowly passed me and hit the still water. It was the first time I had confronted my own mortality and death. I did not particularly like the feeling. It was light, and the enemy were more active than in the hours of darkness. You could now see fear.

AMPLIFIED FEAR 2

We now fast-forward about 10 hours. 2 PARA have by this time squeezed the Argentinians at Goose Green and are edging closer and closer to the settlement. B Company have by now moved forward from Boca House following the magnificent efforts of Phil Neame's D Company (not only is death random in combat, but so is the distribution of medals – if ever a commander deserved formal recognition it was the sadly neglected Phil Neame). B Company were now very close to Goose Green and had just occupied a series of enemy trenches… when all hell broke loose.

The 'all hell breaking loose' is illustrative that in war the psychological has as much impact as the physical. Breaking the will of an enemy to resist is, in most combat, more important than the physical act of killing. Very few enemies fight to the last man – and the Argentinians at Goose Green were no Masada-like force.

The first psychological impact was when our battalion casualty figures came over the radio. They suggested that we had had seven officers killed. There are only about 25 officers in the fighting echelon of a battalion, so this was over 25 per cent. My thought: if we have had seven officers killed, then how many soldiers have we had killed? We must be the only company left (for despite Goose Green being a tiny battlefield we never did see another company during the battle). Field Marshal Wavell once said that 60 per cent of initial reports in war are wrong, misleading or inaccurate. Despite modern communications on the battlefield I believe he is still right. We had four officers killed.

The second impact was physical. The enemy suddenly opened up with artillery, small arms, and a Pucara aircraft proceeded to attack. We were under pressure.

The third impact was both physical and psychological. Suddenly a number of Argentinian helicopters flew in with reinforcements for the garrison. The psychological shock was that prior to the battle, we had been told in our orders that there were no enemy helicopters left on the island. They had all been shot down. Our eyes betrayed the unreality of this false assessment.

If we mix the three physical and psychological impacts together we get a rich soup of fear. For some this was *absolute fear*. Three members of my platoon were seized at these moments of intense fear with an inability to take part in the battle. 'We're going to die, we're going to die!' I heard one say as his body became as small as possible as he hugged every contour of the coarse grass that lay under his torso, legs and head. There is a physiological ability for this to happen; the soldiers call it 'digging in with your eyelids'. There were not enough enemy trenches in the position we had recently occupied, and men now dug in with any implement they could find – mess tins, spoons, anything that could give them some better and deeper cover against what they expected to follow. But we were Paras: the attitude was one of 'come on you bastards, come and take us on' – we were not going to let down those around us or those who had come before us.

The three incidents stopped us dead in our tracks. Up until that moment we had always been on the tactical offensive. Now we were on the defensive, and expected an Argentinian counter-attack. It never transpired, but men took turns all night to man the trenches as we waited the future attack. We were amazed when the Argentinians surrendered the next morning. We did not know that their will had been broken – while ours remained intact – following an ultimatum delivered to them by Major Chris Keeble, the Acting CO following the death of Colonel H Jones.

AMPLIFIED FEAR 3

A few days after the battle of Goose Green, a plan was hatched to conduct a raid on Swan Inlet House. The significance of Swan Inlet House was nothing beyond the fact that it had a telephone link to Fitzroy. In the best case, it might be established via this link whether there was an Argentinian garrison present at both the Fitzroy settlement and Bluff Cove. The plan was simple. Three Scout helicopters would transport 12 men in three groups of four per helicopter. Two other Scout helicopters were to be equipped with the SS11 missile, which would rocket the area prior to assault.

The majority of men on this mission were from my platoon. It meant I got to pick those who had excelled at Goose Green and whose bank of moral and physical courage was still intact. Lord Moran, Churchill's personal physician during the Second World War, had described from his own experiences (in the First World War) that men in battle are akin to a bank account where each action and combat activity uses credits. Soldiers use these credits at a differing rate dependent on their own personal start points. There can come a time where soldiers therefore go into deficit. This can lead in the longer term to PTSD, and in the shorter term to a reluctance or inability to participate further. Identifying these changes is important in managing soldiers and their mental state. Suffice it to say that none of the three soldiers I described as non-participants in the Goose Green incident were selected for the Swan Inlet House mission.

Those who flew in my helicopter included my loyal and great

signaller 'Beast' Kirkwood, and the youngest soldier in my platoon, the recent 18th birthday celebrant, Eddie Carroll. Beast Kirkwood had already shown his own personal resilience and fortitude, for his brother (like Beast a radio operator, in A Company) had been wounded at Goose Green. There is no more profound impact within a battalion than that which occurs when a biological, as opposed to a warrior brother, is killed or wounded. 2 PARA had 14 sets of brothers in the Falklands and a number became casualties. Our company signaller, Corporal Stu Russell, was another whose brother became a casualty. Beast and the others mentally dusted themselves off and continued; the sort of acts that bring meaning to the term 'humbling'.

'Beast' lived his job. Under heavy fire at Goose Green he had sent a radio message to the company headquarters that went as follows: 'Hello 2, this is 23 [2 was the call sign of B Company HQ, 23 was the call sign of 6 platoon] for f*** sake, beam me up, out.' Unfortunately there was no transporter to whisk him from his predicament: he thought he was a likely candidate for the member of the *Star Trek* away team with the red shirt.

The commander of the mission was Major John Crosland. He wanted another opportunity to dust off his black woolly hat and lead. Crosland was an extraordinary officer who never wore a helmet and inspired absolute confidence through his experience, charisma and bravado. It was just as well he was not killed, such was the influence of his leadership on all around him. The orders were given and the Scouts arrived for what we thought was to be a rehearsal. But there was no time to rehearse – we were told we had to go 'now' as the helicopters were a limited asset that would be needed for other tasks. My psychological shift had begun, as we had no idea if there were enemy soldiers on the objective, or what strength we might confront. We would rely on the shock action of the SS11 missile strikes to get us metaphorically and physically over the hill to complete the task.

We took off and flew at about four feet above the ground to mask our signature to any enemy en route. The weather was cold. Beast occupied the skid next to me. We had no doors on the Scouts and we had clipped in and sat on the floor lip with our feet hanging out on the skids, two men on each side. The wind whistled past us as we flew to the objective. My left leg started shaking uncontrollably. I was terrified that I would be useless at the objective; I'm not sure whether it was the weather or my uncertainty about the enemy that led me to that state. It really was like the scene you see with Tom Hanks in *Saving Private Ryan* where his hand shakes uncontrollably but this was reality, not a film.

Fortunately, all turned out well when we reached the objective. My fear subsided and training and instinct took over. There were no enemy at the objective, the phone call was made, and in many ways the significance of this single act has been underplayed. The fact that the phone call confirmed there were no enemy at Fitzroy opened up the southern flank for the leap forward that probably shortened the war by a number of days or even weeks.

And so we did indeed leap forward to Fitzroy, spending another few nights without our bergens and living from our belt order. There were no sleeping bags and we attempted to survive by covering ourselves in the diddle-dee heather from the hills and placing a poncho under our bodies. No one managed to get much sleep. The weather was raw. It made 'Norman the Store Man' and his blankets look like softies, but even a blanket would have been some consolation in the frigid winter of the South Atlantic.

Lieutenant Colonel Jones' death has become controversial for those who like the 'revisionist' school of history. He was killed about 100 metres from where I was pinned down, under fire from my front at Boca House. At the time I knew nothing of the trouble besetting A Company of 2 PARA at Darwin Hill. Although Goose Green was a small battlefield, it is pretty large when you are under fire and, at times, only progressing at 200 or 300 metres an hour. I now know that I could have crawled along the gorse line at Goose Green and helped to unhinge the entire left flank of the battlefield that H Jones sought to unlock. The reality: it might well have been in a different universe, for at that moment I knew nothing of what was occurring seemingly so close to my own position.

Lieutenant Colonel Jones was a hard-driving leader. He personified those aspects that the British army only codified in the late 1980s with the initial publication (somewhat curious since the army was already around 350 years old) of British military doctrine. He was the living embodiment of the approach to operations that sought to shatter the enemy's cohesion and will to fight. He called for an attitude of mind in which using initiative and a ruthless determination to succeed were paramount. The battalion was created in his image – and for that, and the success at Goose Green, he deserved his Victoria Cross. His was an outstanding act of personal bravery. Lieutenant Colonel Jones could never be accused of being akin to a remote 'Chateau General' of the First World War. His own example and death was a return to heroic leadership. One of Field Marshal Slim's other great commands was battalion command: 'Because it is a unit with a life blood of its own: whether it is good or bad depends on you alone.' H Jones could die, assured that 2 PARA was firmly in the 'good' category because of him, and him alone.

Seventeen years after Goose Green I was privileged to be given command of 2 PARA. I was not only their CO. I was now, as H Jones had been, the custodian of all those magnificent officers and men who had come before me – at Bruneval, Arnhem, the Rhine Crossing, the D Day landings at Normandy, and every other battle honour that was part of our blood-stream. I also took something both physical and psychological from the death of H Jones at Goose Green – I never carried a rifle. I always carried a pistol. The pistol was my note to self in both domains – physical and psychological – that my job was 'command' in its widest sense; to cohere all elements of the combat power available to me, and that my job was decision-making to enable these to be brought together. The pistol was my constant reminder of Goose Green. I wanted always to be able to fight a second battle.

I once told this story at the concrete bunkhouse of the derelict Divisional Headquarters where the French had mentally and subsequently physically collapsed following the German invasion in 1940. Professor Richard Holmes (the noted military historian and television personality who sadly died in 2012) was fascinated and agreed with my logic. In the next breath, the senior mentor, a Royal Marine brigadier came up and told me he absolutely disagreed with me. And there you have the diversity of opinion within the forces laid out. Neither is right or wrong – they are just different. Command, and the approach to command, is intensely personal.

There is nothing new in that either. An extract from a 1944 pamphlet by Montgomery contained the following: 'A commander has at his disposal certain human material. He must gain the complete trust and confidence of his men. There is no book of rules which will help him in this matter; each commander will adopt his own methods, and the one best suited to his own make-up.'

2 PARA were tired and bloodied. Goose Green had been a success, but at a cost of 17 killed and 40 wounded. We believed it was now someone else's turn to have a piece of the action. Goose Green had been one of those battles that lived up to the adage that 'when you're short of everything, but the enemy, you're in contact.' It was remarkable how quickly that perception of someone else's turn wore off. After a few days' rest we wanted once again to be in the van of battle, as Monty put it. We wanted to be there in the action at the finish: for the Falklands was to have a defined beginning, middle and end. We wanted to be there at the end. That end would be the battles around the hills of Port Stanley.

For us, this would mean one more battle, at Wireless Ridge, and more nights without our bergens. In this battle we were not 'short of everything'; we had sufficient resources, including direct fire from Scorpion and Scimitar armoured vehicles and indirect fire from co-ordinated artillery fire, not to have to worry too much about the enemy numbers. Battles when you are near the endgame are tense affairs. All the battalion knew this was to be the finish line – the knowledge that makes people ever more worried that they will be killed so close to the end of conflict. Sadly, 2 PARA were to lose three more soldiers at Wireless Ridge. Of even greater sadness was that two of these soldiers from D company were killed by the fire of our own artillery, the grossly named 'friendly fire' that will continue to plague all conflicts because chaos and friction are unfortunate inevitabilities of war. We can reduce the occurrence of such incidents, but we will never eliminate them.

Before we attacked, we occupied a Start Line in ground that could not be seen by the enemy. This was dead ground. In contravention of the rules, but as a reflection of the nervousness before what we knew would be the final push, men cupped their hands around a last cigarette to conceal the glow. A young soldier went up to Corporal Tom Harley, who would win the Military Medal for bravery and was already known as fearless in battle. He inquired of Harley:

'Are you scared, Corporal?'

Harley replied with his hands cupping his final ember: 'Of course I'm f***ing scared. Now get back to your position and prepare to attack.'

This was reassurance for the young soldier that even those thought to be among the immortals had their own emotions with which to contend.

With white flags flying following the Battles for the Hills – Mount Longdon, Mount Tumbledown, Two Sisters and Wireless Ridge – it was time to race towards the capital 'city': the extremely small and parochial quaintness of Port Stanley. We reached it first (the media shots of the Royal Marines hoisting flags over the Governor's house took place some hours later).

I slumped down in a garden at Ross Road West. Major Chris

Keeble, the battalion 2IC, came past and asked me how I was. This was at the same time as my feet spoke to me. This is what they said: 'OK, Chip. You've really abused us in the past few weeks, and we've had enough. You've made us carry ridiculous weight, and given us no shelter for weeks. You've walked us over stone runs and through icy ponds, and rarely even given us a clean pair of socks to relieve our burden. And now we're going to make you suffer.'

I did suffer. Liberation was painful. This formed the basis of my reply to Chris Keeble: 'I did not realise liberation could be so painful.' My feet were satisfied. Now that the fear and the adrenaline had subsided, it was their moment for a little 'me' time at my expense as my feet chuckled in my worn and dirty DMS boots.

A review of the factors for success in 20th century warfare tells us that four factors are predominant: control of the air, shock action, offensive reconnaissance, and surprise. At Goose Green we had no surprise (the Argentinians had been tipped off by the BBC World Service), we had little air support or combat support from mortars or artillery, we had little time or assets for offensive reconnaissance. But we did have a magnificent group of highly motivated paratroopers, dedicated to each other, their sense of history and the destiny of those who came before them, and their mission – and we won. Napoleon is often quoted as instructing us that 'the moral is to the physical as three is to one.' Three times the number of 2 PARA who attacked at Goose Green surrendered from the Argentinian side. If war was merely arithmetic, which it is not – in reality 'far from being an exact science it is a terrible and impassioned drama' (according to the Swiss-born 19th-century war theorist, Antoine-Henri Jomini) – that

74

would mean we were six times as good as the Argentinians. We probably were.

I could now put my less than sharp pencil away.

---

[5] *Memoirs of an Infantry Officer*, Siegfried Sassoon, Faber and Faber (reset 1997 edition) p.4.

[6] This quotation was on the front cover of a School of Infantry exercise named 'Exercise Norman's Conquest' in the 1980s. It came from Lt Col J M McAvity (DSO, MBE) in 1944. It is a useful truism.

CHAPTER 4

THE 'TOMS'

As noted earlier, Parachute Regiment soldiers are known as 'Toms' – an adoption from the Tommy Atkins nickname from the First World War. They like this name, whether they are acting within the law or not.

In Northern Ireland every soldier was required to act within the law. In fact, on all deployments to all operations anywhere in the world, all soldiers are required to act within the law, otherwise we would be no better than football hooligans in uniform. And when you give young men and women weapons capable of lethal effect, there would be even worse consequences than those that occur as a result of recreational football hooligan-type fighting.

The consequences when soldiers do not act within the law are obvious in the age of our ubiquitous media. 'Preservation of reputation' is now akin to a new principle of war. Events such as Abu Ghraib and Camp Breadbasket following the Iraq intervention in 2003, or inadvertent Koran burnings in Afghanistan, should make us all too aware that the recording and transmission of images that inflame and incite are an obvious flank to be exploited by any adversary – and their camp followers. Put more simply, it is also plain wrong.

Commanders love their men, but sometimes-messianic devotion to them should not cloud the fact that although they are the salt of the earth and comradeship is a powerful enabler, they have a great propensity to lie and cheat to preserve their own ass. This is no bad thing of itself, for while we have historically lionised the 'officer and a gentleman', war and conflict require low cunning and guile, deceit and deception, and an approach that unhinges the enemy – it is the enemy who have a large vote in any theatre of conflict. Our soldiers are more than able to adopt these traits in both peace and war.

The bond between officers and soldiers is now a close one. This has not always been the case: neither has there always been a meeting of officer-soldier minds. I was looking at some course notes from an American war college module on 'The Evolution of Military Thought' – which took in the art of war from Sun Tzu to the deterrence theories of Bernard Brodie via other military philosophers of the ages (such as Douhet, Fuller, Liddell Hart, Thucydides, Ardant du Picq and Frederick the Great, Corbett and Mahan), when I came across an additional page. I hope this was mere happenstance, for if it truly represented the views of the only remaining superpower, we could kiss goodbye to the special relationship. The rogue addendum told me that:

An officer should be comely, spratly and above all else, confident in his own dress and bearing. He should, where possible, eat a small piece of meat each morning with molasses and beans. He should air himself gracefully when under fire and never place himself in a position to be shot at. He should eat all his meals comfortably and ahead of his soldiers, for it is he who is more important tactically on the battlefield and therefore he who should be nourished. His hair should be well groomed and if possible he should adorn a moustache or similar facial adornment. When speaking to his soldiers he should appear unnerved and aloof and give direction without in any way involving himself personally in the execution of arduous or un-officer like duties. He should smoke thin panatelas except when in the company of ladies where he should take only a small gin mixed with lemon tea. He should be an ardent and erudite gentleman and woo the ladies both in the formal environment and in the bedroom where he should excel himself beyond the ordinary soldier with his virulent love-making prowess. These I say to you are the qualities of an officer that set him apart from the lay person and the common soldier.'

This 1907 passage from Lieutenant General Hubert Worthington, written while serving in India, is not one that would be recognisable to the modern officer – nor would he endorse the sentiments – bar the final exhortation to excel which is, of course, still absolutely true...

Let me illustrate the guile, low cunning, and yes, deceit, of our soldiers. Acting within the law in Northern Ireland meant that every (well-trained) man was required to 'own up' and to fill in a Complaint Report (COMPLAINTREP) if an occasion demanded it and something had gone wrong with their interaction with the population. We were there to protect the population, and to win their hearts and minds. It was often believed that the natural state of affairs for a paratrooper was to come from the angle of grabbing someone by the balls, hoping their hearts and minds would follow. They are now far more sophisticated and nuanced than 30 years ago, even though the winning of hearts and minds is an overplayed concept. You can lose them quite quickly, but winning them is one of those textbook mantras that in reality is almost impossible to achieve. If you do not believe me, very few people quote Field Marshal Templer's entreaty from the Malayan Emergency (1948 – 1960) that hearts and minds was 'that nauseating phrase that I think I invented' (although plenty of military thinkers will quote Malaya and Templer as the textbook way of defeating an insurgency).

We had a 12-man 'multiple' of three teams of four out on another routine patrol in West Belfast. The patrol ended and came in for its normal debrief when the lance corporal in charge of a 'brick' (mixing our metaphors, a brick was a four-man team within the multiple) declared, 'We think there may be a complaint made against us.'

'Oh yeah?' I replied. 'Tell me what happened.'

'Nothing really happened, boss. All that happened was that we were followed from the time we left the base by three girls who gave us a load of mouth, and questioned our parentage. All I did was put my hands around the groin area of my trousers and say, 'I wouldn't waste it on you.'

'Are you sure that's all that happened?' I replied. 'For if you're lying we might need to get the flying lawyer down to get some legal advice.'

'Naa... that's all that happened.'

I was content with my most excellent fellows and their absolute integrity and honesty. What I hadn't anticipated was that a week later the most excellent fellows were to be interviewed by the police – and under caution. The Royal Ulster Constabulary (RUC) had already completed their interviews with the upright complainants who happened to be the three girls. The troops did not want the flying lawyer; they merely required my presence in the interview room to represent their point of view if things were getting tricky.

The police questioning went along the following lines:

Police (to Soldier 1): 'Did you say to the girls that they needed a good bit of ABC?'

Soldier: 'No, I did not.'

Police: 'Do you know what ABC means in the Parachute Regiment?'

Soldier: 'No, I do not. It's not a phrase with which I am familiar.'

Police: 'What if I was to tell you it means Airborne Cock?'

Soldier: 'I've never heard that phrase.'

Police: 'Did you see the second soldier in your patrol flash?'

Soldier: 'No, I did not.'

Soldier 1 was duly dismissed from his interview to be followed (unsurprisingly) by Soldier 2. The questioning followed exactly the same lines with exactly the same questions and exactly the same responses. There were two further soldiers to be interviewed. After Soldier 2 had given his testimony, I turned to the police and said, 'Stop these interviews now and give me 15 minutes.'

I hastened away to my office, summoned the awesome Company Sergeant Major Brian Dixon, and asked him to furnish me with the three youngest paratroopers from the small NAAFI recreation room.

Jones arrived first at my office.

'Jones, what does ABC mean to you?' I asked bluntly.

'Airborne Cock, sir!'

'Good, now get out.'

Smith was the second to arrive.

'Smith, what does ABC mean to you?'

'Airborne Cock, sir!' he also replied.

'Good, now get out.'

The third and final participant in my cultural observations on the etymology of the use of language in the Parachute Regiment was Bodrington.

Bodders was an effective and good soldier but not best blessed in the brains department. He had the IQ of a tent peg. If Bodders could get the answer, then my thesis would have been proven.

'Bodders,' I started, 'what does ABC mean to you?'

'Uh, I dunno sir,' he replied.

My thesis shattered, he left my office. Ten seconds later, there was a knock on the door. It was Bodders. 'I've remembered, sir!' he exclaimed. I was triumphant.

Soldiers 3 and 4 were next to be interviewed by the RUC. I confronted them. 'Look, I'm not Detective Major Chapman, but I know that you've all been lying through your teeth; now get in there and tell the truth.' They reluctantly acknowledged that they both knew the meaning of ABC, but gave no further truths away.

The interviews concluded. I returned to my office, got all four soldiers in again, and then saw them individually. I really was Detective Major Chapman. One of the things about soldiers is

NOTES FROM A SMALL MILITARY

that if they are going to lie, they need to think through all their responses, and this rarely happens. The more who are involved in an incident, the easier it is generally to get to the truth. So it transpired on this occasion. Once I had cracked the case, I went back down sheepishly to the RUC station attached to our offices and said, 'Look, I know this is technically illegal, but can we start again, and this time the guys will tell you the truth?' They did and the denouement was that the young flasher (who was only 5ft 6in, while the other three patrol members were well over 6ft, although I cannot comment on other parts of their anatomy) was fined £200 under some obscure vagrancy act for exposing his person.

Bodders had been the key to unlocking the problem of the ABC. Fortunately, Bodders served in the era of branch and future internet banking. He, as all soldiers did by the 1990s, possessed a bank account. It was fortunate that he had not joined 10 years previously as this was the era of the 'cash paid' soldier. Cash paid soldiers were simple beasts: if they ran out of money at the end of the second week of the month, they always had a tried and tested alternative option: they would do a deal with someone who had been nominated for a weekend guard duty. The nominated guard (who wanted to go home to see his girlfriend) would 'buy' his freedom and his formerly broke colleague would 'stag on' in his place with an additional £40 or £60 to get him through to the next pay day.

Cash paid soldiers were a dream – they did not have as many credit problems as those who were paid through the bank. The arrival of banking suffrage did cause the army a few problems. It took a process of education to get some soldiers to under-stand this:

'Do you realise that you have bounced a cheque made out to the Regimental Paymaster which is a chargeable offence?'

'No.'

'Why not?'

'I can't have bounced a cheque 'cos I've still got cheques in my book.'

But soldiers did not worry unduly about bounced cheques – particularly if they were close to going on operations overseas, or were serving in Northern Ireland. They still do not. There were many who were killed in action or died by other causes who quietly chuckled as a battalion Paymaster managed to get a bank to write off their credit card and other debts. They may not have cheated death, but somewhere they believed they had cheated the system and had profited from doing so. It is the same reason they pile their plates with food when it is free. Soldiers might leave huge portions of their plated food to go in the swill – but they believe they have got one over the system. With increasingly commercial practices and the introduction of 'Pay as You Dine' into the forces, there is now less food waste – soldiers have to pay to pile food on their plates; the system always eventually wins.

The youngest and newest infantry soldiers are now trained at Catterick. In 2013, I was in the very large office of Major Stuart Morgan, and enquired why his office was so large. He told me that it was to deal with the stream of disciplinary cases that came from converting civilian recruits into soldiers. I was mildly surprised – but probably should not have been – to learn that the majority of the cases were debt-related. My disturbance switched to a more heartening outlook: these soon-to-be-fine-young-men often take on the debt burdens of their dysfunctional families. They may want to get away and make a break, but they also want to help. Their loyalty to their families will translate into a powerful loyalty to their fellow soldiers.

The ABC incident took place while D Company, 2 PARA, were stationed for six weeks at Woodbourne in West Belfast. The company was forward deployed from our two-year residential base of Palace Barracks in Holywood near Belfast Loch. Every base in Northern Ireland was known by a trigram. Palace Barracks was known as PBK, Woodbourne was WDN, while other famous bases included Forkhill (FKL) and Bessbrook (BBK) in South Armagh and the most infamous of all – Crossmaglen (XMG).

XMG was the base that suffered the most attacks, either directly or in the surrounding area. It was out of Crossmaglen that various myths about an IRA sniper grew in the 1990s. Over a 15-month period between August 1992 and December 1993, six soldiers and three members of the RUC were killed in the bandit country of South Armagh or Fermanagh by the so-called sniper. While the reality was slightly more prosaic – there were probably two active IRA Active Service Units (ASUs) and most engagements were from the back of a specially modified vehicle with engagement ranges of 200 to 300 metres – the psychological impact upon the soldiers, whether it was regarded as sniping or not, was great.

D Company were directed to go to the Crossmaglen area in June 1994 to help patrol and hold the ground while the base was being rebuilt. One of the sections of troops under Corporal 'Moose' Miller had a fixed post placed on the ground on the Concession Road. There were six roads that emanated from the village of Crossmaglen, and just about all of them had been used at one time or another to mount attacks – be it shooting, mortar attacks or the Mark 10 Mortar, more ominously known by the IRA as the 'Barrack Buster'. A Mark 10 mortar had killed nine RUC policemen when it hit Newry police station during my first Northern Ireland tour in South Armagh in 1984 – 1985.

The commanding officer (CO) of the unit we were attached to at the time – the King's Own Scottish Borderers – decided to visit the troops. He came across Corporal Moose Miller in his post and asked him what he was up to. Moose replied that he was observing his arcs and that if any terrorist came up the road he was going to get a face-full of 200 rounds of 7.62 lead as his first action from the beloved General Purpose Machine Gun. Moose would then follow that by using applied force!

I do not believe that CO ever came near Moose again. He was too terrified. Moose later became a sniper himself, and he loved the discipline of the art of sniping. During a deployment to Macedonia we knew there were potentially opposition snipers on a hill. It was not our job to confront them, as we were in the country to cement the Lake Ohrid peace agreement, and not to start a shooting match. To ensure that we focused on the job in hand, I therefore drew a 'No Fire Line/No Forward Movement' line on a map during an operation near Radusa. No one was authorised to fire over, or move forward of that line. Moose wanted to know how thick the pencil line was so that he could go as far forward to acquire a potential enemy sniper. Whereas I saw the line as a fine 2H, his eyes interpreted it as a 6B. This soldierly interpretation of a 1:50,000 scaled map would enable him to get about 100 metres closer than I might have anticipated. He was never authorised to fire but he did produce some high quality video of his cross hairs on the head of the opposition sniper, just to let me know that he could.

Moose Miller is a metaphor for why commanders generally love their soldiers. You never had to push Moose or any of his men forward. You often had to try to hold them back. He, and many of his ilk, completed 22 years in the army and served multiple tours in Northern Ireland, Iraq, and Afghanistan (as well as, in his case, Sierra Leone, Macedonia and Bosnia). They did this uncomplainingly, with great humour, under often-intense psychological stress. Men went out – and still do – in all these theatres of operations day after day without thought for their own safety, while the potential to get killed was there constantly. Most of these deployments devolve to 'Corporal's Wars' – and Moose was one of the best examples of the self-discipline, restraint, humour and forbearance that the army can provide. Given the pressures and stresses of operations it is indeed a credit that in all these conflicts the army so *rarely* over-reacted.

If Moose Miller had been in the army in 1975 (he was too young) he is the type of soldier who would have gladly joined the mortar platoon of 2 PARA in campaigning in Angola in the summer of 1975. This is quite a curious thing, as the British army was not campaigning in the recently independent Angola in that year. That being the case, I can neither confirm nor deny that the mortar platoon may have gone for their summer leave for three to four weeks to Angola and by some strange unrelated circumstance ended up fighting as mercenaries for their vacation.

Moose was one of those corporals who learnt their forbearance through analogies. In my first Northern Ireland tour in the 1980s, our mission was clearly defined: it was to kill or capture terrorists. Although we never actually managed to do this from Forkhill or from Crossmaglen – and therefore presumably failed in our mission (Crossmaglen once again received its ritualistic mortaring from the IRA) – this attitude coloured our view. We were quite nasty in our attitude to the locals. This was neither a helpful or realistic approach, given that only politics can unlock the problems of insurgency – not military action, or body counts. We needed to understand the culture, not only of the terrorist but of the civilian environment in which we found ourselves.

By the time I returned to command a company 10 years later, we were far more nuanced in our understanding of the problem. This is what I told the blokes: 'Right men, we are to operate as if you were friendly little Chihuahuas. You are to be like a small fluffy dog that nestles up to the leg of its owner. But if the owner does not like you and starts to kick you, then you are to transform into a Rottweiler and bite the head off the owner. That is how we will work within the population when we patrol, and that is the attitude we will adopt until there is an occasion for you to become the national Rottweiler.' The Toms could take this on board, even if they desired to be the national Rottweiler more than the fluffy Chihuahua.

One of the ungainly young Toms was nicknamed 'big daft Dillon'. He was among a batch of young new recruits to D Company that included Private Proud, Private Hulme and Private Mason. One normal patrol in West Belfast was nearing the Poleglass Roundabout (an infamous place where the IRA would often set command-wire IEDs) when the four-man team intuitively sensed that something was not right. By dint of superb patrolling and a hard and fast follow-up, big daft Dillon and his three fellow soldiers caught an IRA member at the end of a command wire waiting to detonate a bomb that ran toward the roundabout. Ten years earlier, the terrorist might well have ended up in a body bag. Our fine young men arrested him, and he was sentenced to quite a few years in prison. It might have been the smell of the newly laid faecal material in the terrorist's trousers that led them to quickly hand the suspect over to the Royal Ulster Constabulary, or as Dillon put it in his northern brogue, ''E shit 'e-self'.

Let me introduce you to Regimental Quartermaster Sergeant Wattam, for that is who Dillon now is. He has served alongside two of the finest, most professional 22-year veterans of all the British army conflicts in Iraq, Afghanistan and elsewhere during that time – Regimental Sergeant Major Proud and CSM Hulme. I would never call Wattam 'big daft Dillon' again. These young 'boys' all had become awesome professional men; the Jesuits would have been envious of what the army system had managed to achieve.

My return to 2 PARA as commanding officer some five years after your education in the ABC alphabet and kennel-club nomenclature of the Parachute Regiment, produced another challenge of a similar hue. New recruits arriving from Catterick are normally assigned directly to a rifle company. After a period of time they may be asked to 'volunteer' to fill the vacancies amongst the heavy weapons platoons of Support Company. Few volunteer willingly. They are then 'pressed'. During the European championships of 2000, a clutch of new recruits to the battalion were assigned directly to the medium machine gun (MMG) platoon. My logic was faultless: if they could be integrated early in a support weapon platoon, we would not have to undergo the turbulence that occurs when these platoons need more manpower, for one thing that the men do not like is turbulence. Once they have formed their bond within their platoon, to break them apart is akin to ripping bits off their body. Cohesion is everything in the army. It is a force multiplier.

The new recruits in the machine gun platoon were with their

new buddies, bonding and getting cohesive in the Families Bar in Colchester. Now they probably should not have been in the said bar but we can park that transgression for the more meaningful events of that night. Fortunately, the platoon commander, an excellent young officer known as 'Tankers', was not present but his second-in-command, a colour sergeant called Rab Johnson was, along with his most aggressive section commander. Rab Johnson was not from 2 PARA. He had spent most of his career in 3 PARA and had come to us under a disciplinary cloud but the charge could not be proven. He had the nickname of 'Teflon Rab', as he was one of those guys to whom shit never stuck – and so it was to prove in this case.

As happens at all these bonding occasions, there was both beer and finger food, in this case chicken wings. Things got raucous. Teflon Rab first led the men in pissing in pint pots (I'll leave it to the reader to guess the follow-on activity). Shortly after, the men were encouraged to drop their trousers, whereupon the former chicken wings (by now mere bones) and certain orifices became the party game. Perhaps unusually, only one of the new recruits complained about this behaviour.

I heard about this next day and instantly called in the Royal Military Police. Due to their workload it took the RMP two weeks to investigate. In the meantime, the new bloods of the MMG Platoon had been away to the Sennybridge Training area in Brecon with the rest of the platoon, conducting live firing. They returned as everything you wanted about a platoon. They were a band of brothers, they were cohesive, and they were bonded. They were not about to squeal. Apparently, there never was an incident at the Families Bar.

Teflon Rab did not ultimately live up to his moniker, for on completion of his 22 years of army service he followed the golden path towards big bucks by being a private security contractor in Iraq following the 2003 invasion. I am sad to say that he was killed when a vehicle in which he was travelling was destroyed in an IED strike.

The army does not tolerate any of the aforementioned behaviour. I certainly did not. In any transformational or change programme, three things have historically been altered: the organisation, the processes and the culture. The armed forces have been good at changing organisation, less good at changing processes, and worst at changing culture – and the biggest impact is in changing culture.

All these incidents are balanced by other more humbling incidents. The bomb disposal expert who was blown up in Northern Ireland is an example. While defusing a bomb, the device detonated prematurely. He saw what looked like red spaghetti over his visor – it was the pulp of his arm. He passed out. He woke up in hospital with what looked like a tent-like structure over his right-hand side. A doctor came in and was quizzed by the patient as to whether he had lost his arm: the doctor replied cagily and negatively. The EOD expert pushed further.

'Come on Doc, I can handle it. I've lost my arm, haven't I?'

This time the doctor concurred. 'Yes, I'm afraid you have.'

The EOD expert pondered for a moment. 'I don't suppose you want to buy a set of golf clubs?'

It is little wonder that men with fortitude such as this are used to help other soldiers who have lost limbs in combat come to terms with their loss.

The recruitment process for soldiers grades them against a mental aptitude score. It is known as the General Trainability Index (or GTI) rating. The greater the GTI rating the more likely one is to be encouraged to join a technical corps to fully utilise the brainpower identified. Soldiers never cease to amaze with their approach to problem solving. The story of a Yorkshire Regiment soldier in Afghanistan illustrates this point. This soldier was asked to provide a passport photo. He did not have a passport photo to hand so used the unusual approach of cutting out his photo from his passport in order to provide a passport photo. I believe he would score highly for initiative, but lower on the GTI rating.

In the Parachute Regiment this can be variable. There is an attraction to an elite unit that spans all educational and social abilities (a university graduate from my own *Alma Mater* joined the Parachute Regiment as a private soldier in 1980 – he was later killed in a parachuting accident). One soldier who was nearer the bottom was Private Spender. Now I liked Spender – he had lots of good qualities and honesty and integrity were among these. What was absent was driving ability and decision-making. For a short period he was my driver. I had to send him back whence he came (the motor transport platoon – isn't it curious that we still refer to our fleet of vehicles by this anachronistic term?) because he was a danger to me and, more particularly, my wife. Driving to church services for official ceremonies in Colchester and its surrounding villages should not be like the Indianapolis 1,000 race with its attendant crashes. It was almost as if he were determined to combine a Sunday thanksgiving service with a funeral – ours.

So Spender resigned himself to driving, once again, a four-ton truck. Shortly after this enforced change, the battalion was due to move en masse to conduct training for a Northern Ireland tour. This entailed leaving our barracks in Colchester and driving to the Kent coast. Drivers in the army are issued with route cards (this was before the days of Global Positioning Systems). The example below would have been an abridged version of the real route that Spender should have taken:

Take the A12 from Colchester
Exit at Junction 11 on to the M25
At Junction 3 exit on to the M20 etc... etc... until you arrive at Hythe, Kent
Total Distance: 106 miles (one hour, 59 minutes)

This is the route and directions that Spender worked to:

Take the A12 from Colchester
Exit at Junction 11 on to the M25
At Junction 3, inexplicably miss the turn-off and drive the entire 115 miles around the M25 until you come to Junction 3 again.
Now exit Junction 3 on to the M20 and arrive very late at Hythe
Total Distance: 221 miles (four hours, 12 minutes)

Having men like Spender is probably one of the reasons why we like to drive from point A to point B in convoys. Spender wanted to be a traffic cop when he left the army.

All the services have men like Spender. The Royal Naval equivalent is Rating Rumkins – a decent fellow but like Winnie the Pooh, a bear of little brain. Rumkins is distinctive for having a prominent burn mark on his chest. It is almost triangular, with a shorter burn mark on the horizontal edge. It is not absolutely triangular, for at its top end it curves neatly inwards on both sides. Rating Rumkins is the man who attempted to iron his pristine but creased white shirt while he was wearing it and while the electricity was definitely on. Rumkins is another of those service personnel for whom the term 'mission command' and the use of their own initiative is not applicable. He is one of those who need to be given literal instructions, such as 'Iron your shirt once you have placed it on the ironing board, having checked that you are not wearing it.'

CHAPTER 5

FOLLOWING THE FLAG: WIVES, GIRLFRIENDS AND HANGERS-ON

Life is tough for army wives. They contend with the constant upheaval of moving. They even have to contend, sometimes, with being in what they perceive as a war zone. There really were a number of wives who accompanied their husbands on two-year tours of Northern Ireland during The Troubles and were too terrified to leave the barracks. Their husbands might be away for extended periods, and they had to do business with housing staff that might have been trained at concentration camps.

In case you think I exaggerate, the wife of one of the officers working for me in Tampa, Florida in 2011, was moving from her married quarter to Arborfield, Berkshire in June that year (he was due back in England in a matter of weeks). She arrived at the time of the handover to be told that she wouldn't be allowed to move because her husband had to be there in person. Now, call me a traditionalist but Tampa, Florida is a heck of a long way from Arborfield, Berkshire. Refugees often seem to have more status and rights than army wives. The days of 'wife of' still prevail in some quarters (no pun intended).

Here is the sequence of moves that my own bride had to endure: Warminster, Tern Hill (Shropshire), Petawawa (Canada), Camberley (Surrey), Aldershot (Hampshire), Holywood (Northern Ireland), Aldershot, Camberley, Lisburn (Northern Ireland), Aldershot, Colchester (Essex), Notting Hill (London), Catterick (North Yorkshire), Lisburn, Shaston (while I was living in Vauxhall, London, near my gay friends of the Royal Vauxhall Tavern – refer back to chapter one!), and Tampa (USA). This can get too much for some wives, who often demand that their husbands leave the army. Here is how the equation works:

Officer's wife demands husband leaves the army = husband leaves the army.

Soldier's wife demands husband leaves the army = soldier leaves the wife.

Some soldiers get commissioned from the ranks and therefore become officers. They will then fall in to my first category rather than my second. The categories may have become a little blurred in the last few years, given how active the army has been. RSM Gordon Muirhead, who we will encounter in my ramblings on discipline, very kindly wrote me a letter a few years after he had been commissioned telling me that he was sorry, but he thought it was time to leave and seek his fortune in the Middle East. He had spent seven of his last eight Christmases abroad on active service.

My sequence of moves was not atypical of army life. Things are changing, and there is a plan to increase stability for family life under the 'home basing' policy: units and formations will now serve longer periods of time at one location. I welcome this. Given that the government have not invested in the army accommodation for the last four years, soldiers, married ones in particular, will get the opportunity to have stability in deteriorating housing. The 'housing stock' is now owned by a Japanese investment bank.

There are two exceptions to my above rule for soldiers. The first is that my tours in Northern Ireland (where six 'residential' British battalions completed two-year tours) also gave the soldiers time to find, date, get engaged and marry a local girl. What the soldiers did not contemplate was that Northern Irish women do not travel well. Leaving the bosom of their kinfolk to travel to Great Britain did not seem to factor in to their spouse's decision-making. The record for realisation of this was one week: the wife of Private Robden of D Company 2 PARA ran off with another man while they were on their honeymoon in Ibiza.

So, the Northern Irish exception is: Soldier posted from Northern Ireland = wife leaves soldier where wife moves to GB, divorce occurs very quickly and ex-wife moves back to Northern Ireland.

I often wished that the wives of the Toms had heard the lecture I attended in 1977 ('Fanny Kemble – Actress and Friend') by the noted historian of the 18th century, Dorothy Marshall. If they had, they would have learnt never to marry anyone for their virtues, but for their faults. You become tired of your partner's virtues, but if you can put up with their faults, then you will have a successful marriage.

I have already recounted that some wives did not leave the barracks in Northern Ireland. During the Marching Season, when the Orangemen of Ulster put on their bowler hats and with fife and drum march and parade all over NI (there are hundreds of marches of which only a small number are contentious and possibly violent), there were good reasons not to leave the barracks. The 1990s provided some of the most violent episodes in both Belfast and Drumcree.

In 1999 my wife had a choice – remain 'locked down' behind the wire of the barracks in Lisburn for seven weeks while the turmoil played out its merry way, or take the children to visit and stay with her parents for seven weeks. Geinor's parents were living in the Seychelles at the time. Now you might have thought that my loving wife would have wanted to stay to give me moral support in Northern Ireland. She chose to go to the Seychelles.

The second exception to my first rule is those soldiers who meet young women while on six to eight-week exercises in exotic places of the world. The Parachute Regiment used to exercise frequently in and around Fort Lewis on the west coast of America. It is very close to Seattle, and Washington state is a very picturesque part of America and close to the marvellous Canadian province of British Columbia. It is stunning. One of the soldiers met a young lady on day one of Exercise Trumpet Dance and by day 48, when the Brits were due to return home, they were smitten. The engagement was announced with the usual dazzling zircon ring.

Our loving couple then got married. Unfortunately, the wife moved to Aldershot to what could only be described as a tenement block akin to something in the infamous Gorbals area of Glasgow in days gone by. This block was famous to all: Wilhems Park. The combination of Wilhems Park and the American wife's expectation that somebody would pack her produce into bags at the end of a food shopping trip (she used to wait hours), finally made her snap. So, our second exception is that soldiers who marry Americans are always enticed back to America when their wives have had enough:

Soldier marries American after whirlwind romance = American wife (invariably called Sherrie Beth) gets fed up of UK weather and life. Soldier agrees and remains happily married by legally gaining entry to America through his betrothal. They live happily ever after. Soldier becomes an American citizen.

I am pleased to report that Wilhems Park has since been demolished and a Tesco store built in its place. They have glamorous celebrity magazines placed near the tills (as they do in America). They will even pack your bags. The cultural differences between British and American magazines once foxed my mother. She was of the school who, when I was a child, read *Woman's Own*, *Women's Weekly* and *Woman's Realm*. I used to peruse these on a Friday when they were delivered. They were full of knitting patterns, stories on royalty, and instructions on how to bake a cake. My mother was therefore delighted to find *Women's Own* on a newspaper stand during a trip to America. She duly bought it and was quite wide-eyed with surprise at the articles. It was a magazine for lesbians.

Most soldiers settle down and have generally met their soul mate by the time of their third marriage. This is generally via a shared interest. I was thus delighted to find that Sergeant Bob Hilton had found true love on a Second World War battlefield tour while telling an assembled group of the daring deeds of long ago. His first two wives had left him: his third shares his love of the history. He celebrated his honeymoon at Arnhem.

Romance and reality in marrying someone in the army are

two different concepts. One of my fellow officers, Captain James Dalton, was a hunky 6ft 4in paratrooper who subsequently went to the SAS. He met a beautiful young woman who was a top model. She liked the idea of having an all-action war hero on her arm, and he liked the idea of having a top model with very long legs on his arm. I know she had long legs, for at their wedding they were on display more than any other asset. Her dress just covered the essentials of decency. Partying at Stringfellows nightclub in London (her former passion) and married life in the garrison town of Aldershot were not a mix that was likely to succeed in the long term. In fact, it didn't succeed even in the short term. They were quickly divorced.

I am happy to report that I am still married after 28 years. That is not to say that the lovely Geinor (an unusual Welsh spelling and an unfortunate name for young medical and dental receptionists who, perplexed at how to pronounce it, revert most often to 'Mrs Chapman') has not learnt her lesson. She married for love; the second time around she threatens to marry for money. So, if there is a very rich older man who is looking for the girl who graced the 90th anniversary edition of *Country Life* in 1986 as the 'girl in pearls', and because of this featured in the Sunday *Observer* where she was described as 'a modern girl… she has even heard of Aids' – I know just the beauty.

Indeed, there has been a bit of an older-men-fancying-my-wife syndrome throughout our marriage. Within six months of getting married I was posted to Belize. My lovely young bride, far too young to waste away the six months in Warminster, managed to get herself to Jamaica to stay with neighbours who lived between both countries. On one occasion, the former Attorney General of Jamaica took her to a film premiere. The

Attorney General was a delightful and charming man who had been highly decorated in the Second World War while serving as a Spitfire pilot in the RAF.

After the premiere, the innocent Geinor went back alone to the Attorney's house for champagne. Being young and trusting, she thought nothing of it when he put on his Ella Fitzgerald record and asked her for a dance. This was swiftly followed by a tongue 48 years older than my wife's attempting to insert itself into her mouth. Her nanny training now kicked in as she chided him with, 'You're being a little bit naughty and I think it is time to take me home' – which our double Distinguished Flying Cross hero duly did.

My three years of separation from Geinor in Vauxhall did have its consequences. Jenny Jones was a particularly interesting civil servant who worked for me at the time. She had the physique of Jessica Rabbit (she frequently came to work with bandages around her ankle from falling from her stiletto heels) and the 1950s dress style of Sandra Dee. One day I noticed a floral dress that had not caught my eye before.

'Jenny, is that a new dress you're wearing?'

'Yes it is, Chip. Thank you for noticing.'

I went home for the weekend on the train and related my triumph of observation to Geinor. 'What dress was I wearing when we went out last weekend?' she quizzed me. I had no idea. I left for work early on Monday after a weekend of very few words and what is often referred to in the army as a 'deaf and dumb breakfast'.

I first met Geinor in 1984 in Aldershot. On one of our early dates I decided to take her to the cinema in Aldershot. We arrived about an hour too early for the screening of *Police*

Academy (this was before we got through the unfunny sequence that ended with *Police Academy 78*). To fill the time before watching Steve Guttenberg and Bubba Smith rise to their moment of cinematic greatness, I escorted her to the Queens pub for a drink. Corporal Foulkes was in residence, drinking a pint of lager. He had recently had a bad parachuting accident that meant a rod had to be inserted into an upper leg. I inquired how he was recovering. 'Well,' he said, 'do you want to see my scar?' I nodded. He dropped his trousers to reveal a 10-inch scar. He was not wearing any underwear so he also revealed a lot more to my young innocent girlfriend. Despite this, she forgave me for taking her to see *Police Academy*.

The astute reader will notice a bit of a pattern to my postings. There was also a pattern to civilian friends' reactions, too.

'We're posted to Holywood.'

'Wow, you're going to California.'

'No, we're going to Northern Ireland.'

And, 'We're posted to Lisburn.'

'Wow, you're going to Portugal?'

'No, we're going to Northern Ireland.'

It will be no surprise that we had many visitors on our postings to Canada and Tampa, Florida and very few in Northern Ireland.

Despite her many years of 'following the flag', there is still a wonderful naiveté in Geinor's understanding of service life, such as, 'If you have Rear Admirals in the navy, why do you not have Front Admirals?' She once won a shooting competition at the barracks in NI (itself a source of discomfort, for she was an officer's wife, and the soldiers' wives resented this). Her winning shield is very proudly displayed on the wall of the downstairs loo. The army rifle has two settings; it can fire single shot or on automatic. Geinor was not sure which she had been using. 'I don't know if I was firing "machine" or "plain",' she confided after her winning performance. As she had broken every rule of marksmanship by closing her eyes as she squeezed the trigger for each round, I can believe it.

My children always got into the swing of things when we were about to be posted (again) to Northern Ireland. Rosie was 10 and was reading a story in the *Daily Telegraph* about Sinn Féin. She had already lived in Northern Ireland once before. 'I can't quite remember who these people Sin Fin are,' she said. Tom (then a wise 7) came back: 'They're not called Sin Fin; they're called the Provisional RAF.' This perceptive young man will go far. He looks at problems through a different lens – a child's lens. Here is another example. I'd had a hard day at work and to relax I put a Beethoven symphony on the turntable (for younger readers this was also known as a 'record player': I know you might be confused as one of Rosie's friends once told me she had never seen a CD that big before). Tom had been doing music appreciation that week at school: every seven-year-old does *Peter and the Wolf*. He listened intently.

'I like this music,' he said, looking up from drawing the two things he loved to draw – cowboy scenes or building sites. He was ecstatic when he learned that you could combine the two, for he had recently discovered something called 'cowboy builders'. He thought that was great.

'It's Beethoven,' I informed him, and then with a pause to enable him to savour the bars of sweet music added, 'It's Beethoven's Ninth.'

He pondered. 'I like Beethoven. He's a dog, isn't he?'

Rosie became part of the story again in 2000 after 2 PARA had just moved lock, stock and barrel from Aldershot to

Colchester, leaving 50 years of history and broken hearts behind. The battalion was on leave when 1 PARA were warned off for operations in Sierra Leone to prevent a rebel advance. Our sister battalion had a company on exercise in Jamaica at the time and so were short of a rifle company and other specialist elements. While the army quarters were at Colchester, I had just purchased a new house in Shaston and had neither a landline telephone nor mobile phone coverage – despite having a large transmitter in the town, Shaston is one of those black holes for mobile communications. Geinor and I arrived at the prep school when Rosie raced out from her class screaming, 'YOU'VE GOT TO PHONE 2 PARA – SOMETHING'S HAPPENING!' I did, and spoke to the Adjutant, Pete Flynn, who had wisely thought of a cunning way to contact me in the days of house bricks for mobile phones. Pete had been one of my platoon commanders when I commanded a company and he had been both schooled and educated in the way I thought. 'Right, boss, I've already made the following decisions and the boys are already moving.' He was correct on every count.

Pete Flynn also bought a dog around the same time. He called it 'Chip'. He worked in the office next to mine, allowing or refusing access to me. The dog came with him to work, but as I would come running every time he shouted, 'Come here Chip!' I finally had to post him to another job. I last saw Pete Flynn in television pictures. He was standing behind the Prince of Wales during the Queen's 60th anniversary celebrations on the Royal Barge. Pete is now an equerry to the heir to the throne. Chip (the dog) is probably now dead. I was looking to see if there was now a small canine nearer the ground called Charles. I could swear that I saw the Prince of Wales inadvertently turn around a couple of times.

The Americans had a similar problem with names at the Afghanistan base of Bagram. At one time there were six American naval personnel all called Bob who were resident in the same team. Wags would climb on top of a wall and put in a covert watch after shouting, 'Come here Bob!' to see who reacted. There was another common feature of the Bagram Six – they were all shaven-headed or bald. Collectively they were known as the 'Bald Bobs of Bagram'. During the Balkans campaigns of the 1990s many of the interpreters were known as BOB FOCs. This was not in honour of our aforementioned Roberts, but an acronym that stood for 'Body of *Baywatch*, Face of *Crimewatch*' as a descriptor of the Balkan female interpreters.

There are some young ladies who like men in uniform (hence websites such as uniformdating.com). One American lady certainly did, and after a night of dancing and drinking, offered to spend the night with one of the soldiers in Tacoma, Washington state. He duly paid $20 for a motel that she seemed to be familiar with, and had a night of passion. In the morning, the soldier awoke to find all his clothes were missing. His wallet with his money and credit cards was still there but his clothes were gone. Now most soldiers have heard stories of others being 'rolled' and finding that their wallet was gone in the morning, but this was a novel adjustment to the norm. The soldier was not to be discombobulated by his lack of clothes and checked out. The bill had an additional $7 for the sheet from the bed that he was wearing in the favoured toga style. He hailed a taxi. On the way back to camp, the curiosity of the taxi driver was aroused.

'Unusual dress style for six in the morning?'

'Yeah, some chick stole all my clothes last night.'

'What was her name?'

'Chrissie.'

The taxi driver conducted an immaculate hand-brake turn and took our intrepid lover to the dumpster where Chrissie was known to offload her gains. It was her calling card.

The North American continent seems to have a way of coming up with women whose knowledge of the military is even more limited than that occasionally exhibited by my wife. A perk in Canada was that we were able to get duty-free alcohol from the Liquor Control Board of Ontario. To ensure that we were not tempted to sell-on this perk and avoid the taxes, each bottle of wine was stamped 'NATO' and a record kept on a monthly basis of our purchases. At one drinks party held at the height of the Cold War in our humble Canadian abode, the girlfriend of a Canadian officer spotted the large letters stamped on the wine bottles. She politely inquired, 'What's GNAT O?' She had never heard of the collective security organisation that had kept the peace for 40 years. She was also dyslexic to the point where the five-hour drive back to her flat entailed her boyfriend showing her flash cards of what the road signs looked like en route. Most British officers' wives or girlfriends have probably been to university. I don't think I have met any yet who had been – as she had – to the McDonald's University to learn the art of burger flipping.

The great British public is a fine supporter of 'our boys', as are many of the national newspapers. On overseas tours this often leads to curious letters from home. The *Sunday Express* wrote an article on 2 PARA and published the address suggesting the female readership might wish to write to 'A Soldier in Macedonia'. Many did write – and the Toms were grateful for the kind, well-meaning words and greetings from the middle-aged readership of that publication, but wished for something a bit raunchier. Curiously, the content of the letters suddenly changed to exactly the type of letters 'our boys' desired. They were downright filthy, and full of colourful imagery of what the young females would do to our heroes when they returned home. The morale of the recipients soared – they were 'on a promise'. What they did not know at the time was that the august men of Support Company had made up these fictitious raunchy letters and infiltrated them into the theatre postal system where they would be franked and forwarded. The dream dates of our soldiers' lust – the Sharons and Kylies from the county of Lustex and elsewhere – were, in reality, male paratroopers who lived a few camp beds away.

The Macedonia operation also showed how commanders are called upon to have the Wisdom of Solomon – or at least to make what seems like the right decision. 2 PARA were largely a unit of men. Seven hundred personnel had deployed; we had six female soldiers. They were either clerks or chefs. A curious fact, reported at the 5 September 2001 brigade orders group we attended as a subordinate unit, was that 30,000 condoms had been shipped to Macedonia for the use of British forces. I was perplexed. We represented 35 per cent of the British force and had six female soldiers: they and the locals were 'out of bounds'. I wondered who came up with these logistic requests and the scaling per-soldier at our higher headquarters, for we most certainly had no 'input' into the decision.

I also worried that the padre had sown discord in the minds of our soldiers as to what their lonely wives (or girlfriends) might be up to in England. Padre Steele, highly regarded by the soldiers due to his tracking skills learnt from his youth in

Zimbabwe, took as one of his sermons the text from the Old Testament book of Two Samuel, Chapter 11. I am not a biblical scholar in the slightest, but basically the whole of the Israelite army were away campaigning while King David stayed at home. He spied Bathsheba, fancied her and slept with her. She conceived. King David, seeing he had a problem, told his commander to place Uriah the Hittite (Bathsheba's husband) at the point of the next fiercest battle. He did and Uriah was killed. Problem solved. The chapter concludes 'But the thing David had done had displeased the LORD.' I think our Toms could relate to that. I had no idea what the true message was supposed to be.

Our gallant padre tried again at his next field service. This time he took a more reflective sermon from Ecclesiastes: 'A time to be born, a time to die, a time for peace, and a time for war.' It was five days after 9/11. This time he was spot-on. Two months later, 2 PARA would be the first regular unit into Afghanistan.

We had been told that Support Company, the rogues of the battalion, would be represented at the church service by the mortar platoon – the rogues within the rogues. So I was surprised to see a different platoon turn up: the anti-tank platoon. The explanation was simple: the company had collectively decided that the mortar platoon was beyond redemption. Most of the soldiers knew the intent of the sermon from The Byrds' 1965 hit that had used the lament as its lyrics. Padre Steele was an excellent padre. I don't believe the previous padre, who had arrived from another unit, really understood paratroopers and their wives: he wanted to introduce weekly bingo at 1000 hours in the wives club. He did not last long.

Fortunately, there was to be a distraction for the men of the battalion while they were away. England were about to play Germany at football. The result would be one of those few feel-good times that you get from watching England: it was when Michael Owen knocked in a hat-trick for a historic 5–1 victory. But to be able to watch the match we needed a television for the 500 men who resided in one of our two sheds. Sky TV provided a 23-inch version for the noble 500 at the former peanut factory about a week before the match. The men showed their normal low cunning by managing to tap in to a German channel that showed, shall we say, *very* adult entertainment. One of our soldiers complained. I marginally resolved the tyranny of the majority by allowing the 500 to watch their adult channel for one hour a day while the objecting clerk completed a fitness session elsewhere. At the other end of the clerical interest sat Corporal McGowan. She *was* interested: so much so that she purchased six Albanian pornographic movies with the justification that, 'My boyfriend will never forgive me if I don't at that price' (10 Deutschmarks a disc). I have yet to fully resolve the Solomon dilemma of 'what a man (or woman) does in the privacy of a 500-man room is up to him (or her)'.

In a curious twist, and to show the complexities of working in a coalition, the follow-on NATO mission from the Macedonia operation was to have been called Operation Amber Fox – until the French complained that this was the same name as a pornographic website. I had no idea how they knew.

The female clerks and female chefs overtly disliked each other. The chefs disliked the clerks on the basis that the catering platoon had to work up to 16 hours a day, while the clerks swanned around under the protective wing of their company sergeant majors. The clerks were perceived as doing little work, while the chefs worked their socks off – day in, day out without a break. Chefs are always unsung heroes (such as the deliciously named Corporal Onions who had served with me in Northern Ireland). They worked so hard in appalling heat that we decided to give them a day off. The remainder of the battalion reverted to 24-hour ration packs and the Master Chef, WO2 Rigby, produced this superb menu, which illustrates the cohesion of the chefs – regardless of gender – and their dislike of the clerks:

Vanessa & Shez Fishy Knicker COCKtail
(freshly defrosted Skopje prawns in Belgrano sauce)

Fillet Steak Randy Style
(thick chunk of meat served with sauce & shit)
Or
Chicken a la Sonia
(small breasts of chicken not kept on the stove for too long without medical assistance)

Elliot Potatoes
(thick slices served whenever **HE** decides)

Del Potatoes
(right mature spuds scalped on top)

Medley of Chefs
(a right assortment of vegetables)

Clerk Sauce
(thin and weak and no alcohol involved)

Adam and Bruce's Sweaty Boxer Shorts and Crumbs
(finest mature cheese board available in the FYROM)

I have not mentioned mothers. Most soldiers are very young. Before a policy change in the mid-1980s, soldiers could go to war at the age of 17. Private Jason Burt and Private Ian Scrivens, both of 3 Para were killed on Mount Longdon at the age of 17. Their friend, and comrade, Private Neil Grose was killed close by as he celebrated his 18th birthday. Soldiers cannot now go to war until they are 18.

Young soldiers are more likely to receive mail (even if it is electronic rather than physical) from their mothers rather than a girlfriend. It is mothers who constantly write one of the most meaningless (but well-meant) phrases in letters. It is 'keep your head down'. We do, or we try to. Soldiers' mates from home will also tell them to keep their heads down, but this is always followed by '…and we'll have a mega-piss up when you return.' Other meaningless battlefield phrases include, 'Put some f***ing fire down.' We will if we can see the enemy. This is generally followed by 'Get f****ing moving.' We will if it won't kill us instantly.

There is a fine line between courage and suicide. This is best described by remarks made about Captain Charles Upham, a New Zealand double winner of the Victoria Cross in the Second World War: 'Some are under the impression that he was foolhardy and reckless… (but) there was method and cool reasoning in all his actions; he summed up the situation quickly, and his courage and determination ensured success. He never took useless risks and seemed to know just how much he could accomplish.[7]'

Every outer office of senior military or civilian personnel is filled with a variety of personal assistants (PAs). I was fortunate to once have a very hard-working and clever PA called Chardonnay (who you will encounter again later on). Now Chardonnay was more ladette than lady. Indeed, we were quite keen to sponsor her to go on to the television show of that name to transform her rougher edges. By the time she left my tender care she had become wiser and more mature – she had even had the foresight to purchase her own house and to get more money in rent than she was paying for the mortgage. Corporal Chardonnay (for she was in the army) had had a chequered career. She had been up before a court martial as a private and had done time in Colchester prison for taking exception to a young female service member giving her some lip when asked to do her 'room jobs' (the tasks required to maintain a clean and orderly environment in the accommodation). There was a certain amount of violence, and the climax involved a head and a flushing toilet. This had been the making of Chardonnay and followed another incident when she had been arrested by the police in South Wales for squatting on the bonnet of a police car and peeing all over the paint scheme after a drunken Saturday night in Swansea. After a period in the military corrective training centre (jail, or glass house in army slang) she was a reformed and upwardly mobile character.

I liked Chardonnay a lot: she was both very funny and very efficient. One morning, as my time was more precious than hers, I asked her to go to my MoD-provided London flat to let in a repairman to fix the broken boiler. She duly obliged. What I had forgotten to tell her was that my wife was coming to visit. As my wife entered the flat with a curious gaze, Chardonnay screamed, 'WHAT ARE YOU DOING HERE, BITCH? I'M

HIS MISTRESS.' In fact, she did not say this, for by this time in our professional relationship she was on the road to becoming a lady – but she confessed to me that she had *wanted* to say those words. Oh and by the way, she was not my mistress! The last I heard of Chardonnay she had made enough money from her rent to have a 'boob job' – in itself a curious wish, given that she was already on the generous side of ample.

The army consists of young people. They have young wives. This means that each married quarters patch is full of pregnant women, or women with babies and young children. If you cannot abide children, do not venture anywhere near an army married quarters area. It also means many trips to see paediatricians, midwives or gynaecologists. One young wife visiting a gynaecologist needed to visit the loo prior to her appointment. She did so and as (I am told) so often happens in ladies loos, there was no toilet paper. Being ladylike, she had a packet of tissues in her handbag, and therefore used her soft Kleenex in place of the absent toilet tissue. Her appointment time arrived, and she duly disrobed and lay upon the table. A curious doctor looked slightly bemused. He reached for a pair of tweezers. The young wife lost sight of the tweezers as her head was too low to see what was occurring between her legs. The doctor took the tweezers to the bin, when he had to leave the room for a minute, our young wife's curiosity got the better of her. She peered into the bin and there, by itself in the freshly lined waste paper bin, was a postage stamp.

I returned to England from Tampa in late 2012 thinking that the stories from my Florida days were over. Within a week, the headline broke: 'General Petraeus resigns from CIA over affair scandal.' My wife and I turned to each other and said simultaneously: 'I bet there is a Susan Watson angle here.' And indeed there was. Susan Watson is one of those Florida socialites who love rank – the higher, the better. She also loves herself. Here is a real email sent in reply to the standing monthly invitation to the coalition wives coffee morning:

From: Susan G Watson [email address removed for privacy reasons]
Date: 10 April 2011 04:32:56 GMT
To: Chairman of the Wives Coalition Coffee Club
CC: [A list of 70 women, which grew rapidly as it was forwarded in viral proportions]
Subject: Coalition Wives Coffee Morning

I'm sorry I missed the lovely coffee.

My husband, Dr Watson, and I, are in the Middle East where he is teaching the surgeons here how to do large complicated surgeries in which they are not skilled enough to do (my husband invented a lifesaving surgery and teaches it to doctors around the world).

Following our visit to Kuwait, Abu-Dhabi and Saudi Arabia, we will be returning to Washington DC on 3/16 where Commander General David Petraeus will be honouring us at our Nation's Capital on Friday 3/18.

I miss everyone and hope to see you all when I return back to Tampa and Thank You for your support to the USA!

Sincerely
Susan

Had she followed British protocol, she needed only to write: 'Mrs Susan G Watson thanks the wives of the coalition for their kind invitation to the coalition coffee morning but regrets that due to prior commitments she is unable to attend.' It would have saved a lot of wives from reaching for the 'forward' key on their computers in Tampa.

Susan did indeed come back to Tampa from Washington. The next time I saw her she proudly showed me the photos on her smart phone.

'This is me with General David Petraeus; this is me with the Pope.' (In the interests of avoiding a crisis in the Roman Catholic Church, it would be prudent to mention that this was a picture from Rome where Mrs Watson was demurely dressed in black with a mantilla covering her head. She was among a cast of thousands in a basilica rather than in an intimate setting with El Papa.) 'This is me with General David Petraeus and the Queen,' she continued, but then admitted that General Petraeus had, for some unknown reason, photoshopped her into the photo.

I had had enough: 'Susan, do you know that one of the things the Queen and I cannot stand is name-droppers?'

I am happy to report that the American understanding of irony was again as vague as it ever was, as Mrs Watson wound her merry way with her smartphone to the next more-senior-than-me individual she could find to ensnare.

---

[7]From: *The Mark of the Lion*, Kenneth Sandford, Hutchinson, 1962, p104. I was given this book by the fine New Zealand officer, Colonel J G Howard.

CHAPTER 6
NICKNAMES

The army thrives on nicknames. One padre whose Christian name was Derek instantly became 'Derek the Cleric'. A fellow platoon commander called Geoff Weighell (pronounced as per the large sea mammal) became known as 'Sperm', and another whose youthful enthusiasm and energy made him seem like an overactive puppy with four balls became 'Puppy Dog' (as his career progressed this was shortened to the crisper 'Dog').

A further youthful and enthusiastic platoon commander became the 'Boy Wonder' after practising platoon attacks drills on a Norfolk football field on a -5C morning in February, while the remainder of the platoon commanders huddled in our corrugated-iron Nissan huts shivering as we had failed to get the Stalag 15 stove to work. These youthful and enthusiastic platoon commanders were always the ones who joined straight from school. Thankfully we do not have many of those any more: it is quicker to drain enthusiasm when you have cynical graduates. In fact, the 'Boy Wonder' was Chris Waddington: the youngest platoon commander in the Falklands, aged 19, and very brave he was too.

I recently heard of a cavalry officer called 'Bafi' Blair. Apparently this stands for 'B——'s a f***ing idiot' and has something to do with a British prime minister. There have been a number of prime ministers whose surname has started with the letter 'B', including Baldwin, Balfour and two more recent additions in the last 15 years. As a crown servant I was taught to be apolitical, so I will have to leave it to you to make up your own mind which it is – although there is a not-so-cryptic clue to help you in your deliberations.

Cavalry officers seem to have a penchant for giving each other girly nicknames. I knew a regiment that had, serving at the same time, officers called Clare, Gay, Daphne and Charlotte (actually Peter Church but nicknamed 'Charlotte' after the Welsh singer). They even had a Coward, but at least they would look smart on parade as they also had a Needle. During this period they had an air defence battery attached to them with a couple of strapping lads called Gunner Elinor and Gunner Allison. In army terms they provided 'intimate support'. (Intimate support is an official term for those elements of another unit that are attached to a larger unit.)

Even the Parachute Regiment might have been thought to have followed the Cavalry, for 2 PARA had three Camp brothers. In case you are misled, there was nothing 'camp' about them. They were among the finest and cleverest soldiers ever to have served: Tom Camp won a Military Medal for bravery at Goose Green and went on to be commissioned and rise to colonel. John Camp was also commissioned from the ranks. Young but (physically) big brother Billy completed this triumvirate of awesome brothers-in-arms.

One of my great friends as a subaltern (and now a very successful businessman) was Steve Burke. He left shortly after becoming a Major Burke, which he was not. He was known (and still is) as 'Stoney'. This was apparently after the famous (if you live in New Zealand) cowboy character from a television series. It was also because the giver-of-nicknames in 2 PARA was Stan McCord who was of Antipodean origins. I am happy to record Stan McCord's name here for two reasons. First, because I think he is the only officer from the Falklands War from 2 PARA never to have had his name in a book, and second, because he married my ex-girlfriend – the last one I had before I met Mrs C.

Stan McCord was an unusual officer. He would take off for Thailand on every leave period for a vacation, carrying a miniscule bag with one spare pair of socks, one spare pair of pants, one spare T-shirt and his toiletries. And that was it. Given that Mrs McCord may not know of the details behind his travel plans I can say no more, but perhaps the (single-man) philosophy of Stan may give you a clue: 'Marriage is good... because marriage creates widows and divorcees... and they're always good!' But he was the supreme giver of nicknames. An attached cavalry officer was called Captain Lunt. McCord employed his best Spoonerism to rename him 'Laptain'.

I also served with Richard Head. Now what Mr and Mrs Head were thinking when they were choosing names for their bouncing baby boy is beyond my powers of speculation. Richard (we shall call him that rather than the shorter version) wore his name with stoicism – until one night a comedian happened to be the entertainment at an end-of-course party. He exploited the comedic potential of R Head's name for all it was worth. Richard took umbrage with the comedian and reacted in what might be described as a 'physical manner'. *The Sun* newspaper also could see the comedic potential and poor Richard was the front-page headline the following day. It may not surprise you to learn that Richard changed his name and eventually emigrated to Australia; he likes sheep. He was an excellent officer despite his unfortunate name.

There are others whose names invite some sort of curious response. It is probably entirely appropriate that the army has an officer named Julius Caesar. There is even one for the ladies: an officer called Max Joy – I hope he lives up to what I assume is a fine reputation. It reminded me of those girls who I went to school with: they included Lee Pover (say it fast for best effect) who married a chap called John Lee and thus became Lee Lee. There were schoolgirls I thought I might make a romantic play for but never did due to my studious nature, which always left me wondering if Katherine Wood and Susan May really were the stuff of our boyhood dreams and lived up to their names. At least Lt Luckett and Lt Hiscock, who were to be joined in holy matrimony and had considered hyphenating their names, had second thoughts. It was pointed out that if you said Luckett-Hiscock even remotely fast you would forever be in the land of titillation. Any Italian speaking accented English would have had fun with that one.

I was chairman of a selection board as a senior officer at Sandhurst interviewing cadets who wished to join the Parachute Regiment when I came across Jordan Toy. The Parachute Regiment was to have its own toy. It was clear that with a name like that – I immediately had visions of a pneumatic doll named after a well-known glamour model – he either had to be very fast on his feet or a very good pugilist. He was accepted for the regiment. He was exceptional at both.

On most defence databases, it is the norm that surnames come before first names. This is definitely worth taking into account when you name your children. I have found the perfect couple: Max Joy is made for Schear, Joy. I even thought that Jordan Toy's mother was called Joy Toy, but by that stage I might have had a long day; a union between Joy, Max and Joy Toy would have been a fantasy too far. There are those who prosper because of the surname/first name order on forms. Lord, David (a subordinate of mine in the US) was forever getting upgrades from American airlines: they assumed he was part of the British aristocracy.

And then we had Private Eric Erik. Now Eric Erik was from a bohemian sort of family. When he joined the army he had only one name, Eric. The army pay and administrative system could not cope with this aberration and he had to have a surname (or Christian name – take your pick which order you want his name to come in). Now, Eric was mad. No two ways about it: he was definitely missing a few screws. I first met him in Canada, about eight days after I had taken over as CO. He instantly struck one as different. Twenty-four hours after meeting him I inquired of Jack Lemmon, the RSM, who was driving me:

'Tell me about Eric Erik.'

'Ah, I wondered how long it would take you to ask,' he replied.

And he told me the story. Erik was a mess steward (this was

before the days of 'contracterisation'). He was, in all probability, placed in his position so he could be looked after by the warrant officers and Sergeants' Mess. When I say 'looked after' this is because although there is a unique and enduring bond between the junior soldiers, they are not that good at coping with someone who does not meet their model of a paratrooper. This is shorthand for 'he might well have been picked on'. The Sergeants' Mess would ensure this did not happen. He had already been identified as being slightly unusual while he was in basic training. His corporals had fronted up to their platoon commander and stated that he had to be got rid of. The platoon commander interviewed him:

'Why do you want to be a paratrooper, Erik?'

'I want to be an all-action hero, sir!'

He was in. He was, shall we say, mercurial. He was no slouch – he could pass all his recruit tests and he was fit – but there was something nagging about him. Maybe the corporals were right. He joined the battalion in Aldershot and made a name for himself in the following incident. He was out in Aldershot at the legendary Parachute Regiment eatery known as Tony's Fish Bar. Erik knew Tony and Tony knew Erik. Erik was sixth in the queue and paid for his fish 'n' chips. Arriving at the front of the queue, he exclaimed, 'Ha-ha' and did a runner. Now many over the years have 'done a runner' from an Indian restaurant, but it is usually after they have received the goods, and certainly not after paying.

The next weekend, Erik was getting some money from the NatWest cashpoint. The money came out in crisp notes, whereupon he donned a balaclava and ran around with the money, again exclaiming 'Ha-ha!' as he brandished a toy pistol.

I knew he was going to present me with problems.

Fortunately he did not, for in December 1999 he went AWOL. He very generously left a note explaining his reasons: 'Voices in my head, can't cope any more: sorry, Erik.'

I was mildly relieved. We had no inclination to track him down and in time we could discharge him. I thought that was the last we'd heard of Eric Erik, but about 15 months later we had a call from Luton social services. A housing trust required a reference for a former soldier by the name of Eric Laithwaite. The clerical sergeant who ran the discharges of soldiers came to my office perplexed that he could find no record of a discharged soldier called Eric Laithwaite. and worried that his computerised record-keeping was not all it should be. Sergeant Admin knew that I kept encyclopaedic books of events and asked me if I recalled Private Laithwaite.

'Eric Laithwaite, Eric Laithwaite, Eric Laithwaite,' I contemplated aloud in Sergeant Admin's presence before triumphantly exclaiming, 'I know – it's Eric Erik!' It was, and a partially amused yet partially bemused conversation with a young lady from Luton social services followed recounting the legend that was Eric Erik.

2 PARA also had men whose surnames could be exploited for good comic effect. I had my own Private Vineyard. The conversation with cavalry or guards officers would go as follows: 'It's not widely known, but as the Commanding Officer of 2 PARA I have my own Private Vineyard.'

'Really? And in what part of France is your vineyard?'

'No, no – I have a guy called Vineyard, and he's a private.'

I also had my own Private Mountain, my own Private Wood and my own Private Wardrobe, but I'm sad to say that if I had had been a cavalry or guards officer I might have had my own Private Island, and I did not. After all my years of service and injury niggles, I did have two Paynes – only one of whom was (affectionately) known as 'Arse'.

In 1989, Tern Hill Barracks in Shropshire, the base for 2 PARA, was blown up by the IRA. That there were no casualties was due to the prompt actions of the prowler guard who spotted the bombers and managed to engage them – with bullets rather than polite conversation (they unfortunately missed). They managed to evacuate the sleeping soldiers prior to a huge explosion. Those soldiers owed their lives to 'Paddy' Curran and 'Taff' Norris. The Celtic fringes had saved the day. This was just as well, as 2 PARA were already the victims of the worst military atrocity of The Troubles in Northern Ireland, when 18 of their soldiers were killed at Warrenpoint. One of the wounded survivors was 'Spider' Webb.

The Tern Hill bombing was also my first flirtation with the press. I was quite pleased that a report of the incident in the *Birmingham Evening Post* described my telephone conversation as follows: 'A tight-lipped captain said, "Can't explain it really."'

Nicknames even followed people in the international arena. There were 47 coalition nations united at US Central Command at Tampa. The senior Spaniard was a brigadier by the name of Hisario. Now, Hisario had been married (and divorced) three times. He really was 'Hisario the Lothario'. He went on exotic holidays during his Tampa tenure, including the carnival in Brazil. I inquired of him what his trip had been like. 'Untellable,' he replied with a flourish. I last saw him leaving a function for the birthday of Queen Beatrix of the Netherlands with a beautiful young Cuban-American he had been dating for two months. 'She is killing me,' he confided with a wide smile. I am sure he is still very happily alive.

I was once called to the phone after one of the officers who worked for me came in to my office and stated, 'There's a guy on the phone from Germany. He says he knows you, but he says he is called "Your Sphinctum".'

I judged that this must be a hoax call and raced to the phone. 'Hello? Is that "Your Sphinctum" calling?'

'Yes, it is Jorn Finkum from the German army calling.'

A polite conversation followed. Jorn Finkum had been a contemporary at the British staff college. It was the year after the collapse of the Soviet Union. There was much excitement at the college that year over complete revision of the syllabus, with the Brits having recently adopted NATO doctrine. Considering that the British had been part of NATO for over 40 years, that was itself a testament to the army's innovation and willingness to embrace new ideas. Jorn would have approved, for such commonality would eliminate misunderstandings between nations. After all, English was the universal NATO language.

In the US, we lived next to David and Christy Mobley. Apparently Mobley is an unusual name from the southern states of America. I had not come across any Mobleys before. I don't think they had either. When the newly married Mobleys were a couple at a function in the capital of Florida – Tallahassee for those of you who like pub quizzes – the lovely Christy was *sans* her husband and was introduced to a man she had not met before:

'Hello, I'm Christy Mobley.'

'Hi, I'm Curtis Lewis Junior III. Are you married to David Mobley?'

'Yes, I am; we've only been married two months.'

'May I say that what your husband did to my wife's breasts was marvellous.'

Mrs Mobley's jaw dropped but just before she stormed away

to find the sharpest southern knife available to plunge into her husband's heart, CLJ III let it be known there was another David Mobley who also lived in Tallahassee and plied his trade as a renowned plastic surgeon.

Members of the American Air Force all have nicknames that have humorous derivations: they struggle with the derivation of UK nicknames. 'Bunny' James was an RAF group captain serving in Tampa. Bunny was not his real name. The Americans inquired as to the origin of his nickname:

'It comes from where rabbits live,' he told them.

The Americans replied, 'So your real name is rabbit hole?'

In the interests of furthering international educational standards, rabbits live in warrens – a fact the RAF were well aware of when Warren James became 'Bunny' James.

You would be surprised how many odd letters from peaceniks arrive in units when they are deployed on operations abroad. The mailroom received two letters for (the fictitious) Captain Warren Peace. I found this mildly amusing, but it was followed shortly afterwards by one to 'a soldier from Warren Slaughter'. This caused me to think it a spoof too far. But it wasn't a spoof. It wasn't even from Warren Slaughter. The handwriting was terrible but we eventually deciphered it as being from Miss Lorren Slater.

Australians have always been known as 'Diggers' and have always had a swagger about their relationship with the Brits. In the Korean War we fought together in the 1st Commonwealth Division. During the campaign, a British unit was required to conduct a 'relief in place' of an Australian unit. This manoeuvre, by which the replaced unit are sent on to other tasks or some relief from the fighting, is generally completed at night. A young British officer had gone with the advance party to conduct the liaison with the Battalion Headquarters of The Third Battalion, The Royal Australian Regiment (3 RAR). He arrived at the rear of a large defensive position.

'Could you point out the way to Battalion HQ? I've come to liaise on the relief in place.'

'Sure, Ted – just carry on down there, make a right then a left, then a right.'

He made his rights, and lefts and rights, and at each Australian position he came to, the same exchange was repeated. 'Could you point out where Battalion HQ is please? I am an officer with a map and am therefore hopelessly lost.'

'Yeah, sure Ted – just go down there make a right and you'll be there.'

He eventually arrived at Battalion HQ and gave his salutations to the commanding officer.

'I must say how helpful your men were. But they kept calling me Ted, and my name is Charles.'

'Don't worry about it, mate,' the commanding officer replied. 'It's short for "Shithead".'

There are even officers with initials that look like nicknames and thus are given their initials as nicknames, and other officers with the same name, which causes further confusion. I know at least four Andrew Jacksons in the army. Two are in the Parachute Regiment. They are separated in age and rank and so are not too much of a problem, but having two Lieutenant J Shaw's of the same age in the Parachute Regiment at the same time was more of a problem. The only separation was that Lt J A B Shaw had a nickname. Not unsurprisingly, he became known as 'Jab'. At least the Parachute Regiment had the good sense to put the two in different battalions: one in 2 PARA and the other in 3 PARA. This did not stop their mail always going to the other J Shaw. Both served as platoon commanders in the Falklands War and it was rather fortunate that neither became wounded or killed in action – the confusion in notifying the correct next of kin might well have taxed the system.

There are even officers who come with their own nickname-like name, which will of course then get slightly altered to conform to the normal pattern. One such officer was Lieutenant Fairweather, who was known as 'Zero' – the temperature at which water freezes. If he was being particularly stupid this would change to 'Sub-Zero'.

Zero was an immensely fit and strong officer (he was in the squad for a British sports team that won significant honours in the bear pit of international competition) but he was also too trusting. As a platoon commander at 'Depot Para' he was responsible for turning a platoon of day one civilians in to a platoon of week 22 paratroopers. One day his company commander, Major Snook (nicknamed 'Snook Skywalker' by Stan McCord), was coming around to inspect the accommodation (the block). Zero did not have the best of relationships with his immediate superior and asked his corporals for their help in ensuring that the block and most importantly, the ablutions area, were immaculate. He came in 30 minutes before the inspection to do his own walk around.

He looked at the sinks – they were gleaming. He looked at toilet 1 – it was smiling with cleanliness. He looked at toilet 2 – it was radiating porcelain whiteness. Then he came to toilet 3. On the loo seat sat a perfect half-inch, pellet-like turd.

'Is that a piece of shit there? Get it cleaned up!'

'Let's see,' said a corporal, dipping two fingers into the turd and bringing it to his lips to taste.

'You dirty bastard!' exclaimed Zero.

'Calm down, sir – it's only a piece of rolled Mars Bar,' replied the corporal, producing the opened wrapper as evidence.

Zero liked the denouement, and suggested that the company commander would be highly amused by the same wheeze. He would play the part of the corporal in the re-run of toilet 3. History does not record the reaction of Snook Skywalker when Zero played his part with aplomb – with the slight change of projectile vomiting as his two fingers came up to taste the 'Mars Bar'. The corporals had switched the chocolate for a real, Guinness-fuelled turd.

Many officers serving in the British army have Eastern European origins. Their names always get shortened. You will struggle to pronounce the name of Lieutenant Colonel J J P Poraj-Wilczynski, so you will breathe a sigh of relief that he was more commonly known as 'Joe the Pole'. Milos Stankovic was better known as 'Stan'. Then there are others who have equivalent complex names. One such Irishman was Joe McEnerney, known as 'Joe Three Names'. One of Joe Three-Names' friends arrived home one day to tell his wife that Joe McEnerney was coming to dinner that night, then disappeared to the pub to meet Joe. When they arrived back, three additional place settings had been prepared with the required large amount of food for the supposed three guests of Joe, Mac, and Ernie.

There is one thing worse than having a nickname, and that is having your nickname changed to a lower order and less celebrated title. This fate befell the former Mad Dog, the leader of 2 PARA Signals platoon 'away team'. Mad Dog would have his name emblazoned on the Signals platoon T-shirt for their holiday trips to Thailand, not renowned for their cultural bent. There was a defined organisation chart, and

Mad Dog's name was at the top. Everyone else, neatly arranged in a wiring diagram under him, was his subordinate. He was the Top Dog.

Mad Dog and his merry men returned from one such trip just prior to a training deployment to Canada. This included adventure training in the Rocky Mountains. One of the tasks in the extreme white-water rafting element was to jump into a foaming river (wearing a life preserver) from a 40ft cliff. It was similar to jumping out of the door of an aircraft when parachuting. Three times Mad Dog prepared to launch himself over the sheer cliff face and three times his 'bottle' failed him. Sadly, Mad Dog was now and forever 'Soft Puppy'.

Nicknames may even be bestowed late in a career, even on the most senior officers. Field marshals never retire. They are placed on 'Held Strength'. One serving field marshal is The Baron Inge. Before his elevation to the House of Lords, General Sir Peter Inge (as he then was), occupied a number of high-octane positions, which included becoming the commander of 1 (British) Corps at the height of the Cold War in the late 1980s. He had a propensity for sacking his aides and military assistants after their many blunders, and therefore became appropriately named Syringe. He was probably too senior and had frightened too many people for anyone to ever tell him, though. He's actually a remarkably nice man.

You have really arrived as a personality and a legend when you are known by just one name. It is so in politics and other walks of life. If we talk of 'Maggie', we all know who we mean. 'Maggie, Maggie, Maggie, out, out, out' is a slightly uncontrived faux compliment. It just does not work if you try to get the same cadence from 'Tony, Tony, Tony, out, out, out' or 'Dave, Dave, Dave, out, out, out'. It should be a prerequisite that all leaders have two syllables in their name. The army had Cedric. Everyone knew who you meant if you mentioned Cedric. He was a legendary soldier of few words, who, when he was not out fighting the Queen's enemies, got bored easily behind a desk. Many desks had to be replaced as he played with a knife, carving chunks out of them in his ennui.

Cedric was carving and smoking roll-ups in his office when he heard that a MoD policeman in Aldershot had been 'uppity' with a military manned roadblock. This was at the height of the IRA threat in garrison towns. The policeman was uncooperative and believed the troops were three metres outside their jurisdiction.

The police sergeant was called for an interview without coffee, for Cedric was also the Garrison Commander as well as being a fearless leader. A couple of days later Cedric was called to explain himself to the fearsome General Swine-burn (a nickname for, actually, a jolly nice cavalry general). Cedric threw down a letter on my desk. 'You see the shit I have to deal with,' he said. The letter went along the following lines:

Dear General Swine-burn
I prefer to think that rather than calling Sergeant McAssHole of the MoD Police a f***ing twat, what I actually said was that he was being a rather uncooperative person. Neither do I think that my dagger was threatening to him. I was merely carving chunks from the table and had no intention to threaten him.

In one of those tragic ironies of fate, Cedric, after a career spent dodging bullets on the front line and behind those lines, was knocked down by a car after emerging from a cinema. He lost a leg.

Other nicknames are also born out of tragedy, but show the black humour of the soldiers. A young officer was badly injured in a car bomb at Crossmaglen in Northern Ireland in the early 1980s. He died a number of times on the operating table, but was always brought back to life. His youthful good looks had been eviscerated in the heat of the explosion, which melted his face. He endured years of pain and agony to resurrect his career but served a full career until his normal retirement age. David Leigh was henceforward forever known as Crispy Leigh. His party trick was that he was able to shoot horizontal spray from his tear ducts if you upset him: few chose to do so. You had to use his nickname judiciously to avoid this fate.

CHAPTER 7
TRAINING AND EDUCATION

I was always confused by the difference between training and education until I was told that if your daughter came home from school and announced that she had been studying sex education you would understand, but if she proclaimed that she had been conducting sex training you would probably break out a shotgun and head for the headmaster's office.

Many of our soldiers may have joined the army quite soon after coming from the headmaster's office for other reasons. A brigade commander in Scotland received a letter from a headmistress complaining about a group of soldiers from Catterick Garrison. They were in their fourth week of basic training, and she had been sitting in close proximity to them on a Darlington to Glasgow train. It was their weekend break. Our brigadier was about to write his normal apologetic letter when a rush of blood to the head directed his efforts in other directions. He actually wrote: 'Thank you for your recent letter and your concerns about the behaviour of our soldiers on the train. May I beg forbearance for a little longer? We have had these soldiers for a mere four weeks. You had them in the educational world for 11 to 13 years. Please give us a little more time to put right the mistakes and lack of training they have received in the last few years. We may even teach them to read and write.'

We often do have to teach soldiers to read and write – and very successfully. Motivation and responsibility are great teachers. We even have stocked libraries. Most of these are full of wonderful titles – unlike the three books brought to Terry Waite when he was incarcerated for 1,763 days in Beirut as a hostage. The three books he had access to were (the almost useful title of) *The Great Escape*, and the not so useful *A Manual of Breastfeeding* and Dr Spock's *Baby and Childcare*. I learnt these facts during a whole-life learning experience at a lecture given by Mr Waite.

The army is keen on whole-life learning, and many soldiers use their 'down time' when on operations to further their educational knowledge or qualifications. I have seen this in action. The Unit Education Officer (UEO) of 2 PARA conducted maths and English lessons in the evenings for our troops. One evening our august Padre Steele announced that he would be holding a communion just after the UEO was to conduct a maths lesson. This confused the soldiers (in particular the officers), and many had horrible flashbacks to their schooldays and the loathing of 'double mass'.

In the military, education is the business of preparing people to make sense of their individual and collective circumstances. Given the uncertainties, it must be a vital part of preparation for an unspecified war and the generality of other possible operations. Training is the provision of particular skills for the achievement of particular effects, with both individual and collective elements. Exercising is the confirmation of training, an assessment of that training, and its collective progression.

I became a trainer in 1985 when I was posted to the Directing Staff at the Platoon Commanders Division (PCD) at Warminster. Among other things, I was responsible for the mid-course test. Some students always prepared for the test better than others. Among the more memorable answers of the less well prepared were:

Question: 'What is the Russian equivalent of MILAN?' (MILAN was the British anti-tank system at the time and the correct answer was the Warsaw Pact equivalent: the AT-4 SPIGOT.)

Answer: 'Leningrad'.

Question: 'What do you understand by the term "Operational Manoeuvre Group (OMG)"?' (An OMG was a Russian exploitation force designed to punch its way through the NATO lines in Germany.)

Answer: 'Absolutely f*** all.'

And my favourite: 'What is the range of NOD (A)?' (NOD (A) was the Night Observation Device (Alpha) with a surveillance range of 1,200 metres.)

Answer: 'It depends how much fuel Big Ears has put in the car.'

The PCD students, all bright young officers straight from Sandhurst, spent a fair proportion of their time on exercise. I was responsible for their final exercise in Brecon, Wales. I was completing my first course as a DS, which climaxed in a large attack which finished up at X Range, Sennybridge, at about

0800. The final attack went really well, and I smugly congratulated myself on writing a tip-top exercise enjoyed by all. At 1000 I started to get somewhat perplexed, as the two coaches that were due to pick up the students had not arrived. At 1030 I was getting positively anxious. How could this be? I had explicitly sent my Land Rover driver, a young Scots soldier called Hardy, to meet with two white army coaches at the civilian garage at the bottom of Church Hill at 0800.

I was now contemplating my imminent sacking for administrative incompetence. We were *sans* any form of transport, and there were certainly no coaches. At that precise moment, providence intervened as a mounted patrol of the Pathfinder Platoon of 5 Airborne Brigade drove down the training area peripheral road towards X Range. The platoon commander, a friend of mine called John Barrett, was in the lead vehicle. I flagged him down.

'John, you've got to help me out here. There were supposed to be two coaches here by 0900 and there's no sign of them. Can you give me a lift down Church Hill to see what's gone wrong?'

He did. As I approached the top of Church Hill, a wonderful vantage point at Sennybridge Training area, I saw Hardy in the middle distance. He was outside his Land Rover and leaning on the bonnet. Parked next to him were two Wallace Arnold coaches. There were only three vehicles in the entire car park: Hardy's Land Rover and the two coaches. But there seemed to be no rapport or communication between Hardy and the two drivers. We sped down the hill coming to a screechy stop next to Hardy.

'Hardy, what are you doing? Why haven't you brought the coaches up?'

'They're nay white army coaches, sir!'

We raced back to the assembled students and departed for home. There is a lesson here. You can be too specific in your instructions for some types of soldiers, whose ability to see beyond the literal and use their initiative may be slightly less than one would like.

Imprecision of language and expression can sow confusion in war and peace. The young officers can occasionally use too much initiative. 'Right guys, you've done really well today. Let's meet up at the Bath Arms at 7.30 for a drink,' I said, on arrival back at the barracks. At the said time the student body were scattered all over Wiltshire having rendezvoused at the Bath Arms, Warminster, and the Bath Arms at Horningsham, the Bath Arms in Bath and the Bath Arms, Heytesbury.

One of the missing Bath Arms cohorts was Colour Sergeant Ena Ewell. He had also had a misunderstanding with the imprecision of language when instructing a recruit platoon of soldiers. The troops were conducting an early lesson on how to cook the 24-hour ration pack. He was short of time, and applied more hexamine cooking blocks than was normally required to quickly boil the water in the metal mess tin. We all know from our physics lessons at school that metal retains heat, and the handle of the mess tin was hot, hot, hot. This recruit had obviously skipped that physics lesson.

Ena to recruit: 'Take off your beret and pick up the mess tin.'

Recruit to Ena: 'Yes, Colour Sergeant.'

The recruit removed his beret, threw it on the floor and picked up the mess tin – until the point that his skin began to peel from his hand.

Having expressions that have different meanings can have the same effect. 2 PARA were about to fly out on a mission during

Op Bessemer, the weapons collection mission in Macedonia, to help cement the Lake Ohrid peace agreement in 2001. Those who studied their physics at school will know that bessemer is the process whereby carbon, silicon and other impurities are removed from molten pig iron by oxidation in a blast of air in a special tilting retort. The best that the British defence establishment's random computer-generated codenames could come up with for a military mission was therefore Bessemer.

There are plenty of other examples of British army operations in the last 30 years that have had non-military odd names. These have included Op Granby (Iraq in 1991), Telic (Iraq again, in 2003), Banner (Northern Ireland) and Herrick (Afghanistan). I think we need a bit of human intervention in the future. If you are going to die in a military operation, it would at least be a good thing to make it sound that it was a military affair. Although the name is generated by computer, a degree of common sense is sometimes applied to account for local sensitivities – I was not allowed to use the very appropriate Op Incredulous for the notion that the IRA would give up their weapons in the 1990s. These names may suit the British culture, but the American codenames are so much more descriptive: Desert Storm, Certain Victory, Urgent Fury and Destroy-Anything-That-Moves. I think I would prefer to fight under those names.

While in Macedonia during Op Bessemer, my Operations Officer, Captain Gary Wright, became concerned that we would compromise our impartiality during a mission in a small town named Redusa. His angst centred on the graffiti spray-painted on many walls of the town. Each wall had the following painted on it:

UCK
NATO

The UCK (the acronym for the former Kosovo Liberation Army – Ushtria Clirimatare e Kosoves – who had disbanded but joined the Albanian Macedonian rebels) had signed the Lake Orhid agreement, but saw NATO as their protectors. We were impartial. Gary suggested that we would need to take cans of paint to paint this out, for the impact if we were filmed by the press might damage the achievement of the mission. I suggested a cheaper and more effective alternative – we needed to simply spray a letter 'F' in front of UCK. In the event we needed to do neither: 9/11 happened and suddenly the Macedonia mission was (quite rightly) no longer front page news. The news cycle and agenda had moved on.

In 2003, the Brits were once again in Iraq. I was stuck in the MoD. When the war fighting portion of the war was over and the original units who had led the invasion returned to the UK, I asked the Second-in-Command of 3 PARA, Major Mark Christie, what the war was like. His short answer was, 'The war was crap,' but then went on to recount the story of Captain Ned Cameron.

Picture the scene. It is the darkest part of the night before the coming of the dawn. The soldiers of 3 PARA are on edge; they are expecting an Iraqi counter-attack. In their night-viewing devices they spot some Iraqi tanks. With due aplomb and precision they let loose their long-range anti-tank weapons to destroy the Iraqi tanks. The tanks are successfully hit – as they had been in the first Gulf War in 1991. The men of 3 PARA have engaged some rusted relics from 12 years earlier.

It was fortuitous that at about the same time and as the sun rose hard and red into the morning sky, a number of Iraqis were wandering on foot towards 3 Para with intent to surrender. Both sides had some trepidation as the Iraqis closed on 3 Para.

'Drop your weapons! Drop your weapons!' the Brits shouted.

The Iraqis came closer, and as they did so saw the outline of the badges on the right arms of the paratroopers – the Para wings and the green drop zone square cloth that indicated they were from 3 Para.

'You Parachute Regimenti, you Parachute Regimenti,' said an animated Iraqi.

'Yeah, what of it?' intoned our heroes.

'You know Ned Cameron, you know Ned Cameron.'

'Yeah, what of it?' repeated our young paratroopers.

'He my colour sergeant at Sandhurst, he my colour sergeant at Sandhurst.'

'Ned!' shouted a young officer.

And into the sun in one of those quirks of war, Ned Cameron came forward to meet an Iraqi he had trained at the Royal Military Academy some years before. Like me, the Iraqi may not have been too good at bulling his boots and shoes during his tenure at Sandhurst, for the story goes that he was wearing ballet shoes at the point of capture.

Mark Christie and I went back a long way. He was from a statistically unusual family group in that he had two sets of twins. His wife was expecting the second set while his first were still being potty-trained. Mark and Clair Christie were on an accompanied two-year tour in Northern Ireland, and had put the twins upstairs in their shared bedroom to let off steam prior to them gently dozing off. It was the usual raucous chaos from the ebullient boys. Or it was until it went strangely quiet: too quiet for the suspicions of Captain Christie. He rushed upstairs to find a couple of two-year-olds who had decided, after using their potties, to 'experiment'. This consisted of using their hands to smear their youthful excrement over the walls, onto their Teddies, over the duvets, into the recesses of the TV and radio, and across the floor. As this occurred while he was serving in Northern Ireland, it was almost a fitting tribute to the Republican prisoners of a few years before. This was the Christies' own 'Dirty Protest'. I believe this also explains why Clair, when being congratulated by the midwife when she was told that she was to have a second set of twins, instead of bursting with happiness exclaimed a more vernacular single word that rhymes with 'Truck'.

Exercising in the military sense – to 'confirm training' rather than running or conducting push-ups or sit ups – occurred regularly on PCD. The army often trains with live rounds and we did so frequently on PCD. This is not an activity without risk. Our group of instructors was a tight-knit team of seven officers and seven colour sergeants – a happy and cohesive band of brothers. By the end of Exercise Diamond Digger we were down to six colour sergeants. Colour Sergeant Dan Maude was killed when he was hit by a number of bullets. He was one of the safety staff as the students aggressively pursued a company attack. With the confusion and obscuration of the field firing area caused by smoke from setting some grass on fire, he was mistaken when taking up a kneeling position for an enemy target by a platoon of the left flank as he exercised his duties on the right flank. The course was never the same again. The army brought in high visibility vests for safety staff from that moment on.

The bookends of my time as Commanding Officer of 2 PARA also saw the battalion vigorously pursuing live fire training. There is no better preparation for war. On both occasions – in September 1999 in Canada and October 2001 in Otterburn – we somehow managed to hit and injure safety staff. Neither was badly injured – one was hit in the leg and the other in the arm. The curious thing is that when such incidents occur, the army's ammunition technical officers – the experts on ammunition and its disposal – are always called to the scene first to see if there has been an ammunition incident. In my experience, the ammunition has always worked perfectly well – too perfectly most of the time – and it is human error, or people disregarding the rules, that means men get shot during live firing field training. Both safety staff were wearing high visibility vests. It goes without saying that they do not make you bulletproof.

We did not have time on the two-week Territorial Army courses to conduct live firing. The nearest they got to simulating battle conditions was a blank-firing company attack but which included 'battlefield inoculation'. This term describes the use of live flanking or overhead fire to simulate the sound and sight of tracer rounds in proximity to the exercising troops. The loveable general purpose machine gun (GPMG) was mounted on a tripod on a fixed firing lane on top of a building in Imber Village, and would open fire once the students had landed in a valley some 1,500 metres from the objective. The fire would be metres over their heads, but the students would see the effect. The Puma helicopters dropped off the troops, departed, and the GPMG roared in to action. The GPMG had been wrongly sighted. The bullets' 'fall of shot' peppered the landing site of the assembled students. Now, the TA were often criticised as weekend warriors so I am happy to report that on that particular day their use of cover and fieldcraft was of the highest order. They were at that moment the proud inheritors of my men digging in with their eyelids at Goose Green.

Other subjects covered on TA courses included military symbology (the symbols we use on maps to portray units and battlefield events) and the use and description of ground. In military symbology an 'X' on top of a formation symbol represents a brigade, two together is a division, three a corps, four represents an army and five Xs denotes an army group. The number of Xs increases with the size of the military formations. In our small army we no longer have much use for numbers three to five: we are too small to have to worry about their use. After the conclusion of a course, I once asked a female student what she had learnt. 'I now know that one kiss is a brigade, and two kisses are a division,' she replied.

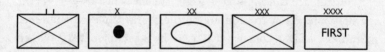

Figure 1: military symbology. From left to right: an infantry battalion, an artillery brigade, an armoured division, an infantry corps, and an Army (First Army represented was commanded by General Hodges in 1944).

It was the same student who had problems with the description of ground. In the army we do not see fields and trees: we see tactical possibilities and ways to manoeuvre. Ground is 'christened' and described from left, centre to right, and from the near, middle and far distance. After three days of christening the ground, she had still not quite got it right. My opening gambit on a Tactical Exercise Without Troops (TEWT) went as follows:

'Sarah, describe the ground.'

I expected the standard 'left, centre, right: near, centre, far'. I was wrong.

'Wet and muddy,' she replied.

Every time the British army has gone to war since the Falklands, I have been on an educational course. During the first Gulf War in 1991 I had the misfortune to be at the Army Staff College. More specifically, I was at Shrivenham, completing the technical training for non-technical officers – Science for Dummies in my case. In 2003 during the Second Gulf War, I was also at Shrivenham, completing the Higher Command and Staff Course. Now that I am finally retired, such a coincidence can no longer occur. Which is just as well, as the army were about to send me on the Royal College of Defence Studies (RCDS) course for a year in September 2010, which would have overlapped our intervention in Libya, giving me a full suite of 'modern wars I have missed due to education'.

At least the TA students had some grounding in the military arts, unlike civil servants. You might think that if there were three single-service staff colleges of the army, navy and air force (prior to the formation of the current college that teaches joint warfare), a civil servant who had worked for the navy for 17 years would end up at the naval staff college. Not a bit of it: he would complete a year in the Army Staff College.

Our naval civil servant found it all most difficult. Life in the navy was simple: you filled up ships with as many stores as you could and sent them to sea. With the army, things were far more complex. He would never simply *visit* the countryside again. Every time he drove anywhere he would be looking at things through the lens of 'good tank country', 'excellent enfilade shoots', 'potential killing area', 'avenues of approach' and 'manoeuvre corridors' and have a keen eye for the possibilities of mobile or area defence.

The Army Staff College has met its demise: it has been replaced by the Joint Service Command and Staff College. After a couple of thousand years of practising, we finally recognised that wars are fought using all ground, air and naval assets. The navy, however, struggle to articulate a role for themselves in land-locked Afghanistan, which is why they are keen to emphasise the role of the Royal Marines who have done a fine job during their Afghanistan tours, but little to justify the role of amphibious shipping in the Hindu Kush.

Education and knowledge are different things. I awoke one January morning in 1991 to the Radio 4 news that the air campaign in Iraq had commenced. The TV rooms were full every night as we watched, as prurient (and cheesed-off) observers from afar. BBC1 TV news was replaying library footage of RAF Tornado jets dropping the JP233 runway denial weapon. This was in the days of low-level bombing before everyone (again) realised that aircraft were regularly shot down when they went in to a wall of missile or flak gunners. A young undergraduate student commented: 'That JSP101 is a powerful weapon.' He had confused Joint Service Publication 101 (JSP 101) – the army guide to writing memos, briefs, and all random sorts of military prose – with a weapon system. He may not have been as wrong as we thought. The time taken to generate the smart munitions that allow stand-off attacks after even minor usage in conflicts such as Libya in 2011, means that often we have shiny aircraft, but with more books than bombs to throw at an enemy.

Army Staff College was at Camberley, in the same grounds as the Royal Military Academy at Sandhurst. The incompetents of 10–15 years before were now senior captains or junior majors. They were all in the top quartile of the army and had been selected for possible future greatness. The shininess of their shoes and pristine creases of their uniform were no longer the prime consideration. Unfortunately, some of the directing staff still believed that they were in charge of benign officer cadets and that shoes and uniform did matter more than operational military planning. One particular colonel had very fixed views on standards. He interviewed a member of the student body newly arrived from Shrivenham with the following:

Directing Staff: 'Well, you obviously don't play much sport. Looking at you, I would say you've clearly had a very comfortable time sitting around lecture halls at Shrivenham. Have you participated in any sporting activity recently?'

Student: 'I've played rugby for Ireland, if that counts.'

This put-down from the extremely gentlemanly Captain Brian McCall – who played in the Ulster team that beat Australia 15-13 in 1984 and was part of the Ireland Five Nations winning team of 1985 – amused me immensely. There are few prizes for guessing the rugby position of the very powerful Brian McCall, although history records that the entire Ulster pack of 1984 went on to play for Ireland.

The same 'traditional colonel' took the same traditional view

Above: P Company – the stretcher race.

Middle: I wait to parachute as Commanding Officer of 2 PARA in 2000.

Below: I stand sixth from right with 6 Platoon, B Company after the Battle of Goose Green in the Falklands in 1982.

Above left: The old and the new. The 50th anniversary in 1994 of the D-Day drop on Ranville, the first French village liberated, with the PX Mark 4 and the Low Level parachute.

Above right: Your worst parachuting nightmare – in twists and entangled.

Below: March 1982. In Belize, anticipating a Guatemalan invasion (Lieutenant Wallis, Lieutenant Hocking, me and Lieutenant Connor). Note the jungle kit and American M16 rifles.

Above: San Carlos Water on 23 May 1982 from 2 PARA's position on the Sussex Mountains after the beach landings in the Falklands. HMS *Antelope* is ablaze in the middle of the picture.

Below: In the British army 'uniform' isn't... With Corporal Jenkins in 2012.

Inset: The Falklands War is over. Myself, Private 'Beast' Kirkwood, Sergeant Bill McCulloch and Lance Corporal 'Bish' Bishop. It's a poor-quality image, but all of us have the thousand-yard stare of men who have been in combat.

Left: In the Falklands. Private Eddie Carroll and Private Jim Moodie – the youngest and oldest Toms of 6 Platoon. Carroll turned 18 en route to the Falklands.

Right: Once a PARA, always a PARA.

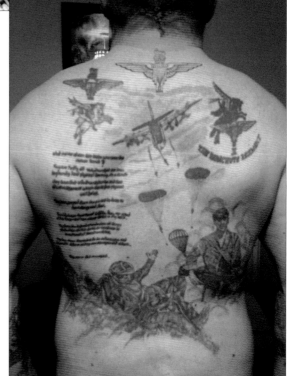

Above: Corporal Moose Miller – my metaphor for a PARA soldier.

Middle: Support Company, exiled to the 'open prison' of Privassion camp in the jungle of Belize, in 1983, ensuring remarkable cohesion.

Below: In Belize as Commanding Officer of 2 PARA with Major Mark Christie and Captain Gary Wright in 2000.

Left: An inclusive army – celebrating the Hindu festival of Diwali with Geinor in 1999.

Right: 'Mad Dog' contemplates becoming 'Soft Puppy' as he fails to jump.

Above: Macedonia 2001 – the 2 PARA Falklands survivors from 1982 still serving. Two have since been killed working for private security companies in Iraq. A third has also died.

Middle: Equality and diversity. With my bodyguard and driver in Northern Ireland in 2007. The female military police officer is the bodyguard.

Left: Nepal 2001. If you think you are having a crap day, consider how much worse it could be – carrying a three-piece suite on a mountain 12,000 feet up.

Above: Brigadier Peter Wall and I plot, in 1999, how he will head the army as Chief of the General Staff by 2012. Both of us will have to shave off our moustaches as part of the plot.

Below: All you need for command – a pistol, a map, a radio, a staff... and a Frenchman on your left.

on the cleanliness of footwear. He may not have been cognisant that we were no longer Sandhurst cadets. But we were certainly more subversive and would not put up with such pedantry. The student body had a secret weapon – the scurrilous student publication. Spurious orders could be issued to slay such pedants as in this extract from an army operations order.

Mission: To ensure the correctitude and fastidiousness of Staff College students in all phases of classroom exercises.

Code words:

Serial	Code word	Meaning	Issued by
(a)	(b)	(c)	(d)
1	KIWI	Directing Staff commence recces	Colonel D Division
2	SHOESHINE	Discovery of unclean footwear	Inspecting Directing Staff
3	KILLJOY	Commence student discipline	Colonel D Division
4	PARADE GLOSS	Standards achieved	Commandant (on authorisation Colonel D Division)

Fortunately for my career, I was in B Division, and my shoes were excused the zealous gaze of D Division staff. Moreover, I would be posted to the Airborne Brigade upon graduation, where such things took second place to thinking about tactics and operations.

In the era of the Cold War there was always a slightly bizarre conclusion to the Army Staff College course. Maybe this really was the era of the gifted amateur. If one visited the

American Staff College at Leavenworth, or the German Fuehrungsakademie, there would be an immersion in great feats of strategy and a war game that manoeuvred large-sized elements of corps, armies or even army group strength formations around a large scale map of Western Europe to defeat the Fantasians (in reality the Russians). The Army Staff College concluded their course with a pantomime. I think it was *Jack in the Beanstalk* in my tenure. I watched from the audience, being a recalcitrant who would not have a role in this charade. My wife had a major role, applying green make-up to Jack's legs. Believe it or not, the head of B Division of the Staff College was none other than Colonel Dick Wittington.

I am happy to report that the pantomime is no longer a feature of the conclusion of the course: war-gaming and the operational art are once again taken seriously, even if the days of corps, armies and army groups are far behind us and the scale of British operational abilities is a fraction of what it once was. Montgomery commanded 12th Army Group in the Second War World War; General Rupert Smith commanded merely a division in the 1991 First Gulf War; we now struggle to go beyond a large brigade.

I had the privilege (and responsibility) of becoming an instructor at the Army Staff College. It was getting near the end of the course and the students were in a frivolous mood on a visit to the Pentagon. One student (this was 1998) asked a senior four-star American general, 'When do you see Joint Vision 2010 being implemented?' The course tittered. The answer was obvious and the UK commandant's face contorted into pure hatred for the offending student. Now, the US general had not heard of Joint Vision 2010, and an aide quickly whispered the salient points in his ear. The general's reply was a masterpiece: 'Son, I have enough problems with 1-9-9-9.' And that is true. Our ability to predict what the world will look like in one year, let alone five or 10 years is at best uncertain. That is why I liked a more relevant question asked during the trip, which was: 'What is the most difficult question I could ask you, and what is the answer?'

The commandant at the Staff College was a major general with a brilliant mind. He once appeared in an article of a national magazine that looked at the top thinkers of the country. He was one of the 50 top thinkers in the UK and was referred to as 'the keeper of the army brain', and I believe he was. I'm not sure if the army is only allowed one brain in line with Lloyd George's comment that military intelligence is a contradiction in terms. He knew everything about everything. This included the exact formula of what height to hang pictures on a wall. The unfortunate 'House Member' – the officer responsible for such things when the Staff College moved from Camberley to Bracknell – got all too familiar with this detailed level of knowledge, as he constantly filled in holes and repainted walls from his incompetence at 'guessing' what the formula was.

General Keeper-of-the-Army-Brain (K-O-T-A-B) had also been the author of the mid-1980s pamphlet on British Army Doctrine. He was a very clever general who we all admired for his intellect. Whether our very clever general espoused the modern British army command philosophy that he had written about was another matter. Let me explain. The modern British army is based on attempting to follow the 'manoeuvrist approach'. This is a tactic in which shattering the enemy's overall cohesion and will to fight is paramount. It calls for an attitude of mind in which doing the unexpected, using initiative and seeking originality is combined with a ruthless determination to succeed. The command philosophy that must underpin this approach is called 'mission command'. It demands de-centralised control. We have moved away from pre-scripted solutions – the enemy has a vote. To do this successfully, subordinates should be told what to achieve and why, rather than what to do, and how.

To test the student body's understanding of such concepts, the 1997 course was undertaken at Fort Benning in Georgia, in order to complete all its operations of war studies utilising the huge area of land that America offers and which was laid out before us. If you tried to do this in the UK you would unfortunately bump into the sea after quite a short time in any given direction, and as not too many nations have invaded the UK since 1066 this is not very convenient from an offensive learning point of view.

One particular study was centred on a 'Staff Ride'. This is an in-depth look at a real historical battle, visiting the ground on which the actual event was fought. In this case it was the American Civil War Battle of Chickamauga of 1863. Until you live in America, you do not really get a feel for how the Civil War still divides people. A wealthy car dealership owner during my tour in Tampa refused to take $50 notes because they had pictures of General Grant from the Army of the Union. She held him responsible for Sherman's scorched earth policy in his 'drive to the south'. Our car dealer was an older Southern Belle who really did believe in The War of Northern Aggression on the southern Confederate states.

Major General K-O-T-A-B, whom we met earlier, was to come and visit my syndicate of students, who were due to present before heading off to another group. I had primed my group and did my usual summary at the end, quoting the great philosophers of military history to make my points about the timeless elements and continuities of warfare through the ages, and further deepen the understanding of my students. General K-O-T-A-B was delighted. He thanked me for my contribution and duly went to hear the next group. This was led by Lieutenant Colonel Dick Crombie of the Royal Signals. His syndicate presented their findings and Dick summarised, whereupon General K-O-T-A-B launched a broadside at them for their lack of understanding of command at the tactical, operational and strategic levels of war. Major Mark Christie (he had by now been promoted) came away grunting, 'Mission command and de-centralised control. All this General K-O-T-A-B understands is D-A-F-T: "Do as you are f***ing told."' The last time I checked, Colonel (as he now is) Christie was writing... doctrine.

Despite our adoption of new philosophies for command and war, some things still seem hard to get through to some higher elements of the army. I am, of course, not a subversive, and do believe in discipline. But I do think it stretches the imagination to be told as late as 2005 that, 'saluting is not being treated as a decisive weapon system'. Although nearly 100 years separated the above remark from Sassoon's incredulity at being told that the bayonet was a similar decisive weapon in 1914, he would have recognised it for its idiocy. In Sassoon's case, the bayonet-loving Highland Major's star turn in the schoolroom was 'afterwards awarded the DSO for lecturing'.[8] We promoted our saluting guru, General Anachronism, to the highest ranks and knighted him.

To convince you that I am not a subversive and believe in

discipline, I refer to an incident with my operations officer, Gary Wright. Complex airborne or helicopter operations require an air adjutant to do the manifesting of the troops and liaise with the helicopter or air transport commands. We had one of the best air adjutants – Captain Spencer Ainsworth – although there was an occasion when he had manifested 792 troops and could not account for one individual. Manifesting of all personnel and accounting for them is necessary in case an aircraft or helicopter is lost in action. All 792 troops were on parade and had been loaded on the parachuting 'chalks' for the port and starboard sides of the aircraft. Still we could not find who was missing. Ainsworth berated the chalk leaders from a high podium. Two hours later it dawned on him that the missing individual was... him!

On one operation, Ainsworth was away manifesting and leading the planning with B Company, 2 PARA, who were about to insert into an area with the French Foreign Legion. He had already done the planning for a separate battalion operation. The out-load of 2 PARA led by Ainsworth had gone faultlessly. Forty-eight hours later, the battalion mission was drawing to its conclusion and the helicopter extraction would follow. This was the conversation with Gary Wright, the Operations Officer:

'Ops, Ainsworth's been left behind to complete the French operation, and the helicopters are due in 20 minutes. Ensure that they are called in precisely and in accordance with the plan.'

'But sir, I've never been an air adjutant and wouldn't know what to do.'

'Stop flapping[9], Ops, I know you're flapping, because you're calling me "sir".'

There was no point trying to confront General Anachronism with the realities of modern warfare. He was stuck in the second generation of warfare, between the chariot and the rifled weapon. He did not seem to realise that modern warfare relied more on the power of the microchip and processing potential than on the range of a bayonet. (The range of a bayonet is either: 1. Depends on how long your arms are. 2 Very close. 3. Bloody close.) Neither did he appreciate that the potential of offensive and defensive cyber warfare might well be crucial in the future. Or that army or joint-service units of all three services now relied on a collection of capabilities that needed to be cohered, including the exploitation of the fourth dimension of space and satellites. The British adopted their command philosophy and 'mission command' from the Germans. The fundamental German command tradition is that officers *must* think two levels above their rank and command and therefore *must* disobey their immediate superior if the higher intent demands it. This very idea would have been anathema to General Anachronism; thereby reasserting the British dislike of anything that seems an infringement of the concept of authority.

Saluting is part of drill. And at one end of the scale of combat activity is drill – a precise, automatic ritualised response to a given stimulus. In psychological terms it represents conformity and a restriction on an individual. At the other end of the scale is tactical skill, or military art. This involves judgement, intellect, calculation and cunning (plus 'character' on the battlefield). It is not automatic in the sense of drill. Fortunately, I came from the part of the army that embraced the latter, and where mutual understanding and common perception led to the ability to cope with any unforeseen eventuality. We did not see the bayonet as decisive.

MAJOR-GENERAL CHIP CHAPMAN

General Anachronism must have missed the last 70 years of warfare. We were schooled that 'manoeuvre theory is about amplifying the force which a small mass is capable of exerting; it is synonymous with the indirect approach.'[10] None of this was new. It was precisely what Liddell Hart had written about prior to the Second World War with such maxims (as applicable for cyber and other capabilities domains today as when they were written) such as 'no general is justified in launching his troops to a direct attack upon an enemy firmly in position' and 'instead of seeking to upset the enemy's equilibrium by one's attack, it must be upset before a real attack is or can be successfully launched.' Today, we call this 'preparation of the battlefield' so that the distribution and transmission of means fulfils the ends of policy. Perfection of strategy would obviate the need to use General Anachronism's bayonet at all.

The Territorial Army students brought an interesting and different civilian perspective to life and work – including the psychological perspective. One of the students told me that what we were teaching them was a waste of time during a two-week course, because the brain does not function according to being receptive to the principles of this or the principles of that. It is cognitively able to learn better if one is a storyteller. The brain can remember these stories and an individual can then extrapolate the lessons from the stories (rather like this book). Her lesson to me: it is not what we teach, but how we learn that is the important test.

I put this to the test many years later when I followed a senior Home Office official in communicating about counter-terrorism at a Staff College module some 15 years after I had taught the perceptive TA student (who happened to be a psychologist by background). The Home Office official gave his pitch about the government's **counter-t**errorist **s**trategy (note the bold letters), the wonderfully named CONTEST. He went through the four principles (which you will encounter later). I followed him in the presenting order and gave my pitch. It was still morning. I guaranteed to the students that they would remember my mnemonic for ever more but would have forgotten the principles of CONTEST by lunchtime. I was right.

Al Qaeda was the predominant threat at the time. I wanted to inform the student body what Al Qaeda was, and what our response should be. This begat AQUATIC SEA COVES. Again, note the bold letters: **A**l **Q**aeda **U**n-Islamic **a**ctivity **t**argeted against the **I**nternational **C**ommunity was the AQUATIC part (though most terrorist violence is actually perpetrated against fellow Muslims). The response to the problem – for we should always look at the source rather than the symptom of a problem – became **S**topping **E**xtremist **A**ctivity, and **CO**untering **V**iolent **E**xtremist **S**trategy (thus, SEACOVES). I was rather proud that I had learnt something from a TA student. It illustrated what a free-thinking officer I had become.

The British army has always had training teams around the world conducting British Military Advisory and Training Team (BMATT) missions. These teams help to build the capabilities of the recipient nations and are useful in furthering the UK's 'soft power' objectives and influence in the world. One such mission was in the very warm climes of Kuwait in the late 1980s and early 1990s. When you get off a plane in Kuwait you are hit by the heat. It is best described as like having a hot hairdryer permanently shoved up one's nose. It is that hot.

One of my friends, a tough Scot called Alex Boyd, had the misfortune (as it turned out) to be part of the Kuwait mission in 1989. He was training the Kuwaitis in logistics. His wife and family were with him, living the military expatriate dream for a couple of years. The dream turned into a nightmare in August 1990 when Saddam Hussein invaded. Alex and his family were captured by the Iraqis and 'put in the bag' as the colloquial expression goes. They were incarcerated. In an act of generosity (for this, read propaganda) Saddam released Christine Boyd and the children, who disappeared back home to an undisclosed address in the UK. Alex was kept a hostage. At Christmas 1990, the Iraqis wished to show what fine fellows they really were. They instructed Alex to phone his wife and invite her to come to Kuwait for Christmas. Alex had no idea where his wife and children were living. He did the know the address and phone number of his mother, who lived in Glasgow, and using all his canny Scots wisdom he managed to get through to her. His conversation went along these lines:

'Hi Mum, it's Alex speaking. I'm being well looked after in Iraq. I've only lost four stone. You tell Christine that if she comes to Iraq for Christmas I'm going to give her a big Glaswegian kiss. Do you understand?'

The Iraqi guards of our truculent Scot were beside themselves with glee that such fine greetings had been delivered to reinforce the propaganda they wished to portray. But Alex's mother knew exactly the meaning and power of the colloquial phrases used. She knew that a 'Glasgow kiss' was a term for being head butted, and that Alex was warning her that there was no way that Christine should come to Iraq. She did not.

I am happy to say that Alex's enforced slimming diet finally ended and he was released, even if there were a few occasions where he thought he was going to suffer more than the odd rope-burn when he had a noose put around his neck. The great Alex Boyd was one of those guys that we would now refer to as 'resilient'.

---

[8]Again: from *Memoirs of an Infantry Officer*, Sassoon, Faber and Faber, 1997 revise, p.5

[9]'To flap' – to be uncertain and disquieted; to speak more quickly and to raise the pitch of the voice by an octave. Wright did splendidly. Ainsworth became a civil airline pilot when he left the army.

[10]*Race to the Swift*, R Simpkin, Brasseys, 1985. This was the theoretical book of choice on warfare when I attended Staff College.

CHAPTER 8

DISCIPLINE

Given that soldiers are devious and cunning, they enjoy certainty in discipline. Shades of grey are exploitable commodities for soldiers. If they are given an inch they will take the proverbial mile. Nothing illustrates this more than the thing that probably causes more of our discipline problems in peace than anything else: drinking or, more appropriately, drinking alcohol to excess. It is a good thing that once deployed to conflict zones, most bases and troop operating areas are declared alcohol-free, or we would fight ourselves as well as the enemy.

There are three types of drunks in the world. In fact I now know that there are five, for they should include the idiotic drunk and the emotional drunk. I am grateful to my female political advisor at CENTCOM in the US for pointing out the latter: she tells me she is more likely to burst into tears once she has had a few drinks. Fortunately, I never had occasion to see this phenomenon in action.

Anyway, back to the three types of drunk – the happy drunk, the sleepy drunk and the violent drunk. I wanted the happy drunk to bring the sleepy drunk back to barracks, and would always tell my troops that if they were a violent drunk I would lock them up in the glasshouse (military jail) for 28 days. The powers of a commanding officer to send someone to Colchester Military Corrective Training Centre (MCTC) are quite wide. This certainty of discipline worked. When soldiers came on orders (the disciplinary process) after an evening of mayhem I would ask them what type of drunk they had been. No soldier will directly admit that he is a violent drunk, and their vocabulary in finding alternatives to the term became quite wide-ranging. The most popular was somewhere around the term 'aggressive drunk'. This was close enough for them to understand that they would shortly turn to the right without passing 'Go' and spend the next 28 days in alternative employment. It worked. We really had very few disciplinary cases.

While the reader uneducated in the ways of the military may be surprised at the powers of a commanding officer to imprison a soldier for a disciplinary infraction, these have been downgraded over the years – but booze is always a recurrent factor. This extract from the journal of Captain Robert Cholmey's batman (we do not have those now either) prior to the Battle of Fort Duquesne in July 1755 illustrates my point:

'We had a Genll Coart Marshall. One soldier was tried for disartion and sentenced to suffer death. Three more was tried for stealing a Barrel of Beer in the Cuntry and Was Ordered 300 lashes a man with the Cat of Nine Tails.'

Three points arise. First, one would recognise the above in the educational attainment and spelling ability of some of our soldiers. This is a failure of the educational system, not of the army, which does a remarkable job in fixing this over the tenure of a soldier's career. It could be that the army recognised this failure of the system long before anyone else. My essay topic given to me at the Commissions Board in 1977 was: 'Has compulsory reorganisation of education led to a decline in standards and increased violence?' Second, we are no longer allowed to administer the cat-of-nine-tails. Third, it may not surprise you to learn that we lost the battle of Fort Duquesne.[11]

The Parachute Regiment had their own equivalent of 'a Barrel of Beer in the Cuntry' during the period when Aldershot was their home base from the late 1940s until 2000. Every Saturday lunch time from 2.30 onwards, a collection of soldiers would gather in the grassy park between the Trafalgar and Queens pubs with a few bottles of wine to bridge the gap between the pubs' lunchtime closing and the evening's opening hour. This was before the days of almost universal 24-hour pub opening times. More importantly, it was in the era of wine bottles with corks. With the recent introduction of screw-top wine bottles I fear that the art of successfully opening a wine bottle without a corkscrew may be lost. In the interests of keeping the flame of this ancient army technique alive for posterity, here are the required steps:

1. Push cork into bottle of wine with thumb.
2. Remove shoelace from left or right shoe (those truly skilled would already have a piece of parachute cord to hand).
3. Knot shoelace at one end, and insert into wine bottle with knot entering neck first.
4. Ensure shoelace is below bottom of floating cork.
5. Pull shoelace. Knot will tighten against cork and enable cork to be successfully removed.

In April 2000 Airborne Forces sadly left Aldershot to begin a long-term relationship with Colchester. After 50 years, the men were very familiar with the lay of the land in 'The Shot'. It would take them a while to find the same equilibrium in Colchester. I know this to be so, because during the soldiers' summer leave in 2000, I was called to a meeting with the Licensed Victuallers of Colchester to be berated about the unexpected pub etiquette of our men. (To show my own sobriety I only accepted an orange juice as my refreshment.) I had already placed a number of pubs 'out of bounds' prior to this. I came away suitably chastised and determined to deal with the consequences of any future incidents. This became known as my 'special offer'. Using a rarely used rule, I applied to our superiors for extended powers. These meant I could now lock up any miscreants for 60 days. The men came back from leave and I got them on parade to tell them my September special offer: all the pubs would be back in bounds because I trusted them, but anyone who was a violent drunk would be locked up for 60 days. I think they found their equilibrium from that moment on, and we had a happy, incident-free autumn and winter.

Our young lieutenants in Colchester at least did not have to fulfil some of the onerous duty officer tasks that were part of the ritual of living in Aldershot. Most units in the army, including those in Colchester, no longer have their own unit guardrooms. They are now forbidden from looking after their own prisoners due to health and safety, and duty of care considerations. This makes the worries of the youngest subalterns less than they were in the halcyon days of the early 1980s when the duty officer's orders included:

(1) Tour the camp with the battalion orderly sergeant.

(2) Visit the guardroom and inspect the prisoners, once by day and once in the evening. Check if they have any requests/complaints and sign the visits book (*while ignoring their requests, for they are all guilty bastards who have been locked up for being miscreants*).

(3) Mount the guard and piquet as ordered.

(4) Be prepared to attend any disturbance in Aldershot that affects the battalion (and pray that you are not on this duty over the weekend).

This was code for 'avoid the Globetrotter pub (known as the "GT") at all costs'. The GT was a subterranean den so packed that people were literally bodysurfed over the heads of the masses to get to the washroom/loo. Non-airborne forces were generally ejected by the fastest route. It closed down. Whether this was due to licensing law infractions, violence, lack of safety exits or just because the floor was pretty sticky I cannot recall, but it was immensely popular. In reality, the Royal Military Police would have had to utilise the resources of the whole of the southeast of England before a subaltern would risk his life at the GT.

(5) Attend the Restrictions of Privileges Parade at 2200 hours. Soldiers on show clean are not to be awarded extra parades. If they are in bad order they are to be placed on report by the battalion orderly sergeant.

The wonderful company character of Private Street would always seek to redefine the limits of the process. His turnout would be fine – but in the words of the eulogy for an offending soldier, 'His eyes were glazed; he smelt of alcohol, I knew that he was drunk.' Strasse (as he was affectionately known) never quite worked out that Murray Mints did not disguise the smell of recently consumed whisky – which he liked (a lot). Strasse was wounded in the Falklands.

Working with allies can also induce its own cultural and disciplinary challenges in the equality and diversity field. Here are two examples. 2 PARA were on exercise in Fort Lewis in Washington state. It was the era of the IRA, and of 'tiger watch'. Tiger watch was designed to always have a designated sober soldier to look for suspicious characters and packages in a bar while his comrades were partaking of some libation. After a raucous night at a country and western bar, the soldiers came out a shade worse for wear to be confronted by the US military police, of which the lead spokesman was a young female. She was slightly perturbed by the behaviour of the British troops, but our designated hero assured her everything was fine, as he was on tiger watch. It was: until he made the error of saying, 'I bet I know what you do with your truncheon at night,' and was promptly arrested for sexual harassment. I would like therefore to nominate him for my idiotic drunk category, and ask you to 'pass' on the slight detail of his sobriety.

A collective group of idiotic drunks is well illustrated by the six paratroopers who were making their way back from the pub one evening when they came across two characters, who they did not like the look of, promenading the other way. They followed the normal protocol of these occasions which commences with 'Who are you looking at?' before some serious fighting ensues. Our six paratroopers were beaten to a pulp. This included Private Steve McConnell, who had been dragged by his ankles from under a car, where he had attempted to escape the carnage.

Two days later, Steve McConnell was in a different pub and came across the aforementioned two characters. This time the conversation was slightly different: 'Hey guys, maximum respect for the kicking you gave us the other night. What are you doing in Aldershot?' Steve McConnell and his five amigos had picked on the two army full contact karate champions.

During the writing of this book, my wife reminded me that I should add that there is a sixth type of drunk – the lecherous drunk. Here is why. We were invited guests at the Corporals' Mess Christmas Ball. It was quite late, but not that late (there were still about two hours to go before the fights broke out). Of course, everyone knew me, but they did not all know my wife. I was conducting my normal sweep around the tables talking to the corporals and their wives. This, unfortunately, left my wife alone for a while on our table. Corporal Waller, well on the way to becoming a happy drunk, spotted this attractive lady all by herself and sat down to chat. In the interests of decorum, it would be wrong to record the conversation verbatim, but if you rearrange these words you will have an understanding of his offer: 'Fancy outside a you coming do f*** for?' She laughingly declined and he moved off. Somewhat flattered (but rather taken aback) that she was still in the 'top totty' category (although she may have misinterpreted this) she mentioned the incident to the RSM when he returned to the table. The night went downhill for Corporal Waller from that moment on.

There is also a lecherous drunk who appears once a year – yes, it's 'Airborne Santa'. Airborne Santa is generally a Senior NCO who has been nominated to deliver the Christmas presents at the Officers' Mess Christmas party. He will arrive with a 'Ho, ho, ho', distribute his presents, stay on, get very drunk and try to chat up the girlfriends of the youngest lieutenants. One particular Santa attempted to cycle home at three in the morning across the acres of football fields in Aldershot known as Queens Avenue. Those with a modicum of medical knowledge will know that balance is controlled via the inner ear or cochlea, and those who know Aldershot will agree that cycling across Queens Avenue is hard enough in the summer, let alone in December. Airborne Santa's cochlea and legs were not communicating very effectively and he tumbled off his bike and fell asleep. At six in the morning he was roused from his slumbers by the police. He briefly awoke and stated, 'F*** off, I'm Airborne Santa.' In the spirit of co-operation the police departed. Airborne Santa slept on.

As a CO in Colchester, the proximity of the MCTC to our barracks was a bonus, saving quite a lot of Her Majesty's fuel in transportation costs. It also had a further bonus when I came up with a devious scheme to sign a soldier *out* of his corrective training to go on operations. Corporal Franks was involved in a bad GBH incident when he was an instructor at the recruit training centre at Catterick (not with the recruits, I hasten to add). Alcohol was undoubtedly involved. What most soldiers fail to realise is that while they now generally fight in close proximity to the establishments they have been drinking in – pubs and nightclubs being the favoured battle pitches – this also gives a really good CCTV coverage of their misdemeanours and aids in their conviction.

Corporal Franks was duly sentenced to serve in the MCTC. We were about to go on operations and he was a mortar fire controller of some excellence. I managed to find an obscure regulation from the Manual of Military Law dating back to the 1860s that allowed me to sign him out on probation as long as I guaranteed that he would remain in my care. I was now his best friend. Twenty-five days into the operation in Macedonia – and three days before Franks would have qualified for his NATO medal – I realised that I was not the army's best friend.

The bureaucratic gnomes in some personnel department back in the UK went apoplectic and ordered him to be escorted to a plane to return at once to his former berth at the MCTC. I received no plaudits for my initiative, bar the respect of those who mattered – the soldiers of 2 PARA.

The forces are not a drunken savagery across the board, and alcohol has less of a place than it did. We no longer have Friday happy hours. I even feel quite sorry for the Royal Navy for losing their rum ration. A naval officer friend, who was originally a rating, told me of the impact of this on the Petty Officers' Mess. One Friday night he was on duty and was told by the petty officers of the ship on which he was serving to go to the victualing store and get a number of bottles of Brasso and muslin cloth. He was to continue his travels to the galley to get bottles of orange juice and loaves of sliced bread. The captain of the ship was probably ecstatic, believing he would have a gleaming ship with all the brass glowing superbly. He would be disabused of this notion. What the Petty Officers' Mess was actually up to was distilling the Brasso through muslin cloth, draining it through the sliced loaves to filter the impurities, and then having a Brasso-and-orange party on Friday night. They wouldn't wake up until Monday morning. For those of an experimental nature, this falls firmly into the category of 'do not try this at home'.

The same naval officer was in Northern Ireland in a headquarters appointment some years later. One night he was visiting 8 Infantry Brigade in Londonderry. His specialist subject on *Mastermind* would have been Heavy Drinking: he wasn't proud of it, but he was good at it. He could animate a mess bar with his tales and bonhomie. He could lead a bar full of officers to alcohol, from which they were not in a position to extract.

When the brigade commander saw the officer in Lisburn the following week, he told him that he had done something that the IRA had failed to do in 30 years – single-handedly destroyed the Command, Control and Communications of 8 Infantry Brigade for 24 hours.

My favourite acronym encountered during my career has to be MARILYN. This report from the 1980s stood for Manning and Recruiting in the Lean Years of the Nineties. I have no idea or recollection of what the report actually said, but I marvelled at the inventiveness of the acronym. The reader might be baffled by the acronyms of the army, but will not be alone in this respect. To even the balance, here's a story of the confusion that can reign between all three services. Each service has its own glossary of terms, which can mean different things to each service. This can be illustrated by the term 'secure a building'. If you mention the need to secure a building to the Royal Navy, they will turn off the lights and lock the doors. If you were to say the same thing to the Paras, they would storm the place and kill everyone inside. If you were to give the order in the RAF they would take out a five-year lease on the building. This goes to prove two things: first, the need for a common glossary and lexicon, and second, don't f*** with the Paras.

I had briefed the press using this analogy in the summer of 1993 prior to a large airborne exercise called Roaring Lion. It was reported in the *Armed Forces Journal International* in October 1993, in the section headed Darts and Laurels, Note Worthy, and Stray Voltage. Just beneath it was a report stating: 'A recent confidential British army report notes that about 30 per cent of army personnel have been, or are, frequent users of drugs.'

'That would explain the mistakes of [the UK's] Options for Change [defence review],' quipped one officer, hinting facetiously that some members of the Army Board may have been on drugs when they decided on force structure cuts. Some would argue that not much has changed in every subsequent review.

The services are equal opportunities employers, and embrace equality and diversity. We have gone in the last few years to wearing our rank slide (for there is now only one, rather than one on each shoulder) in the centre of the body mass just above the chest cavity. This is unfortunate, as 15 per cent of the services are now female, and the eye is inevitably drawn towards the centre of the chest area to check someone's rank. As my wife has frequently told me since embracing the push-up bras of Victoria's Secret: 'My eyes are up here.'

Twelve years after the 'idiotic drunk' incident, the largest combined airborne exercise between the UK and USA held for some years at Fort Bragg led to a major diplomatic incident. It seems we still had not learnt our lesson on interaction with our American colleagues. A British paratrooper stood in the aircraft door (in the number one 'first out the door' position, where the wind sweeps through the aircraft when the jump doors are opened). The jumpmaster, who is responsible for the dispatch, timing and cadence of the stick of 32 paratroopers, happened to be an American female. The normal drills applied, with one addition. See if you can spot the addition:

'Action stations' (the men dress as far forward as they can so as to follow closely behind the man dispatched in front of them when 'Go' is given).

'Red on' (the men bring their arms across their equipment and get all pumped up).

'Green on' (the men ready themselves to commence their exit on the jumpmaster/dispatcher's cue).

'Kiss the jumpmaster' (number one in the door plants a kiss on the check of the jumpmaster).

'Go' (the men exit the aircraft).

Despite all the above, the men are MAGNIFICENT. I would not normally write in capitals, but more than the average soldier does, and in particular it seems, those ex- soldiers of a former generation who choose to correspond with the commanding officer. These letters are regular and have a constant theme. They almost invariably include a cutting from a national or local newspaper which includes a picture of a paratrooper wearing his beret one or two inches towards the left ear, and therefore not in accordance with Queen's Regulations that demand it be worn over the centre of the left eye. Sideburns creeping below the required length comes a close second in the correspondence stakes. These photos are invariably circled (always in red ink) to make the point. The WONDERFUL men of the GREATEST GENERATION will then proceed to tell you that standards have slipped from their day and that the regimental sergeant major needs to 'get a grip' or the world will IMPLODE. They always state that RSM Jack Lord would never have allowed such slackness.

I was berated under the cover name of RSM Jack Lord on so many occasions that you might find it worthwhile to understand why. RSM Jack Lord was one of the legendary RSMs, latterly of 3 PARA, and at the Battle of Arnhem in

1944 he was part of General Urquhart of 1st Airborne Division's staff (as his bodyguard, once 3 PARA were rendered non-effective). He was also the RSM at Sandhurst for something like 15 years from 1948-1963, and a subject of the *This is Your Life* TV programme.

He was wounded at Arnhem and sent to Stalag XIB, now part of that wonderful British army garrison town of Bad Fallingbostel in Germany. At one point he complained to the Germans that Red Cross parcels were not being distributed. The Germans agreed to the request to commence distribution – as long as the British prisoners showed them due respect and saluted German officers. Lord agreed, but there were murmurings of discontent among his prison committee members for this apparent capitulation. Lord then went outside to demonstrate what he meant. He promptly found a German officer, saluted with his ramrod efficiency and said: 'Bollocks'. The German, taking this to be a form of greeting, replied 'Bollocks' back. And so for the remainder of the war in Stalag XIB each side talked a lot of bollocks to the other.

RSM Lord always began his address to a new intake at Sandhurst by saying, 'Gentlemen. My name is Lord and my initials are JC. That doesn't stand for Jesus Christ. He is Lord up there and I am Lord down here!'

I was fortunate to have two outstanding and completely different sorts of RSM: the 6ft 4in 'steady, boys, steady' type personified by RSM Gordon Muirhead, and the 5ft 6in theatrical former English gymnast of RSM Jack Lemmon (his real name was Richard). The height issue is an interesting one in films portraying soldiers and heroes. Those of you who have seen the film *Zulu* will recall the 'steady, boys, steady' company sergeant major who, like RSM Gordon Muirhead, was a man mountain. In reality, CSM Bourne at Rorke's Drift (who died on VE Day in 1945) was only 5ft 2in. Similarly, Peter O'Toole, 6ft 5in, portrayed Lawrence of Arabia in David Lean's legendary film when Lawrence was, in fact, only 5ft 5in. Jack Lemmon died of cancer in 2011, aged only 53, and he would not mind me saying (using one of his favourite RSM phrases) that he has now had 'more time off than Rip van Winkle's bedside lamp'. For me, he was taller than Peter O'Toole.

A further example of our MAGNIFICENT soldiers is worthy of retelling. The 2006 Tour of Afghanistan (the British Army was quixotically on Op Herrick 4 by this time)[12] was notable for being one of those classic examples where our military 'means' did not match the 'ends', or what was thought could be achieved. And the 'ways' were going to involve a bloody tour for the hunkered-down Paratroopers who fought like tigers to successfully stop themselves being overrun by 'Terry Taliban' – the 21st-century equivalent of 'Fritz' – in minor and less than always relevant bases in Helmand province. The allusions to adversity and 'being like Arnhem' have been commented on many occasions since. While this is what our great soldiers relish, it is no indication of good strategy. But on to the achievements of our MAGNIFICENT soldiers...

A few days after 3 PARA had occupied a series of patrol bases, the administrative captain of 3 PARA – a representative from the Adjutant General's Corps (AGC) – arrived by helicopter to conduct a minor administrative task. He would be in and out in 30 minutes. Due to the intensity of the fighting and the lack of helicopters, this would actually extend to seven days. The AGC captain, Greg Ehlan, was a fine airborne warrior of long standing. During the first elongated 'contact' with the Taliban, he manned the ramparts of his isolated outpost in true Beau Geste style and engaged Terry Taliban. Two soldiers fiercely defended the position immediately to his left.

'What you doing, sir?' enquired a quizzical young soldier.

'Engaging the enemy,' came the obvious reply.

'Two points, sir. First, if you fire that many rounds we're gonna run out of ammunition, and second, fuck off – this is Tom's work!'

There is nothing that our soldiers, the Toms, like better than a good scrap. We would obviously prefer this to be on the field of battle rather than in a town centre, but occasionally we have to acknowledge with an unfortunate resignation that soldiers and fighting are a historic and continuing combination.

Our soldiers are not only MAGNIFICENT, but they are also MOTIVATED beyond belief. In 2000, an intervention was required in Sierra Leone. 1 PARA were the lead parachute battalion group (LPBG), the quick reaction UK force that would go to prevent Freetown, the capital, being overrun by blocking the rebel advance on the Aberdeen Peninsula. Unfortunately, 1 PARA had a company deployed overseas in Jamaica: they were a company of 110 men short. Not a problem – call your mates in 2 PARA and see if they will provide.

We did provide, thanks to D Company under Major Andy Charlton, a humorous and aggressive but compassionate leader. I was out of communications range due to moving house with no mobile or landline. When I eventually raced back after getting the message (you have already met Rosie and learned how) I asked the adjutant, Pete Flynn, where all the officers were.

'Well, boss. They've gone down to the air mounting centre at South Cerney to get on the plane and fight with 1 Para.'

'But we're the next unit in line for other contingencies. If they all desert their posts we'll have no capability. Get them back!' I barked.

It was too late in many cases. Most were already Sierra Leone bound. I did manage to prevent two officers from boarding the plane. They paraded in my office to be bollocked for their actions, but quietly congratulated for their motivation. One of the officers who managed to slip my grasp was Lt Osman Alashe. Oz was brand new and had not even completed his platoon commander's battle course. He was in Sierra Leone illegally, but had sold his competence in five West African languages as the reason he needed to go. In reality, he was a public school educated, charming, well-spoken Brit of African descent who had played a wonderful line in bullshit to secure his first medal.

Andy Charlton wanted to motivate his men to be absolutely sure they knew the enemy they might be up against. He rotated men through an orphanage in Freetown to see the young orphans who had had their limbs cut off by the rebels. This was more than enough motivation, as if more would be needed, to ensure that if the rebels foolishly decided to come they would be engaged with maximum force. They wisely desisted.

The 212 men of 2 PARA returned some six to eight weeks later. As a duty of care, and to ensure that the men had not been affected by the sights they had witnessed, I called in the military psychologist. He was to determine if any of the men were outside clinical norms and might need some counselling. We used a control group to verify the results. It did not surprise me that they revealed a mild but higher level of depression among the men of 2 PARA who had *not* been deployed.

There are occasions when officers also come under the disciplinary spotlight. How they are dealt with is partly determined by where the crime or misdemeanour takes place. The most expensive painting in the Officers' Mess of 2 PARA is *The Bridge at Arnhem – The Second Day* by David Shepherd. This painting became recognisable worldwide, gracing the cover of the bestselling book *A Bridge Too Far* by Cornelius Ryan, on which the film was loosely based. The painting is now worth many tens of thousands of pounds. One night three young lieutenants were clowning around and throwing beer cans at each other when a couple of misdirected Carlsberg cannons pierced the canvas. Our most expensive painting was now battle-scarred.

The adjutant reported the crime to me next morning just before he marched in the three culprits. The solution was simple: the officers would alternate as the battalion duty officer every day until the painting was restored to its former glory and hung back on the wall. As this would take some time to achieve, the young officers undertaking these extra duties become known as 'the subaltern's friends'. Our three culprits might just as well have been drinking very expensive champagne in copious quantities on the night of the crime, for that is about what it cost them. A few choice bottles of Laurent Perrier 1976 would have made for a cheaper night.

One of our intrepid three subalterns had the misfortune to compound his error a few months later. I arrived back after three weeks away in Nepal to an angry phone call from the head of the army intelligence training centre at Chicksands. He told me that one of the three Laurent Perrier amigos had failed to turn up for his intelligence course, and that he did not think he was best suited for intelligence work. I was out of touch on the situation and defended Lt Crelltan: surely he must have confused the timing on his course joining instructions? Unfortunately, it was week three of the course and Lt Crelltan was making a habit of not turning up on Monday mornings. I had to concur with the analysis of the intelligence community. Lt Crelltan was duly dispatched back from the course. I had no choice but to remove him from the battalion. He was to suffer two punishments, the second perhaps even worse than the first. He was to go to Londonderry for six months, and to work with a battalion from the Foot Guards.

We do have boisterous, but utterly professional, officers, and mess nights can be great affairs of cohesive bonding – but also of rivalry. My first-ever regimental dinner night as a lieutenant involved the almost obligatory 'mess rugby' following the conclusion of dinner. We had supremely fit officers, in very expensive mess dress uniforms, attempting to get a rugby ball (but a scrunched wad of newspaper would do just as well) from one end of the mess to the other against an opposition who were trying to do the same going the other way. No one ever scored. Four officers broke bones, and there were the usual blood injuries in abundance. We were a few months from going to war, and had broken four officers. I banned mess rugby when I was commanding 2 PARA. Having people ready for contingency was more important to me.

As one becomes more senior in the army, there is more disciplinary interaction with civilians. So it was for me in

Northern Ireland in 2006 – 2007. I was often called upon to be the 'deciding officer' in multiple cases. I became known as the 'sacking brigadier'. Of course I was not – I never sacked anyone. That term had negative connotations and was not allowed to be used. I could 'dismiss' people, though.

Now, I have been fortunate to have been healthy and fit throughout my career, and have rarely had a day off sick for the reason that... I was rarely sick. With high motivation and a strong work ethic, I have never really understood the notion that there are days that people can have off 'sick' and that many view this as an entitlement. The following three stories might give you an indication of why we have a budget deficit in the UK. They all involve cases of 'sickness absence management', although if you follow the chronology you might agree with me that there was not much management.

Mr Green-Liquorish was one of few ethnic Rastafarian chefs in Northern Ireland. He was coming to see me as 'deciding officer' on his case in August 2006. Mr G-L had started as a chef for the forces in 2003. He managed to pack 143 days off sick in 2003 and followed this with 146 in 2004 before he went long-term sick in October that year with work-related stress. Now, being shot at, or seeing your mates get wounded or killed in combat, is quite stressful; burning the mashed potato is not quite in the same league. He had attended a Divisional Review Board (DRB) in December 2005, which recommended dismissal. I concurred. I dismissed him. He received £15,000 in full compensation.

Mrs Brown came to see me the following week. Her case was not so bad, and there must have been a modicum of management, for she had only been sick since February. Sitting at her desk had been very stressful. The DRB recommended her dismissal for long-term sickness. I concurred. I dismissed her. She received £11,500 as full compensation.

Mr McArdle was the next to appear before me, in mid-October 2006. He had been long-term sick since September 2004. His level of attendance had been unacceptable since 2001. His interview was the opportunity for him to make a final representation. His absence had arisen also as a result of stress arising from a disciplinary case. The DRB recommended dismissal. I concurred. He received £4,500 in compensation.

After my dealings with the civilians of Northern Ireland, I was to be posted to Iraq. I never made it. Due to a social-disciplinary indiscretion by a senior officer I had to quickly move to another job in London. Just prior to this, I was having one of my final lunches at the house of the General Officer Commanding in NI, Lt General Nick Parker, and mentioned to the assembled guests that there must be some unknown reason why I was moving so quickly to take over – some reason at that time unbeknown to me.

A colonel present at the lunch thought it might have to do with 'trousers down' dalliances, recollecting the story of when he had been fortunate to follow the officer in question for a one-year attendance at the Australian Staff College. Most staff colleges have a scheme whereby foreign students (and a Brit in Australia is still a foreigner) are allocated both a military sponsor and a civilian sponsor for the year, to show them the ropes. In my case, I had sponsored a Zimbabwean student at Camberley, Zinzi Bube. I think he thought I was his slave. I gave him my spare bike so he could cycle to work with the rest of us. He thought that demeaning.

The colonel arrived in Australia and was completing his pre-course administration. He asked for any advice, as he was the sole Brit on the course. 'Yes, please don't f*** the wife of your sponsor.' His intuition about the officer I was called upon to relieve proved correct.

I have to confess that I was myself guilty of (inadvertent) sexism. I was giving a series of lectures to a Territorial Army staff course at Camberley on the estimate processes. There were two lectures of 90 minutes each, punctuated by a 20-minute coffee break in the middle. After the first lecture, three of the female students came to see me and said, 'We haven't understood a word you have said.' I spent the coffee break trying to break down the nuances of the deductive decision-making of the British army for them. I missed my coffee. At the end of the second lecture I made the fatal error of saying, 'If any of the women in the audience haven't understood what I've been saying, please come and see me.' We always retired to the bar at the end of the day to talk about what the students had learnt. Content with my performance, I arrived at the bar before the students. Five minutes later I was pinned to the wall by a female United States Marine Corps major, who berated me for my blatant discrimination and gender-specific comments. Suitably chastised I went home, where my wise wife also told me the error of my ways. I should, of course, have said, 'If *anybody* in the audience has not understood what I have said, please come and see me.' I still believe the USMC major fancied me.

During my time at Tampa I came across a story concerning the USMC that the British army would rather have enjoyed. You would be amazed at the number of soldiers who have, over the years of my service, apparently slipped in a shower resulting in a black eye. It really is something those officious people in the health and safety industry should be alert to. Our USMC colleagues, or at least four of them, were outside a store collecting for the Toys for Tots programme when a thief exited the shop with a laptop under his jacket. The marines stopped the man, but one of the USMC personnel was stabbed. The police and an ambulance arrived at the scene to take the marine corporal to hospital. The thief was also transported to hospital with two broken arms, a broken ankle, a broken leg, several missing teeth, possible broken ribs, a broken nose and a broken jaw: injuries sustained when he slipped and fell off the curb after stabbing the marine, according to a police report. I rather hope those nice policemen of Augusta, Georgia are twinned with our common-sense bobbies who dealt with Airborne Santa.

General George Patton is known to have said, 'You are always on parade. There is no such thing as "a good field soldier". You are either a good soldier or a bad soldier.' To spare the blushes of a real regiment, I will call the unit I am about to describe the Loamshire Regiment. In fact, nearly all of our training at Sandhurst was based around this fictitious regiment. We also never fought the Soviets on an exercise, but always fought either Orange forces (we were blue and hence friendly – unfortunately this is where the phrase 'blue on blue' comes from when fratricide occurs) – or we fought the Fantasians.

One hot sunny day I had occasion as a brigade commander to have my attention drawn to the front page of the *Sun* newspaper. The article recounted the violent exploits of a soldier from the Loamshires who had been in civil court. The regiment had pleaded with the judge not to jail him, as he was a 'good soldier', for an incident that was on the more grievous side of grievous bodily harm (GBH) than most. He was let off by the lenient judge with a large fine.

I had bothered to view the CCTV coverage of the incident and was not amused by the ferocity of the assault on a poor civilian. I phoned the commanding officer and inquired what he was going to do, for this was a sergeant. In fact he was only an *acting sergeant*. The nuance of this is that he is really a corporal who holds a temporary rank. Any unit worth their salt (and a regimental sergeant major and commanding officer should have known this) would have instantly thrown him out of the Sergeants' Mess and reverted him to the rank of corporal. This was the third such violent act by the said 'good soldier'. He had been court-martialled for a similar assault on a soldier only some three years before and had been demoted to the rank of lance corporal. To have then flown through the ranks back up to acting sergeant was extraordinary. The CO chose to do nothing.

This was an example of messianic devotion to subordinate troops leading to poor decision-making from the CO: he is still a lieutenant colonel seven years after the event. After this incident my mind returned to Field Marshal Slim's rephrasing of a Napoleonic line that, 'There are no bad regiments, there are only bad officers.' There may be veterans of past wars who will shout that the incidents I have described are DISGRACEFUL and WOULD NEVER HAVE HAPPENED IN OUR DAY. They would, and did happen.

It has been a long time since there was a mutiny in the British army. The last one involved 13 (Lancashire) Battalion The

Parachute Regiment in Malaya on 14 May 1946, at Muar Camp, when 250 soldiers went on 'strike' to protest the conditions in which they were living.[13] No officers or non-commissioned officers took part. This was an early episode of something that in the last couple of decades has been called the Tom's Liberation Front or TLF. Sentences were passed on 243 of the paratroopers, with most being sentenced to two years' imprisonment with hard labour and to be discharged with ignominy. Although death was still on the statutes for mutiny, the ringleaders received five-year sentences, with presumably an even greater ignominy. In one of the first examples of 'support for our boys', the entire population (1,614) of Cuxton in Kent and 10,000 from Gravesend petitioned against the sentence of two of their residents who had been caught up in the mutiny.

We have not had a mutiny since. There have been various inter-unit battles late on Saturday nights, of which the 3 PARA versus 1 Royal Irish score-draw in Tidworth in 1981 springs to mind. I believe around 30 soldiers were court-martialled for violence that night. A police dog was even concussed from a blow, and the street lights became useful vertical aids for the Royal Military Police to which they could handcuff the fighting soldiers as a means of breaking them up. Bizarrely, both units had a respect for each other after that incident.

The reader may chastise me for the incorrectness of this chapter's title, believing that it should have been called 'Ill Discipline'. But discipline is rather like war. Most of war is pretty boring and involves waiting around for real excitement or terror to occur. Discipline occurs naturally in the army and is a matter of course most of the time. Discipline is a function that happens routinely and is in the ascendant. Men behaving well is the natural state, so you can rest assured that most of the time the army is not really like a bunch of football hooligans dressed in uniforms: the army is well disciplined. Thomas Hardy wrote: 'War makes rattling good history.' Ill discipline is the same: it makes for good stories.

However, discipline can quickly change to ill discipline. Just over 200 years ago, following the victory and capture of Badajoz (Spain) in 1812, Wellington's army went on the rampage:

> What scenes of horror did I witness there. They can never be effaced from my memory. There was no safety for the women even in the churches; and any who interfered or resisted were sure to get shot. Every house presented a scene of plunder, debauchery and bloodshed, committed with wanton cruelty on the defenceless inhabitants by our soldiery. All of this from what had been, twelve short hours previously, a well-organised, brave, disciplined and obedient British army.[14]

In 2013, soldiers are remarkably brave, disciplined, and obedient. You have no reason to lock up your daughters.

---

[11]From *Braddock's Defeat*, ed Charles Hamilton, University of Oklahoma Press, 1959.

[12]For descriptions of more interesting examples of cultural differences see page 138.

[13]Recorded in Hansard, Vol 427 pp 34-42, 8 October 1946.

[14]I am grateful to (then) Captain Dan Dandurand of the Canadian Forces Military Police (who I should have put in the nickname chapter for his marvellous name) for pointing this out to me when he served as my brigade provost officer. It is from *Watchdog – A History of the Canadian Provost Corps*, by Andrew R Ritchie (University of Toronto Press, 1995 p.5).

CHAPTER 9

FOREIGN TRAVEL AND ALLIES

THE PROLOGUE

Personnel in the forces love to travel. Most soldiers do not own a passport before joining the army – and they have a great capacity for losing them – but once they have one, they do like to use it. They prefer this to be on exercise, where they might get some 'rest and recuperation', for a chance to see the host country rather than on back-to-back operations. In Macedonia, Bootsy, from the machine gun platoon, had inscribed on the back of his 'bazaar folding chair' (the item of the tour purchased for $8 from the American commissary in Camp Able Sentry by hundreds of soldiers): 'Same shit, different country.' Soldiers often have a sense of déjà vu.

The bazaar folding chair, incidentally, did not meet the Californian Bureau of Home Furnishings flammability requirements, according to its technical bulletin 117. More importantly, such was the surge in purchases of bazaar folding chairs (and other items) that the Americans banned further British use of Able Sentry. The Brits thus lived up, once more, to the name often given to them by the Americans of 'The Borrowers' (from the books of Mary Norton). Some have suggested that it may actually have had something to do with the Toms' small 'day sacks' being filled with supposedly free cans of coke and Hershey bars that led to the ban.

Apparently, there are 300,000 people in the UK who have visited 50 or more countries. Now, I have only been to 49, so I want to know who these people are. Until I stumbled upon that statistic, I used to think I was fairly well travelled and had witnessed explosions and coups in some of the shittiest countries in the world. It is no wonder cruise liners are so popular: I guess that they are the reason that so many have travelled so widely. Perhaps the 300,000 figure includes senior military visitors who also love to travel, when often there is absolutely no need to do so bar a desire to collect Airmiles from Avios or BA, or to satisfy their own vanity of importance.

As you can imagine, my posting to Tampa in the Florida sun became 'Viagra for visitors'. We had a succession of visitors who failed to follow the wonderful CENTCOM commander's dictum that if you were contemplating being a visitor you should 'patrol with a mission, otherwise you become a pain in the butt.' I hate to disappoint our civilian taxpaying colleagues, so you might wish to know that many of your taxed pounds are being spent on such vanity without any 'output oriented business objective' (you will learn more of such matters in chapter 10). Once you get beyond the 'bureaucratic-speak' in such phrases, you might consider it more simply as I do: as a waste of public money with little or no process or governance behind it. Bad or non-existent governance is a universal business problem – starting with the financial sector. In order for you to frame any future questions to your MP on such matters, here are a number of principles that are worth knowing. Governance should follow:

Propriety and regularity

Prudent and economical administration

Avoidance of waste and extravagance, and

Efficient and effective use of available resources

In my desire to serve the taxpayer wisely in the above cases of visitors to the Florida sun, there were three options for their accommodation in Tampa. They were as follows:

Option 1: We had a spare 'swing flat' that was used when our permanent staff were changing over (more cost efficient than using the hotel in option 3). When the British staffs were not in occupation, this swing flat could be used by all visitors from the UK – free of charge.

Option 2: American military bases have wonderful on-site accommodation all around the world that can be hired for around $50 a night. MacDill Airbase in Tampa has, unsurprisingly, the MacDill Inn. Here is a brief description of what is on offer, from the *Temporary Military Lodging Around the World* book: 'One or two bedrooms, private bath. All units include kitchen, telephone, refrigerator, complete utensils, TV/VCR, air conditioning, daily housekeeping service...'

Option 3: An expensive hotel for three to four times the cost of option 2.

The reader will probably guess which was the most popular option. If you can't, it was option 3. I think you could hear me tear my hair out when the civil servant responsible for the budget at our higher headquarters in England stayed in the expensive hotel (option 3) because it was (bizarrely) more 'convenient' (it wasn't). I even offered to put her up for free in our house. I called that Option 4. So: four options, two of which would cost no money, and most visitors went for the most expensive option. It is little wonder the UK budget is in a mess.

RUSSIA

Most people's lives are punctuated by certain major events. Generally, these revolve around something like getting married, a death in the family, or the birth of a child. I would like to add to this 'visiting Russia in the period following the fall of the Berlin Wall and the collapse of the Soviet Union'. The reasons for this are simple:

Not many folks are forced to drink vodka for breakfast, lunch or dinner.

Not many folks have parachuted with the Russians after they have had vodka for breakfast, lunch and dinner.

Not many folks have been birched (legally) in a sauna by the KGB while drinking vodka after dinner.

Not many folks have broken up a fight between a Russian lieutenant general (and hero of the Soviet invasion of Afghanistan) and the senior visiting British officer.

Not many folks have been worried at my (then) tender age of 32 that they were going to have a heart attack because their metabolism was absolutely shot to pieces by being forced to drink vodka for breakfast, lunch and dinner.

Now that I have your attention, an explanation is warranted.

A very forthright and charismatic officer in 5 Airborne Brigade called Mark Harding-Rolls (obviously known as

'Roller', and of course with a double-barrelled surname he was a cavalry officer) had managed to secure a trip to Russia for five officers of the brigade in 1992. This was a period of uncertainty for the Russians. Their world view and place within the world had been shattered by the collapse of the Soviet Union.

We were hosted in Ryazan, the home of the Russian Airborne Academy. On our first night we experienced the initial vodka indoctrination. We toasted everything under the sun (we may have even toasted the sun, as we ran out of joint Russian-British interests after about 20 shots).

At about two in the morning, three of the Brits (including me) very foolishly asked if we could join our Russian hosts for physical training in the morning on their 'Airborne Playground', a series of assault course-type obstacles where they honed their wonderful physiques – or at least they all looked wonderful on their postcards. To our surprise they concurred. We dragged our bodies out of bed and at the appointed hour duly waited for our hosts. There was no sign of life anywhere in the camp. Not wishing to waste the opportunity for some PT while in Russia, we decided to unilaterally complete a 45-minute run outside the camp – which we did. However, as soon as we left the camp, the gate guard phoned the commanding general to inform him that the Brits had exited. We were suspected of being spies and were never allowed to leave the camp again on our own.

Our confinement to camp meant that we were denied the free will to pick what we could drink and when we would drink it. There was only one drink, and it began with the letter 'v'. It also meant that we could not choose when we would sleep. Our British general did come up with a cunning wheeze one day to outwit the Russian entourage accompanying us. We were taken to see the poet Yesenin's birthplace in Konstatinovo, and to be told about every artefact in every glass case pertaining to the local hero. Now I knew about Yesenin. I had even been to the Royal Opera House at Covent Garden in 1981 to see the Kenneth MacMillan ballet *Isadora*. Yesenin was married to the famous American ballet dancer Isadora Duncan in the 1920s (she died when she was strangled with her own scarf while driving a Bugatti).

General Not-Interested had no desire to see another Russian museum. Yesenin and the ballet were not in his fields of interests. He informed his Russian hosts that while touched by the desire to be shown around the museum, he would get more from the cultural experience if he were to have an anthology of Yesenin's poems and be allowed to read them on the verdant hill overlooking the nearby River Oka. The Russians complied. The remainder of the British party was duly told about every exhibit in minute detail. The tour concluded. I thanked the Russians profusely for their informative and fascinating insight in to the life and times of the great poet Yesenin. Further, I informed them that General Not-Interested was overcome by emotion at being at the birthplace of the noted Russian poet Yesenin. Outside, General Not-Interested slept soundly on the banks of the Oka without ever having opened the book.

Our final day saw us decamp to a training area to see the Russians complete a series of tactical manoeuvres – and to gain our Russian parachutist wings with our famous vodka-induced jump. The night concluded with a gala dinner in our honour. The dinner was all going well until the speeches. With the cumulative impact of six days of vodka coursing through his veins – and, disappointingly, not a honey trap in sight – the British general asked his UK interpreter (a Major Hambledon from the Moscow Embassy who, very confusingly for the Russians, was the spitting image of Lenin) to translate directly. He did. This included: 'Tell the Russian general that I do not like him and have not liked him all week.' I demurred, shaking my head. The Russian general reciprocated in similar terms, and the scene was set for them to disappear outside for a fight. The walk to the doors coincided with the Russian Airborne folk band, who had been quietly playing their hippy-hippy-hoppy-hoppy tunes, breaking into (in English) Stevie Wonder's classic love tune 'I Just Called to Say I Love You'. You couldn't have made it up.

Thankfully, the fight was more a 'vodka handbags at dawn' affair than you would see outside a British pub. The next day we all parted friends on the banks of the Volga. The Russians quite liked me, although they thought I was the political commissar sent from England to keep the wayward general in check. They wanted to keep me for re-education.

JAPAN

Following the Second World War and the occupation of Japan under General MacArthur, the Japanese constitution had been changed so that they were only entitled to have self-defence forces. In light of this, I was sent to Japan to instruct, alongside the Japanese Ministry of Foreign Affairs (MFA), at a peace-keeping seminar.

The MFA were generous hosts, and to show us the Japanese culture we were inevitably taken to a karaoke bar. Now, a Japanese karaoke bar is not like karaoke in a British pub. It consists of a large padded room with a screen the size of a large wall and a phone book-sized book of every song from the inception of the gramophone from which to choose. The first song from our hosts, in perfect English and surprisingly tuneful, was an emotional rendition of 'Bridge over Troubled Water' by Simon and Garfunkel.

The background shots on the screen to the bouncing ball over the English words to the song showed a Japanese girl in a kimono, twirling an umbrella, and walking along a beach. The second song, 'Walking on Sunshine' by Katrina and the Waves (the last UK Eurovision winner in 1893 if my memory serves me correctly) similarly showed a Japanese girl in a kimono twirling an umbrella walking along a beach: a different girl on a different beach, but there was definitely a theme going on here. By the time of the third song, the seditious Sex Pistols' 'Pretty Vacant', we were in 'let's rev it up' mood. Once again we had a version of a girl twirling a kimono walking along a beach. That was the default and little varied background to all the songs: it was visual Muzak.

Later that night, with our evening supposedly over, we decamped with our hosts to a Japanese bar that had just closed. There were no other customers. Thanks to the leverage and esteem of our Japanese Foreign Office hosts, they managed to get the bar to remain open. The Japanese bought their usual (bottle of) whisky (each) and settled down once more to re-start their karaoke. As traditionalists, they commenced again with 'Bridge over Troubled Water' (and this was some years before it became reality with the giant earthquake and tsunami of 2011).

Our senses dulled by the replayed scenes of geisha girls twirling parasols, we had an inevitable sense of déjà vu. This was only relieved when a Japanese Imperial Army song from the Second World War was suddenly the track of choice. There were to be no more geishas. The karaoke screen was now ablaze with scenes of Japanese soldiers storming all over positions with glistening fixed bayonets and raising the flag of the rising sun. There were Zero fighters strafing enemy positions. There were Japanese Foreign Office personnel now on top of the tables, ramrod straight and rhythmically clapping and singing along. The three assembled Brits looked knowingly at each other, thankful that the Japanese constitution had been changed, for it seemed at that moment that the Samurai and warrior character of the Japanese had not.

A visit to the Kamikaze museum in Tokyo gave further proof to my observation, for it is a pretty scary take on history. If the Japanese ever perceive the Chinese to be a threat, I do not think it would take them too long to rediscover their martial roots.

I like the Japanese. They are generous hosts, and were among my favourites of the nations represented at Central Command in America. I was once taken out for a nine-course dinner by them. I struggled manfully through it and did not eat for another two days. I left to go home at 10 o'clock. Our Japanese hosts went to a bar (presumably for some karaoke), and a couple of hours later started eating again. I will credit the Japanese with great culinary and drinking stamina.

BANGLADESH

I travelled to Bangladesh a number of times. This is a fairly new country. It was born out of war with Pakistan in 1971 and the East Bengal struggle for independence produced three million casualties. These sorts of figures put into perspective all the casualties the Brits, US and Europeans have suffered in the last 50 years. Henry Kissinger said that the Europeans are 'post-combat, post-casualties and post-caring'. While this is largely true for Europeans, he did also say that the Brits are quite unusual, as they still quite like fighting. The Toms of the Parachute Regiment can happily relate to the thought of Kissinger.

It may surprise you to learn that 80 per cent of Indian restaurants in the UK are, in fact, run by Bangladeshis. Here are a few other notable facts about Bangladesh, proving that I was paying attention at Bangladesh National Day celebrations in March 2012:

Eleven of the greatest natural disasters in history have occurred in Bangladesh – quite a lot in a 40-year history as an independent nation.

It is the only country in the world where the composer of the national anthem also composed the anthem for another country (India).

Bangladesh is the size of Florida but has the seventh-largest population in the world (167 million).

There are six seasons in Bangladesh.

I always travelled to Bangladesh conducting counter-terrorist work, so my tourism facts are about all I can tell you – apart from the fact that travelling with a military escort to Dhaka airport while there is a curfew is a very fast way to get around, due to the absence of any other traffic. For one reason or another, I cannot see the UK Highways Agency adopting this as the solution to the traffic flow on the M25.

BELIZE
Belize is a small country in the Central Caribbean. I commend

to you Marie Sharp's Belizean Heat as a favoured hot sauce. But we were not in Belize for six-month tours in the 1980s and 1990s to partake of Caribbean cuisine and sauces. We were there to deter the Guatemalans from invading the former British Honduras. The Belizeans, a mixture of cultures, are really nice people, and pretty laid back. 'Don't rush the brush' was the frequent refrain from the civilian workforce who had that wonderfully relaxed Caribbean take on life.

My first tour, following on from the aborted 1982 adventure that saw an about turn and march to the South Atlantic, occurred in 1983. The battalion was spread between Battle Group North in Holdfast and Airport Camp, and Battle Group South in Salamanca and Rideau Camps.

We deployed in April 1983, only nine months after returning from the Falklands War. In many ways it was an uneventful tour of jungle patrols, and live weapon firing, of guards, of relaxing in the sun when not out on patrol – and of a one-month exile for Support Company, 2 PARA, in a remote area called Baldy Beacon. I was now a member of Support Company.

Support Company were (still) the rogues of the battalion, full of real characters and old sweats. It had the most experienced men of the battalion, but was not known for being as laid back as the locals. Every six-month overseas tour (and this included Northern Ireland) attracted an entertainment show from England. In the 1980s this was known as the Combined Services Entertainment (CSE) show. The format was pretty standard – a dancing troupe, some singers, a few comedians, with the addition, at Rideau Camp, of a riot during the performance. The riot would have scored highly on *Britain's Got Talent*: it was stylish and had a loose choreography of flying bottles and flying fists. It was a novelty act rarely seen in entertainment circles. Unfortunately, the result of the riot was not to be judged by Simon Cowell but by Lieutenant Colonel David Chaundler, the Commanding Officer.

Lieutenant Colonel Chaundler's judging was as ruthless as that of Mr Cowell. For his poor leadership, the officer commanding the company was not to progress to boot camp but to be booted – straight back to the UK after being relieved of his command. His 'backing band', Support Company, would be banished to Baldy Beacon for a month to live under canvas in the heat after contemplating their misdeeds during an 84-mile forced march to the area of their banishment, which had as its sign at the entrance the black-humoured welcome of 'Privassion Open Prison'.

As is the manner of these things, and of soldiers in adversity, the march and living in the middle of nowhere strengthened the resilience and cohesion of Support Company, who were far stronger for the experience. It brought them together in the way that only the seeming injustice of collective punishments can. They were not humiliated but resolute, and had a marvellous time, relieved of the tedium of routine, guards and the daily bull of a normal camp. Thus the forced march and banishment followed what is known as the 'law of unintended consequences'.

There is a maxim from the era of National Service that goes: 'If it moves, salute it. If it doesn't move, pick it up. If you can't pick it up – paint it.' Belize is the only place where I have actually seen this in action. I did see people paint grey stones with whitewash for a royal visit. This was not a Parachute Regiment edict, but a Belize garrison edict. The Parachute Regiment might, at best, have washed them. This is also why garrison headquarters and the troops who work for garrisons are generally known under the rubric of 'Rear Echelon Mother F***ers', or REMFs.

I returned frequently to Belize throughout my career, for it provided marvellous jungle training. If you can survive, look after yourself and fight in the climatic conditions of the jungle, you can do so anywhere. I went about four times from the UK when I commanded 2 PARA. I always took Captain Gary Wright, my operations officer, with me. Air travel to Belize from the UK entails changing planes at Miami. Every time we transited through Miami, Captain Wright would get taken aside for the yellow 'Marigold glove' strip-search treatment. After our third trip he became exasperated that Cuban illegals could seemingly pass through the airport unhindered, while he, an ally of the USA, could not, and inquired why he was always stopped.

The explanation was simple. He had a marker on his computer record that showed that he had transited through Nairobi on the day the US Embassy was blown up in the late 1980s. Whatever Wright did, he could not erase that geographic fact that would forever be on his record. Now I was mildly reassured that the power of the microchip could allow such computing power to be brought to bear, and this has increased exponentially since 9/11. I am still reassured by such facts, but it has all been done without much of a hint of public debate. We are the most watched society in the world.

The 2,000-man British garrison of the 1980s is now around five-strong. I suppose this proves that relations between Belize and Guatemala have improved so much that a British military presence is no longer required – and that the Belize Defence Force have been effectively trained. Deterrence allowed normal diplomatic relations to be established. There was always a low probability of conflict. There was also always a low probability of running into armed drug smugglers. There was a high probability that if you did, particularly in 1983 (only a year after the Falklands) that the battle-hardened troops of 2 PARA would ruthlessly dispatch you to meet your maker if you challenged them with weapons. It came as no surprise that the promoted Sergeant Manny Eisermann and the men of 6 Platoon did just that.

BURKINA FASO

I also travelled to Burkina Faso in West Africa, but it was on counter-terrorist work, so I cannot tell you much about this. But Burkina Faso is worth mentioning for two reasons. First, it was known as Upper Volta until 1984, and second, it has the most brilliant name for a capital city that can be employed in pub quizzes. It is Ouagadougou – pronounced 'Agadoo'doo'. Despite the seeming complexity of the name it is easy to remember, for it is very similar to the infuriating song of the 1980s called 'Agadoo' which is about pushing pineapples, shaking trees and grinding coffee!

I have now sent you a subliminal message by which to remember the capital of Burkina Faso, and challenge you to get the lyrics of 'Agadoo' out of your mind within the next two hours. I was amazed to find during my research that 'Agadoo' is only the fourth most annoying song of all time, and I can relate to the song voted the 'most annoying'. In December 1982 I had a bad car crash when I skidded on ice while driving on the A303 in the UK. This caused my car to roll three times down an embankment before coming to rest upside down on its crushed roof. I lay conscious and contemplating my death when the fine men and women of the Hampshire Ambulance service reached the car. I implored them as their first act to switch the radio off, for I could think of nothing worse than dying while 'The Birdie Song' blared in the background. They complied, and I thankfully lived: going to heaven while the 1981 Tweets song played would have been a trip via hell.

Oh, by the way, there is a problem in the region within which Burkina Faso sits from the terrorist organisation known as Al-Qaeda in the Islamic Maghreb, or AQIM.

SAUDI ARABIA

There is no country that has more antipathy towards Iran than Saudi Arabia. It is a curious country to have as an ally. It is a bizarre mix of parallel societies, where the sight of abayas and face coverings being torn off to reveal rather attractive women underneath the yards of formless black cloth is evident on any Gulf Air flight from Saudi Arabia (the reverse is true on flights back to Riyadh from London). It is the largest importer of Johnny Walker Blue whisky in a dry country. I was not surprised to hear on my travels that a UK diplomatic bag labelled as 'a grand piano' led to a frantic call from the customs hall to the British Embassy to inform them that 'you need to get to the airport; your piano is leaking.'

Women cannot drive in Saudi Arabia (I mean they are not *permitted* to drive, rather than the age-old debate that women *can't* drive). I was not sure therefore what I was to make of a protest drive by 43 women in 2011 as part of the Arab Spring. I was even less sure what to make of the fact that two men were arrested in Riyadh at the same time for driving while dressed as women. Homosexuality is banned in Saudi; apparently it does not exist in the Islamic world (despite a curious Middle Eastern proverb that 'women are for procreation, men are for love'). I guess the same applies to cross-dressing.

It was my concern for the gay community of Saudi that led me to fear for the decision-making of 'Gay Gav', who was a personal assistant in the MoD. I only became aware of Corporal Gay Gav of the RAF when I was stopped at his desk on my way to talk to his boss – we never passed more than 30 seconds together. I was thus surprised while we were smoking a cigarette outside a bar during a leaving function in London to realise how camp he was. Cigarette finished, I returned and questioned Chardonnay, my PA.

'Gav's a bit camp, isn't he?'

'Camp? He's queer as a nine-bob note. And all his mates in the corner over there are too.'

She proceeded to educate me in the ways of the world. Gav was an exponent of the modern communication age and even had a 'Gaydar' (a gay version of radar) app on his phone that would bleep when in close proximity to other gay men using the same app. He was posted to Saudi Arabia. I trust he still has his head on his shoulders.

Gav McCoy served with me in 1984. He too was gay. This was quite a feat, as before 1994 a homosexual act by a member of HM Forces was a criminal offence, and homosexuals were deemed (almost like women at the time) to be 'incompatible with service life', despite there being no bar to military service in any other NATO army (less Turkey and the USA within the Alliance). Some 15 years later I was asked my views at a focus group on whether we should allow gay personnel to serve in the armed forces. The Italians probably had it right: a gay (or straight) identity is not an issue;

unwanted predation is, and it is the same issue for predators of a heterosexual persuasion.

So, I knew two servicemen who were both gay and called Gav. If you were an idiot, you might conclude that all men called Gav are gay. This would be to misunderstand and confuse correlation theory, which is also different from causation – the same problem that small-minded people have when they state such absurd notions as 'terrorists are Muslims, therefore all Muslims are terrorists.' This is sometimes seen as a particular concern for Saudi Arabia, from where 15 of the 19 hijackers involved in 9/11 originated. In fact, Saudi has a very successful and proactive de-radicalisation programme – just don't expect them to be socially liberal, as the following stories illustrate.

In 2010, a fatwa was issued by a Sufi cleric, Dr Tahir Ul Qadri. This fatwa was a 600-page dismantling of Al Qaeda's violent philosophy and was widely reported. Good news. At the same time, the press did not pick up on another fatwa by the leading Saudi cleric Abd al-Rahman, in which he ordered the killing of Muslims who allowed the sexes to mix freely in the workplace or educational institutions. This fatwa came on the back of the opening of the non-gender-segregated King Abdullah University of Science and Technology. These two examples – Dr Tahir Ul Qadri is from the non-Saudi Sufi tradition while Abd al-Rahman is from the Salafist-Wahhabist tradition – show us that much of the current struggle is within Islam, and between modernisers and traditionalists.

The UN adopted the Universal Declaration of Human Rights in 1948. All signatory states agreed to promote 'universal respect from and observance of, human rights and fundamental freedoms for all without distinction as to race, gender, sex, language or religion'. I'll give you one guess as to a country that abstained from the vote. I share the values that the UN promulgated, but beware politicians who talk of them too openly. I did not only have to go to a focus group on whether we should have homosexuals in the army in 1999; a far worse fate awaited. I had to go to a focus group on 'The Human Rights Act 1998 – Implications for Army Policy'. This told me to be aware of a possible increase in the number of redresses and grievances arising from perceived 'rights violations'. I no longer needed to surround myself with tactical experts and advisors; what I needed was a platoon of lawyers. They would answer the mysteries of the Act as they pertained to the army. This included such scenarios as:

A soldier refuses to perform a regular night guard duty on the basis that it interferes with his right to private and family life under Article 8. This is not a breach. It is a regular part of a soldier's duties. Force protection is a fundamental part of the army's role.

A soldier refuses to engage with the enemy in combat on the basis that his right to life under Article 2 of the Act is to be breached.

A soldier refuses to perform five press-ups for a minor misdemeanour on the basis that it is inhuman and degrading treatment under Article 3 of the Act.

If you are in doubt where I and the rest of the army stand, refer back to Barbie and Warhammer. Maybe the Saudis do not have it as wrong as we sometimes think. Nevertheless, I hope I live to see the time when women can drive in Saudi Arabia, and that there are more accommodating freedoms that do not see people condemned to death for apostasy, and for such heinous crimes as blogging. It is, of course, for the Saudis to determine the speed of any future transformation – should it occur. Saudi is not on my list of countries that I would urge you to visit, unless you are taking part in the Hajj as a religious obligation, for it is regrettable that the spiritual struggling in the ways of Allah – *jihad* – have been so violently corrupted in its recent meaning by fundamentalists.

THE USA

America is awesomely powerful. Its military has capabilities that would beat the next 10 most capable nations hands down. It is a military that invests in the infrastructure and architecture for modern war. If you wish to confront the USA in state-on-state conflict, you are on a losing proposition. In America, 'scale' has its own multiplication factor.

We tend to forget how big America is. It is 2,571 miles from New York to San Francisco. Despite some differences between who is a liberal (they are *all* liberal in California, even though Reagan was once the Governor) and who is a conservative, an American in New York and an American in San Francisco can relate to each other. If you flew from London to Moscow you would only cover 1,550 miles; it is a similar distance to Istanbul and London to Cairo is only 2,180 miles. We find it difficult to relate to the views of people living closer to us than do the Americans on either side of their continent. It is remarkable that America is so unified.

Americans feel the need for constant change. They do not look back. Clothes, cars and the military change frequently. They learn quickly and adapt even more quickly. In 2012, the US military disbanded the Joint Force Command because fighting as one force combining all the capabilities the US military machine possessed was deemed to be so ingrained as to make the need for a separate command no longer valid. The UK set up its own Joint Force Command *in* 2012 because no one here was the champion of the architecture, infrastructure and enablers that are so crucial in modern conflict. Change in America is seen as a positive in all spheres of civil and military life. As the Americans say: 'You may not like change, but you'll like irrelevancy even less.'

General Mattis, a steely warrior monk (and who always seemed to me to be the spitting image of George C Scott's portrayal of General Patton in the film of that name) headed US Central Command (CENTCOM) from 2010 to 2013. He was a brilliant intellect but also a wonderful mangler of the English language. 'Blinding the UAVs to discombobulate them' and 'Do not assume the automaticity of UK support' were two of the examples where I winced at how our two countries had grown apart linguistically since the Royal Marines burned the White House to the ground in 1814.

General Mattis personified the work ethic of the Americans. He lived to work. The Americans live to work. To have one week off in the US military was unusual; to have two weeks off was downright suspicious. The Americans would work tirelessly in CENTCOM until an issue was solved. Often this meant all night. General Mattis once chastised the Chief of Staff, a shaven-headed major general named Karl Horst, at a meeting at three o'clock in the morning. He urged Karl to manage the work/sleep patterns of the staff, as 'no one should be expected to work more than 18 hours a day.' The Americans expected swift answers, and had the connectivity with their information systems to get them from anywhere in the world.

On one occasion they needed to liaise with a British officer from a headquarters in England. It took five days to get the answer. The US headquarters at CENTCOM were baffled by both the reason, and the mixed metaphor, for the slow response: 'Sorry you couldn't get me. I have been a guinea pig into a clinical study into allergies following wasp bites. Having been suitably stung I am now back at the desk.' The Americans simply could not understand this – neither could I.

The US relationship with China will become their most important long-term bi-lateral. It is described in the term 'strategic pivot' (even though that nomenclature scared the horses and has since been reclassified as a 'strategic rebalancing'). But the UK remains its most important ally. At the core of this are the military, nuclear, intelligence and diplomatic relationships and a willingness of the UK to use hard power when required. We are still a military that has not been paralysed by a willingness to avoid fighting when required. But size does matter. As we further reduce the size of the British military, two trends that are already seen in America's view of the UK will be exacerbated. First, their use of information technology and their communications architecture has advanced to the stage where we are becoming irrelevant and unable to compete in attempting to take on independent operations (or even to talk and communicate with them in future operations). Second, US officers know little about UK capabilities and show even less interest in learning about them. The 'special relationship' will be less special.

Allies are important to the US. They wish to be seen to be good multi-lateralists. 'Never forget that Tonga has the same number of votes in the UN as the USA,' as they like to say at

CENTCOM. Nations do not have friends, they have interests, and America will always ruthlessly target those who seek to harm its interests. If you are a superpower, then there are times when you need to, and should, act like a superpower, but perhaps not all the time, for the world could occasionally do with a touch of light relief. America is still the indispensable nation – damned when it does take action (based on 'realist' foundations of foreign policy), and damned when it does not (such as overtly in Syria, where the moral precepts of Woodrow Wilson are often used as the yardstick for the need for US action). It cannot win, whatever it does. It deserves to be given a bit of a break.

The US are fantastic at doing 'change of command' ceremonies – and make much of retirements. One famous departure at CENTCOM involved a two-star army major general leaving after many years of mobilised service following 9/11 (recalled to active duty from the reserves from being an executive in a defence company for *nine* years). The Americans do have a habit of mobilising their reserves in a far more ruthless manner than the British. The retiring general wittily said that his speech would follow the 'three Bs'. He would 'be brief, be brilliant, and be gone.' One and three-quarter hours later he was still going – he even thanked his dog and all the pets he had owned during his life – leading to involuntary shuffling in the ranks, a collective lateness for all sorts of meetings that very senior people should have attended, and a complete misunderstanding of what his three Bs were supposed to mean. I believe General Mattis mentally called in an air strike.

The military has a fondness for threes, fours or fives. There are the three Bs (above), the four Cs (Confirm, Cordon, Control,

Clear – how to deal with bombs in Northern Ireland) and three Ds (Defeat, Disrupt, Dismantle – that's al Qaeda). There are even the five Ps (Prior Preparation Prevents Poor Performance), often elongated to six Ps with the addition of a rude lavatorial word between 'prevents' and 'poor').

Government ministries have now got in on the act. The Home Office Counter-Terrorist Strategy is also based around four Ps – Prevent, Prepare, Pursue and Protect. The military threes, fours, and fives are based around simple things on which to hang a procedural automatic response in the adrenalin-filled moments after an incident. Some of the government soundbites are due to the fact that they often treat the population as idiots. Instead of 'the people have lost trust in the government' we have too often reversed this to become 'the government has lost trust in the people.' You can see this in the things we have had legislated for us in the last 10 years. I was sitting on my 'risk assessed' chair when I wrote this paragraph bemoaning the fact that I had not been invited to a SALAD (Senior Army Leaders Away Day).

IRAN AND OMAN
General Mattis used to say there were three things that kept him awake at night: 'Iran, Iran and Iran'. Ever since the Iranian Revolution in 1979, the UK has been portrayed as the 'Little Satan' to the USA's 'Great Satan'. It was not always so.

In the early 1970s, the British army was fighting an undeclared war in the Dhofar, a region of Oman. One of the participants was my boss from 1992 to 1993, a legendary SAS commander: the famous Cedric from our earlier survey of nicknames. Cedric was an unusual officer; he smoked his own roll-up cigarettes and was famous for his taciturn nature, though maybe not quite as taciturn as that other famous counter-insurgency expert whose books we all studied in our formative days, General Sir Frank Kitson. His reticence was legendary. At a dinner, he was sitting next to a lady who bet that she could get more than three words out of him. 'You lose,' replied Sir Frank. When General Kitson was commandant of the Staff College, the chief of staff was skipping down the corridor with carpet samples for his office. 'What you got there then?' enquired an unusually loquacious General Kitson. 'Your carpet, sir,' replied the colonel. 'Bit small, isn't it?' replied Sir Frank.

Anyway, Cedric had just passed SAS selection and was helicoptered out to a jebel in the Dhofar to meet and lead his SAS troop. The Iranians were friendly forces at the time and were securing the base of the jebel with a battalion of soldiers. The British have never been fantastic at languages and sure enough the army had a lack of Farsi speakers. In an act of prescience, the SAS had sent one of Cedric's troopers, Vince, to learn it with a professor of Farsi at Cambridge University – it cost the army tens of thousands of pounds.

After 24 hours on the jebel getting to know his men and being briefed on the situation, Cedric announced to Vince that it was time to go and talk with the Iranians. They arrived and looked around the defensive perimeter.

Cedric: 'Vince, tell the Iranians I'm unhappy with the siting of some of the claymores and the layout of the defensive position.'

Vince thought for a second then shouted, 'THE CAPTAIN SAYS...' thus once again proving the inability of the English to converse in a foreign language.

The impact of the support that the Iranians provided is still evident. Sultan Qaboos is still an ally because of the blood debt that the Iranians paid to help secure the future of Oman during the Dhofar conflict. The Iranians lost 600 soldiers killed in action. I suspect they will lose a lot more in the next one to three years if and when they are visited either by the Israelis or the Americans. Unless there is a 'grand bargain' over the Iranian nuclear issue there is the potential for a 'grand' (or 'petite' depending on the likely scale) war. It is almost that binary. 'Jaw, jaw' still remains a better option than 'war, war'. You will quickly notice if such an event ever happens, because the price of a gallon of petrol will go through the roof, making the 1973 petrol price levels after the Yom Kippur War look like the good old days. The survival of the Supreme Leader in Iran is bound up with propagating an anti-US posture: the mullahs in Iran really are a mad bunch.

AFGHANISTAN

A stolen Afghan National Army (ANA) Ranger vehicle was eventually discovered parked on the side of the road by a joint Afghan National Army and Afghan National Police (ANP) patrol with NATO advisers. The ANA were wary of approaching the truck, thinking it might be booby-trapped. The ANP did not want to deal with the vehicle either, so the ANP decided to blow it up with a rocket assisted projectile (RPG). As the ANP prepared to fire, the advisers were yelling at them to consider another course of action (such as explosive ordnance disposal). The RPG gunner somehow had a premature firing – a 'negligent discharge' – with the RPG. The rocket missed the truck and struck a tree next to it. The tree fractured, causing a suicide bomber to fall out of it onto the truck, detonating his bomb and thus making the booby trap on the Ranger vehicle blow up as well.

That just about sums up Afghanistan. Dr Johnson is probably most famous for his remark that 'When a man is tired of London he is tired of life.' I have yet to hear anyone make the case that 'The man who is tired of Lashkar Gah is tired of life' or of Helmand province for that matter.

There has been only one year since the Second World War in which British forces have not lost a man killed in action in combat or on operations somewhere in the world. In that year, 1968, we were neither in Afghanistan nor Iraq. Come to think of it, neither were we in Vietnam. I often liked to goad my American colleagues with the query:

'People often wonder why the Brits were not involved in the Vietnam War. Do you know the answer?'

'No, do tell me.'

'The Viet Cong were doing very nicely on their own, thank you very much.'

Harold Wilson, the Prime Minister at the time, may have got it right in rejecting calls for the UK to participate to stop the (now known to be false) assumption that there would be a series of dominos if South Vietnam were to fall to the communists. We only suffered the Grosvenor Square riots in 1968, protesting against *US* involvement in the Vietnam War. In Vietnam, it was the year of the Tet offensive, of massive casualties, with the profound impact that had on public and policy opinion. The US was apparently always winning in Vietnam, despite the fact that they failed strategically. The same case is now made for military operations in Afghanistan: we were always winning. I trust this is seen to be true.

Afghanistan is prone to what has been termed the 'supermarket theory'. You can 'pick and mix' with your facts. It is like a supermarket, in that if you have a recipe, you can quite easily roam the aisles to find the right ingredients to make your dish. So it is with Afghanistan. You can see Afghanistan through any prism you want: counter-terrorism, counter-insurgency, counter-narcotics, nation building, economic development (the panacea of a modern Silk Road and the utilisation of Afghan minerals to create a new society is always just around the corner), or human rights development. The policy-maker gets to choose the paradigm to fit the message he wants to deliver at the time.

I was an expert in the theology of Al Qaeda. I can quote to you the 'single narrative' that underpins their views. I am word perfect on Al Qaeda and their desire to remove the apostate regimes in the Middle East, to remove the influence of the West in the Middle East, and to re-establish their perceived caliphate. We went to Afghanistan originally to remove Al Qaeda after 9/11. That objective was achieved long ago – the Afghan Taliban are not global *jihadists*. So, ask me what our narrative is in Afghanistan and the answer is: I haven't got a clue.

Whatever measure you use to view Afghanistan, it was expensive, in both 'treasure' and lives. A further 59 names were chiselled onto the National Memorial Arboretum in Staffordshire in 2012 to represent those who were killed in action in 2011. These followed the 112 names that were added the year before. A further 44 Afghanistan combat deaths were chiselled into the memorial in 2013. Ten more were finally added in 2014.

By the end of 2014 we should have ceased combat operations in Afghanistan. We will be in the 'transformation decade' to 2024 (although it is always useful to know into what you want something to transform). That will take us up to a commitment of something like the Thirty Years War (1614 – 1648). That war ended with the Treaty of Westphalia, which set the future of the sovereign state for the modern era, and included the rule of law where all are treated equally, and a culture of peace. Let us hope we can return to both 1648 and 1968.

There is a further military maxim that I have not yet introduced. It is: never get separated from your kit. In 2010, I travelled to Bahrain to take part in a conference on board a Royal Fleet Auxiliary ship. As I was a newly promoted major-general, the naval stewards had 'upgraded' the bunk I was to occupy. My cabin still had the name of the original occupant on the door, but such fripperies were of no concern to me.

After two days of deep thought with various top-level commanders from around the deployed UK 'footprint' from Iraq to Afghanistan and the Falklands to Diego Garcia, it was time to go home. Those who were serving in Afghanistan had the RAF to take care of them and would leave three hours before those travelling elsewhere, who would take a BA flight to London.

To ensure the out-loading of all the luggage went smoothly, the ship's staff transported all rucksacks and bags from the cabins to the fleet of cars. With great efficiency we set off in four Range Rovers for Bahrain International Airport. At the airport everyone got out and located their luggage – except me. We stripped all four vehicles to the bone to locate my bags, picking up four parking tickets for extending our stay beyond what was reasonable in the drop-off positions. Then it dawned: due to the name on my room door, my bags had been flown to Afghanistan. My world consisted of what I stood up in, and a handkerchief. My passport, wallet and all my means of being a modern man had been stripped from me. For 48 hours I lived on a Royal Fleet Auxiliary ship with just my handkerchief until my kit was flown back for our reunion. Thus, as my wife likes to tell me, my kit did more time in Afghanistan than I did.

CANADA

I love Canada. It has two seasons – hot and very cold/snowy. You know where you stand in terms of Canadian seasons. Why the Brits make a big song and dance about the weather is therefore beyond me, for we really do not have many variations in our seasons. Unlike North America, we have no tornados and no hurricanes. Our weather is (comparatively) benign. But as this book is written by a Brit, it is only right and proper that I make some allusion to the weather: the reader would expect no less.

I spent 21 months in Canada on exchange with the Canadian Airborne regiment at a place called Petawawa. I would not expect too many people to have heard of Petawawa, even less know where it is: three hours west of the capital, Ottawa, by road. Now you know.

In winter, the Canadian army goes about its business covered in white camouflage and wearing snowshoes while towing their supplies on a toboggan. Canadian winters are very beautiful. When it is not snowing, there are vibrant blue skies. I once parachuted into the Arctic Circle (at a frigid -45 degrees) to conduct an exercise around Rankin Inlet to prevent the wily Russian Spetnaz Special Forces from seeking to destroy the joint American-Canadian early warning system. I think the Russians possessed stand-off munitions by this time, so the concept was ever so slightly flawed. Rankin Inlet is an Eskimo settlement. Or it was an Eskimo settlement until we had to start changing the nomenclature of the indigenous peoples. I think we now refer to the natives as Inuit, and that Rankin Inlet is now an Inuit settlement.

These confusions about the native peoples also cross the border into America. When I was a boy, we played Cowboys and Indians, and referred to the Indians as Red Indians. I recounted this on a visit to San Francisco. The young tour guide thought I was referring to the Indian sub-continent. The native Americans have now gone through a couple of re-brandings from 'American-Indians' to the latest, 'First Nation Peoples'. The Inuit may even have been rebranded as First Nation. I can't keep up.

The Canadians frequently refer to the British as 'shit-eaters'. They seem to think that we eat deep-fried toast and deep-fried Mars Bars. This is quite a statement for a nation where a seven-course meal consists of a six-pack of beer and a slice of pizza. I know this to be true: holding a refined supper or dinner party in Canada can be a challenge. This begins with the phrasing of an 'At Home' card and the instruction line: 'Dinner: 7.30 for 8'. We hosted many a dinner party where the plates of our guests were surprisingly full after the meal. My wife's cooking is rather good, so I was not sure what had gone wrong. I learned that Canadians would eat their 'tea' at around five in the afternoon, so their bellies were full by the time they arrived. My main interlocutor in calling Brits 'shit-eaters' was a splendid Canadian officer called Mark Skidmore. As my son grew, he was able to avenge this affront to our nation by renaming him 'More Skidmarks'. I rather liked that.

During my time in Canada the country was going through a bit of a crisis. The often-festering constitutional issue raised its head once more between the French-Canadians of Quebec and the Anglo-Canadians (resolved at the time by the Meech Lake Accord). Canada is officially bi-lingual. Given the size of the country, this makes it a challenge to get your head around if you live in the wilds of Alberta several thousands of miles away from the French-speaking province.

The Canadian army was also going through a crisis. Canadian society is quite liberal. Their defence forces (they had officially got rid of the individual services) were focused on peace-keeping only. Let me give the Canadians credit: they have rediscovered the fighting spirit that they displayed in both World Wars in the manner of their conduct in Afghanistan. They deserve no less; man-for-man, the Canadians were really good and tough soldiers. The Brits should know, for one of the other quibbles of our Canadian cousins was that 'The Brits would fight to the last Canadian.' I think this came from our propensity for wiping out the Newfoundland Regiment on several occasions in the First World War. Newfoundland did not become part of Canada, as the tenth province, until 1949.

It is no surprise that at Beaumont Hamel in France is a monument to the Newfoundland Regiment. It is sovereign Canadian soil. The Newfoundland Regiment took the second highest casualties of any regiment on the first day of the Somme on 1 July 1916 with 684 killed or wounded in action. They were not even in the first wave to attack. To have such a scale of casualties would represent a campaign of some years' duration today. We never lost that number killed in Northern Ireland over 38 years, in any of the Gulf Wars, in the Falklands, or even into our second decade in Afghanistan. It will not surprise you to learn that the thoughts of the Newfoundland soldiers as they went 'over the top' were on less highbrow matters, since a noted lady of society in the capital, St John's, had thoughtfully stated that she intended to marry the first VC in the regiment. 'Buxom Bessie or a wooden leg' was the supposed battle cry as Newfoundlanders were led to their slaughter. Bessie never did get to marry a soldier.

CHAPTER 10

THE MINISTRY OF DEFENCE

The Ministry of Defence is a curious place. My own curiosity lasted over five years in two stints, the first of two years and the next of three. I went through the backsides of three pairs of charcoal grey trousers in my second iteration – that is a lot of bottom-sitting time.

I should have known this was to be the fate of my trousers when I found a note I had inexplicably written in a 1977 diary. It recounted a conversation from 1919 between Birkenhead[14], the Attorney General, and a much-medalled general who had spent the First World War sitting in the War Office (as the MoD was then known):

'General, you have a lot of medals.'

'Yes, Mr Attorney. If I get any more I shall scarcely know where to put them.'

'Put them where you earned them, General – on your backside!'

The MoD, like most of Whitehall, is somewhere you can be stabbed in the back and the chest at the same time while someone smiles at you. I was given a dressing down for the lack of passage of information on an incident over a weekend by a senior RAF officer in my chain of command. I would not have minded, but I had arrived for my first day in the job: I do not mind being held accountable for anything if I am actually in a job and responsible, but this was too much. The RAF officer was someone who I was worried that I might have a future 'character clash' with (if you are a subordinate you will always lose in such circumstances). I managed to avoid this by finding out that the RAF officer did not have a character to clash with. He put me in mind of why the army, when it evacuated from Crete back to Alexandria in Egypt in 1942, felt let down by the RAF. The RAF had, for good strategic reasons, abandoned the island and fallen back to Egypt, leaving the army with no air cover. Quite a few fists were thrown in the direction of the most junior service when the troops reached Egypt. The RAF acronym suddenly stood for either 'Rare as Fairies' or 'Ruddy Absent F******'.

What do you need to know about the Ministry of Defence? The first thing: repeat after me, 'The minister is always right, the minister is always right, the minister is always right.' You will by now understand that the minister is always right (even if he is wrong). That is why we have political control of the military. I may not understand democracy but I'm prepared to fight for it, but it would be helpful to be given clear strategic guidance and objectives for any campaign.

The minister requires political-military advice (from the civil service) and military advice from the service chiefs. The minister is, after all, a politician. It does not matter if you follow the Jeremy Paxman School of Philosophy applied to politicians, which goes along the lines of 'Why is this lying bastard lying to me?' This is similar to the old adage that you can tell when a politician is lying because his lips are moving. It does not matter, because the minister is always right. And the minister is always right even if he is a *new* minister in a *new* government that has replaced a party of a different hue and knows nothing about defence. When this occurs, the minister has only six to 12 months to blame the previous government for being incompetently wrong and for leaving everything in a complete mess, before he is blamed by the opposition for being incompetently wrong and should of course resign. Each government will seek to push this six to 12 month period of grace (as they see it) as far to the right in terms of time as they can safely seem to do while maintaining their credibility. Then, horror of horrors, they have to take responsibility and make their own decisions.

It is from this paradigm that the most useful of political-military weapons derives – the blame thrower. This is capable of squirting malice and venom over a wide arc; it never runs out of ammunition, and is generally most excellent at evading the enemy that goes by the name of responsibility.

In the case of the Ministry of Defence, we do not require too much political help for leaving things in a mess from one administration to another, for it is also a political axiom that indecision is the key to flexibility. Given that an extraordinarily large number of people work in the Ministry of Defence you may find this indecision incredible. That would be to misunderstand the nature of this 'all-consuming bureaucracy, a paper octopus squirting ink and wriggling its tentacles into every corner. Unless pruned with an axe, it will grow into a fakir's mango tree, and the more it grows, the more it overshadows the Minister or the General.'[15]

There is another useful maxim: 'If you have good people and bad processes, bad processes will win nine times out of 10.' The real panacea is to combine the first axiom with the maxim. You will then have a combination of well-intentioned good people with bad processes who fail to make a decision. We generally call this 'government'.

My first MoD internship occurred during the 2003 Iraq War, while we were already campaigning in Afghanistan. At the time, defence was having terrible troubles with the SA80 A1 rifle, which had replaced the beloved SLR as the personal weapon of all soldiers. It had a propensity to gobble sand. The SA80 also presents an enduring problem for someone, like me, who is left-handed and predominantly left-eyed. It can only be fired right-handed (using the shoulder for the butt of the weapon). The SLR could be fired from either shoulder. As there were quite a few urban operations in Iraq, this exposed the firer, more often than he would like, to enemy fire if he happened to be turning a corner to the right. Turning a corner to the left gives the body a lot more cover. It is rare in warfare in urban areas to have to conduct only left-handed turns around street corners. As the SA80 actually is not supposed to be a sand-eater but a weapon, the weapon was problematic, so much so that the SA80 became known as 'the Civil Servant' – it doesn't work and you cannot fire it.

Now this may not be a true reflection of the Civil Service and I have had some wonderful suited comrades, but there is an element of truth in the 'doesn't work' or at least the caveats on working. I had an ebullient and talented POLAD (political advisor) in Tampa called Chris Kitchener. She was a civil servant grade B2 but maintained a spreadsheet, for she was only mandated to work 37.24 hours per week before she received overtime payments. I want to know what crazy negotiators come up with .24 of an hour. She also discovered that if you work with the three services, 'uniform is not'. You could count up to eight pairs of different boots at each morning meeting of 10 people.

The mandatory 37.24 hours is a lot less than the European Working Time Directive maximum of 48 hours. I know this because the RAF and RN Search and Rescue force (SAR force) had a civilian comparator to benchmark against. Benchmark is one of those words that you absolutely must drop into a meeting to ensure you have a chance of winning MoD Bullshit Bingo, ticking off the current buzzwords on a small card. Current favourites include 'blue skies thinking', 'delivery' (a curious notion as I thought that postmen did this, and slightly different from the 'short term deliverables' which is also in vogue),'horizon scanning', 'resilience', 'paradigm shift', 'strategic fit', 'results-driven', 'think outside the box' et al. The simple requirement is to tick off five buzzwords in one meeting and shout 'bingo'. As one player described it, 'I feel that the game has enhanced the overall quality of meetings per se on a quid pro quo basis and that employees have been empowered and added-value in the big picture enabling us to stretch the envelope and really move the goalposts in order for us to play hardball leaving us in a win-win situation.'

If you are unlucky enough to be in a department or on a floor in the MoD that does not deliver (at least not on time and on budget, such as anyone in procurement), you might be one of those who comes away after a two-year tour of complete bafflement uttering the oft-used phrase: 'What the f*** was that all about?'

Fortunately, I was in the Operations Directorate, so I never had to suffer the above misfortune. But I had my favourite phrases about the MoD, such as Churchill's that 'meetings are events where minutes are taken and hours are wasted' (I think the collective noun must be – or should be – 'a virus of meetings') and for those in procurement, 'if Moses were a committee, the Israelites would still be in Egypt.' If we had an equipment programme named 'Moses' I am sure it would still be on the drawing board, or at least be in serious danger of cancellation due to cost overruns.

Harold Macmillan, Prime Minister from 1957 to 1963, once said that there are three organisations you should never contemplate having an argument with: the Roman Catholic Church, the Brigade of Foot Guards, and the trades unions. In my time in the MoD I was involved in taking on both the Brigade of Guards and the trades unions. We managed to ameliorate the impact of the trades unions in their strikes, but there was absolutely no chance of messing with the Brigade of Guards. Both were involved, to some degree, in my time as the strategic planner during the national fire strike in 2002 – 2003.

The MoD knew that the Fire Brigades Union (FBU) was contemplating industrial action and were asked by the Deputy Prime Minister, John Prescott, to come up with a contingency plan that would involve the armed forces providing emergency cover, so that lives would be saved. We could never hope to replicate the professional and in-depth expertise of the ordinary firemen, but with training and an organised plan we would be able prevent loss of life.

This was a big undertaking and our strategic planning showed that to provide national cover would require somewhere around 19,000 troops from all three services. I was undertaking this work on behalf of the Vice-Chief of the Defence Staff. He was an RAF air marshal with a fearsome reputation. He was so disliked in the RAF that if you ever used his name in any RAF Officers' mess, you had to buy a round of drinks. To avoid such a situation, he was known under the sobriquet of the 'Scottish Air Marshal'. I think he actually rather liked me: he once wished me a 'Happy Christmas'. Unfortunately, it was Christmas Day and we were both in the office working, for not only did we have a national fire strike we were also contemplating the 2003 invasion of Iraq, for which we would have to find another 38,000 troops on top of the fire commitment.

The Scottish Air Marshal's approach to time off was very similar to that of the Americans. The only slight irony at CENTCOM in Tampa (to talk of irony with most Americans is itself an irony) is that a large headquarters that sees itself at war has the following conversations, mainly on Friday afternoons: 'Have a nice weekend, see you tomorrow' or 'Have a nice holiday, see you tomorrow.' All militaries talk of 'battle rhythms': I have yet to hear anyone talk of vacation or holiday rhythms in the same way.

To commence our emergency fire planning, we took the Military Tasks (MTs) laid out in the Defence Strategic Guidance (DSG) document and mapped the 'must continue' standing commitments that the three services had to conduct, setting them against lower priority tasks that might temporarily cease. At the top of our 'list to continue', I put as the most important military task the uninterrupted submarine patrols of the strategic nuclear deterrent. I was wrong. The most important military task was the continuance of the ceremonial duties of the Brigade of Guards. They were untouchable. Every time I went to a briefing at the Cabinet Office Briefing Rooms (COBR), nestled within 70 Whitehall, I passed some of the Household Division in their boxes under the arches at Horse Guards. While tourists saw the spectacle of four men in finery, I only saw a mental image of a missing Green Goddess crew. We justify this under the title of 'fabric of the nation' (the Canadians conduct the task outside their Parliament in Ottawa with students).

The Green Goddesses were the key to unlocking the strike. These 50-year-old fire engines were owned by the Home Office. The armed forces merely manned them. Why were we able to bring about the move back to work? One of the planning tools we have (based on Clausewitz, our favourite military philosopher) talks about an enemy's 'centre of gravity' (not that the FBU were the enemy, but the methodology we used was the same).

So, if understanding the problem is everything – Einstein is quoted as saying that if he had one hour to save the world he would spend 59 minutes defining the problem and one minute coming up with a solution – the FBU needed to have 'the ability to use strike action as a coercive tool'. But we were an alternative, and the Government was not going to give in. The Fire Brigades Union therefore had no chance of succeeding in their strike aims. The same would have been true in the fuel disruption of 2012. The last decade of military involvement in 'disruptive challenges' has largely been around four Fs: fuel, floods, foot-and-mouth and fire. The Chief of the General Staff at the height of these, General Sir Mike Jackson, used to double the number of Fs to eight by his use of more vernacular introductions in each case.

Politicians like to wave their hands and say 'make it happen'. They also, more dangerously, sometimes like to say 'make it legal'. There are limits to the creativity one can come up with for certain circumstances. For example, I had to explain to the Minister of the Armed Forces why we could not put Tornado fighter aircraft at the City of London airport during the Olympics. The laws of physics apply. If an aircraft requires 10,000ft of runway to take off and the said runway is 2,000ft shorter, there is an obvious problem. This can only be solved by going elsewhere to another airport, or demolishing the infrastructure of the financial capital of the world to extend the runway at a cost of a squillion pounds. The minister did not like the explanation, telling me to 'make it happen'. I am happy to report that the particular minister lost his seat in the 2010 election – and we never did raze Canary Wharf to the ground.

Politicians, of course, should not be expected to act any other way than politically. An opposition leader in Israel, Tzipi Livni, was defeated in mid-2012 within her party. The ensuing analysis: she was an intellectually honest thinker and a brave leader, but a poor politician. We are not sure what sort of politician we want in the UK either. The power of the American politician to fight for his own constituency benefits is never more evident than in the defence field.

It has become a truism that when Western nations go to war that treatment of the wounded must conform to 'the golden hour'. This states that the wounded have a good chance of survival if they receive surgical treatment within that time frame. It is a sensible rule. It is not based on clinical reality, but comes from a Maryland politician lobbying for a number of field hospitals to be placed in his state: this politician coined the phrase. It is used in Afghanistan and drives the laydown of the helicopter force to extract casualties. It was used in the Falklands. In one of those horrible phrases that sanitise the reality of combat: failure to achieve these norms can lead to 'negative patient outcomes'. You might know this more prosaically as meaning that men die.

The Ministry of Defence fulfils two functions. It is both a higher military headquarters and a department of state. Both sides can forget this. I think Prime Minister David Cameron was right when he told the service chiefs after their squabbling over the impact of Libya operations in June 2011, 'You do the fighting, I'll do the talking.' There is something unseemly about the service chiefs airing their dirty laundry in public. They may not intend to do this deliberately but there are few organisations as 'leaky' as the MoD. The email, the contacts with journalists and the photocopier are three of the most dangerous weapons in the modern era. We would do well to remember that political control of the military is a given in a democracy, and that the sage words of Alanbrooke, whose statue with the words 'Master of Strategy' on the plinth graces the Whitehall side of the Ministry of Defence, are still very relevant: 'If you insist on being damned fools, sooner than fall out with you, which would be fatal, we shall be damned fools together, and we shall see that we perform the role of damned fools damned well.'

It is slightly curious, given the political control of the military, that it is Alanbrooke, the master of strategy, who surveys Number 10. It should be the other way around. Alanbrooke understood about political control of the military and also that part of his job was to enable the 10 per cent of Churchill's ideas that were genius and filter the 90 per cent that were bonkers. Perversely, on the Embankment side, there is a statue of General Gordon of Khartoum. Most readers will be familiar with Gordon from the 1966 portrayal of him by Charlton Heston in the film *Khartoum*. I have always found it odd that there is a statue of Gordon – who was absolutely beyond political control, which led to Gladstone having to dispatch (too late as it happened) a rescue mission – outside the Ministry of Defence. Perhaps it is there to subliminally remind us of the tension between the MoD as a department of state and as a higher military headquarters.

Having told you that Alanbrooke was a 'Master of Strategy' it would be wise to tell you what strategy is, as it is the most widely used, most widely misunderstood and most wrongly used term across government. It is not news headlines, nor is it chasing the short-term deliverable, where activity is confused with progress and defined strategic outcomes. Alanbrooke's strategy is this:

'Determine the aim, which is political: to derive from that aim a series of objectives to be achieved; to assess these objectives as to the requirements they create and the preconditions which the achievement of each is likely to necessitate; to measure available and potential resources against the requirements, and to derive from this process a coherent pattern of priorities and a rational course of action.'

I have this definition in the back of every notebook that I have carried with me over the last 10 years along with a reminder that: 'Strategy is not policy and policy is not strategy. Policy states what is to be done, or sometimes what is not to be done.'

The problem of leaks has become so bad that we now resort

to the slightly ridiculous. There is a sensitive country where if leaks were to get out would be bad news, both internally and in the wider international forum. I have changed the name to prevent leaks. A colleague had the following conversation:

'We want you to write a covering brief for the paper that is going to the Secretary of State for Defence on what our policy should be on FANTASIA.'
'Fine, but where is the paper? I haven't seen it.'
'That's correct. You are not allowed to see the paper because it is highly sensitive.'
'But how can I write a covering brief for a paper I have not seen?'
'You know what's in the paper anyway.'
'So why can't I see the paper?'
'You can't.'
'So you want me to write a brief on a paper that I cannot see but which you think I know the contents of anyway?'
'Yes.'

He did not see the paper, but still had to write a brief explaining the contents of the paper that he had not seen.

Every time there is an incident of some magnitude (and many occasions when there is not), the Cabinet Office Briefing Room Alpha (COBRA) is activated to bring all government departments together to fix the problem or return an emergency to a steady state. I attended COBRA meetings on many occasions.

To indicate to you that our former colonies learned the lessons of acronyms well from their former British masters, some readers may be familiar with the Indian CoBRA, which stands for 'Commando Battalions for Resolute Action'. These units are employed against the Naxalite uprising in the Indian state of Andhra Pradesh. If you are familiar with these things, then I believe that you could consider yourself to be a counter-terrorist or counter-insurgency expert, and are currently reading the wrong book.

Presentation and media concerns play a big part in the considerations of the UK COBRA. In December 2002 there was the potential for an Al Qaeda rogue ship to disperse a chemical-biological cloud over southeast England. It is almost inevitable that these sort of crises start at about three o' clock on a Friday afternoon – and this one fitted that pattern. If a ship is travelling at X knots an hour, and it is in the Bay of Biscay which is Y distance away from the coast of the UK, it does not take the brains of an archbishop to work out when it is likely to become a threat. This is the kind of basic time and space (X and Y) calculation that the services are good at. Forces are not sitting ready to go; they are at Notice to Move (NTM) and you have to bring them down to readiness to execute a mission. It is therefore not a good thing for the military blood pressure when the first 45 minutes of this particular COBRA meeting was taken up by a discussion of what should be said to the press. We were anxiously looking at our watches – we needed to rev up the intervention force. Eventually a decision was made, and an intervention on the ship did take place – it was carrying nothing more than bananas. Given the intelligence, it needed to be searched, and for seven days a thorough search among a rapidly rotting cargo of browning bananas revealed nothing more sinister than... rotting bananas.

This obsession with the press almost as the first agenda item is not to underplay the importance of the press or the need for governments to be media savvy. The worry is that short termism triumphs over longer term strategy. A Pakistani brigadier once told me that there is no such thing as strategy any more, only crisis management (or 'crisis muddle' as he put it in relation to the perennial problems encountered in Pakistan.[16]) He may well be correct.

Exercising for terrorist intervention scenarios was a regular occurrence. Ministers were always involved, for they are responsible for signing-off on the risks. One particular scenario involved a 747 wide-bodied jet that had been forced to land by the RAF, and the SAS were required to conduct a hostage rescue after terrorists had seized the plane. David Blunkett, the Home Secretary at the time, was the minister in the chair. He was required to decide if he would authorise the operation. The Special Forces cell in COBRA was required to articulate the risks. A young Special Forces colonel commenced his brief: 'As you can see on this PowerPoint slide...' You could have heard a pin drop – Blunkett could – but being blind, the one thing he could not do was view a PowerPoint slide. His guide dog shook its head in exasperation.

PowerPoint is the curse of the modern world. Even more so in America where 'slide-ology' has been taken to new heights: forget the message you are trying to convey, it is more important that your font size and palette colours are correct. It was not always so. In the early 1990s, we were still living in the world of the 'slide pack' – colour transparency slides in a circular carousel for briefings to senior officers. The CO of a Para battalion was about to conduct such a brief to the General Officer Commanding (a lieutenant general) in Northern Ireland. He started his brief, but the carousel refused to budge. He pressed harder and harder – all to no avail. The brief was a spectacular flop. Once the GOC had departed, the CO had the slide pack escorted to the 25 metres firing range. He then proceeded to blow the slide machine to bits with a shotgun. He was still wearing his puttees.

Presentation is almost everything. There are handling plans for everything and embedded in every brief. Here is a handling plan announcement made during Barack Obama's presidency: 'The main communication aim for this period is to convince target audiences that the campaign has made significant progress on the way to a successful conclusion and that a continued effort will achieve ultimate success.' It would probably be against the Official Secret Act to reveal the time and place of this wizard plan, but for the purposes of our lay audience it could be Iraq, Afghanistan or Libya, because it says something that, at some time, could be said about any or all three of those operations.

The Ministry of Defence also regularly produces 'top-line messages'. The next four lines are a real example about terrorism – one of them may have been falsely inserted:

Line 1: Terrorism is a real and serious threat to us all.

Line 2: Terrorists are criminals and murderers. They attack the values that we all share.

Line 3: We all need to work together to tackle the terrorist challenge.

Line 4: I kid you not.

Most government departments are obsessed with the news headlines. Goebbels, the horrific master propagandist of the Nazis, described the press as 'a piano on which the government could play to influence the public in whatever direction current policy might make desirable'. It is a moot point whether this description has now been reversed, and it is the press who are playing the tunes. My eyes always glaze over when we get to the 'something must be done' approach[17] that comes from politicians scanning the media – the so-called CNN factor – which almost always turns out to be the basis for bad policy and decision-making.

Just before a decision was made to intervene in Bosnia, Prime Minister Margaret Thatcher came to speak at the Staff College. The commandant was SAS hero Mike Rose who had commanded 22 SAS in the Falklands. He was no shrinking violet. She asked him his opinion of what we should do in Bosnia.

'Well, Prime Minister, there is no strategic interest at stake for the UK. We might enable some humanitarian support for the non-governmental agencies, but in the words of the German Chancellor, Bismarck, at the 1878 Congress of Berlin, it's really not worth the bones of a Pomeranian Grenadier.'

He was about to be hand-bagged. 'How dare you be so lily-livered! We should bomb the power stations, we should bomb Milosevic, we should bomb the bridges – we should really take it to that awful dictator Milosevic. Are we promoting cowards to be generals these days?'

General Rose was suitably chastised. The following week the Secretary of State for Defence came to speak to the college. He asked Mike Rose the same question: what to do about the Balkans? Mike Rose knew the answer to this one: 'We should bomb the power stations, we should bomb Milosevic, we should bomb the bridges – we should really take it to Milosevic.'

The Secretary of State looked aghast: 'Are we promoting mad men to be generals these days?' Mike Rose had failed to realise the truth that was revealed to me by a very senior civil servant and a further useful political maxim: 'Consistency is the hallmark of a shallow mind.'

It seems there is a crisis in the defence budget every year. In my final MoD tour we were conducting a review into 'Counter-Terrorism and Resilience'. Some of our colleagues in the security agencies believed that it was Byzantine that we charged them for our services when we provided them with support. There were many budgetary transfers between departments. In the back of every book I have kept since that time I have also always written the following:

> The notion that the MoD should swallow its own smoke is frequently encountered, but the budget is not structured to flex in that way. We do not have a non-core programme budget. Our non-core programme budget (i.e. for operations) is the Treasury Reserve. And when the Reserve doesn't want to cough up, we find it hard to identify resources. The scale of the defence programme means that when we have a financial problem it tends to be a big one – because the elements that cause the problem, such as Category A equipment programmes (those over £400m), but also service pay, pensions and fuel costs, are on a scale that few outside the department can comprehend. So, if counter-terrorism and resilience were to have a higher priority, then a rational judgement would need to be taken on which areas of activity we were prepared to forgo in consequence, or we need to put in a bid for more resources at the next Spending Review.

Let me decode this for you:

1. Getting rid of a few coffee machines in the MoD is not likely to do much good in a budget of over £36bn. It is not a major cost driver.

2. The service chiefs sit on the main board, fight for their individual services (and therefore for the shiniest and most expensive new equipment programmes), which always have a cost overrun. They therefore cannot act corporately for the benefit of defence as a whole.

3. Going to war or on operations overseas is paid for from the Treasury Reserve. Unfortunately there is no such thing. With the mismanagement of finances in the last 10 years, the Treasury Reserve is borrowed money – the Chinese or other foreign nations and their sovereign funds are paying for our wars, and we will owe them lots of money in the future for the debt interest payments.

4. There are few real levers in defence because the discretionary money in the defence and single service budgets is very small. That is why we always target the wrong things to cut when the budget is tight – such as recruitment, training, education and travel (but not wholeheartedly, because the video conference is still not as sexy as travel).

5. Getting rid of manpower is the easiest way to 'cut costs' (and accounts for bizarre decisions when the army/navy/air force is undermanned, as money is rarely set aside to pay for a fully manned service of any of the single services.

6. The budget is generally in a mess. The current government is trying to make a good fist of solving that problem, but balancing the budget has little to do with understanding the delivery of military capability. The National Audit Office report of 10 January 2013 confirmed yet more equipment cost overruns in both time and money.

7. Hence, I leave the army when it will be down to its smallest size since the post-Napoleonic Wars days. (The Army 2020 is a date rather than the remaining number of

personnel left serving although even the current figure might reduce further.)

8. It will be a small military. There is a book title in there somewhere.

The army sent me on a senior finance course a few years back. Although no one is ever truly incentivised to save money, I have saved millions over the years. No one gave me any thanks for it – it merely upset those who had been on gravy trains. Let me explain with three examples.

One of my responsibilities as the last Chief of Staff in Northern Ireland was to 'call out' the part-time Royal Irish. This was a legal mechanism. But there was no need to call out the part-timers. The amount of patrolling conducted with the PSNI had tailed off to nothing, and could be conducted by the regular army garrison as we wound down toward the end of Op Banner (the army support to the RUC/PSNI from 1969 – 2007). I did not call them out. I would not call them out to sit around drinking tea. I was firmly and forever more in the Royal Irish's 'enemy forces' paragraph from then onwards.

Arriving in Tampa I came across a couple of extraordinary letters justifying an arcane allowance I had never heard of, called 'Special Messing Allowance' (SMA). I only found the letters by trawling the computer files, for no one was likely to brief me on their moral turpitude. The justification went as follows: 'We all receive SMA at the rate of $54 per day (-ish). We are meant to feed ourselves by eating out for all meals (as they think we are living in hotels) and this is the line we take when SMA is reviewed.'

For eight years, the British defence establishment had been living in rented apartments. When you consider that the official (rather dull) rule is that, 'SMA is a contribution to assist eligible service personnel to meet necessary additional costs when they are without access to service messing or *self-catering facilities*, and have no option but to eat in commercial retail outlets' you might sense my anger. Our apartments most certainly had kitchens. Rather like living in Florida in the hot and humid summer months, a kitchen (along with air conditioning) is considered to be almost a human right: we all need to eat. I will leave you to 'do the math' of 30 days in a month multiplied by $54, divided by the exchange rate of $1.62 and multiplied again by many personnel to give what this equated to in budgetary terms. This produces the equation of:

$$\frac{\text{taking the piss}}{\text{people have lost their moral compass}} = \text{righteous indignation}$$

Defence had wasted £3.5m in Tampa alone from 2003 onwards on an immoral and illegal justification for an allowance. No one thought this was wrong. I stopped it. I called it 'fraud'.

Military machines are unbelievable consumers of fuel, and it is one of the military's major cost-drivers. In 2010, the American military spent $15bn on 5bn gallons of fuel, $13bn of which was for military operations (principally in Iraq and Afghanistan). A frightening 80 per cent of all ground movements in Afghanistan were concerned with fuel delivery. I thought one of the strategic outcomes of 9/11 would be the equivalent of the Manhattan Project (the one that split the atom to develop the first nuclear bomb during the Second World War) to reduce our reliance on fossil fuels and Middle Eastern oil due to the volatile nature of that region. While you may have bought yourself a hybrid car, it has not really happened as I thought it would. Despite any environmental concerns, fracking makes geo-strategic sense. The UK remains vulnerable, not because of oil (we import most of that from Norway), but because of the liquid gas that we import from Qatar – and the inter-connectedness of the world's economy.

I gave evidence in front of the House of Commons Defence Committee (HCDC) on a number of occasions in Westminster. They often struggle to find a quorum of three or four people. It will not surprise you that when the same committee visited Tampa during my time to investigate US attitudes towards Afghanistan, it was a surprisingly quorate visit. The full complement of the committee – somewhere around 12 people – came to Florida. I can't even remember if their report had any value. It may not have mattered.

A recent innovation outside the MoD building on Whitehall has been the building of a 'pen' that allows protesters to be appropriately marshalled and contained, and from where they can shout and wave placards. This is not for protests against the MoD: it faces Downing Street and the orientation is such that the chants and bodies are directed at the heart of government. It shows peaceful protest in action. The loud chants are guaranteed to put you off your work. Most of these are probably baffling to the average tourist or London passer-by.

Here are two examples. On 14 February 2012, the first anniversary of the occupation of the Pearl Roundabout in Bahrain occurred (the Pearl Roundabout had been the symbol of protest for democracy in Bahrain during the Arab Spring). In sympathy with this, the Bahraini British diaspora protested. The bemusement of the passer-by in this instance centred on trying to 'guess the country flag': few had a clue what they were looking at. The next day the Somali diaspora (or rather their women and children) protested. Their placards and slogans were 'Ban Khat from UK' and 'Khat: it is a lethal drug'. Most Brits, in this case, were probably bemused by the lack of formal education and that people could not spell 'C-A-T'. In most of the world 'Khat' is spelt 'Qat' (one of the few words beginning with the letter 'Q' that is not followed by a 'U' and so is immensely beneficial in Scrabble). I have actually chewed Qat in the Yemen with some elders in an Al Qaeda-infested street in the capital city of Sana'a. I was not versed in the art of Qat-chewing (this was official government counter-terrorist business, and I was in the company of the British Ambassador) and made the mistake of swallowing it. If the weed is not banned in the UK, may I suggest that you never follow my Qat-swallowing example? You are supposed to take it out of your mouth after savouring the mildly narcotic effect.

It is for politicians to decide if the armed forces go to war. It is never, nor should it be, a military decision – stand fast Gordon of Khartoum. I was fortunate to fight in the Falklands War. Our more recent interventions in Iraq and Afghanistan have been not been decisive (there is never a decisive battle in an insurgency). So to remind our politicians (and maybe the military fraternity too) for the future, here are five differences between the Falklands War and the Iraq and Afghanistan interventions:

1. In the Falklands, we won and we won quickly. It was state on state conflict.

2. It was a popular war: our territory had been invaded.
3. There was no ideological element to it, other than patriotism.
4. Even though there may have been some acts that might have strayed from the Rules of War, because of points one and two it was not deemed in the public interest to open the wounds.
5. The object of war is a better peace. It is not to go to war for the sake of going to war.

Thousands of years ago Herodotus spoke these words: 'No one is foolish enough to prefer war to peace: in peace, children bury their fathers, while in war fathers bury their children.' We would do well to remember these words.

---

[14]F E Smith, later 1st Earl of Birkenhead (1872–1930) and a close political and personal ally of Churchill.

[15]This is a loose paraphrase of a quotation from the 1930s given to students of the Staff College in 1991 when the War Minister and size of the octopus was considerably smaller.

[16]I believe this may originally have been said by Robert McNamara, who was one of the architects of the US Vietnam strategy in the 1960s.

[17]General Sir Rupert Smith gives an excellent example of this on pages 311 and 312 of his book *The Utility of Force*, Penguin, 2006. He describes a conversation between the MoD (him) and the FCO in 1994 regarding Rwanda.

CHAPTER 11

GENERALSHIP, COMMAND AND LEADERSHIP

The most hotly debated topic on my American Pinnacle course (the highest course for senior leaders in the US Army) followed a comment from a United States vice admiral that went as follows:

> Listen up shipmates, there are three things you need to know about senior officers:
> 1. Four star officers make shitty teammates.
> 2. Four star officers' staffs make even shittier teammates.
> 3. If in doubt refer back to point one.

I am not sure that my observations of senior US officers would lead me to conclude that that is true – it may be more so in the UK. There are differing demands on leaders at different levels. You may recall what I learned from the death of Colonel H

Jones VC at Goose Green: I carried a pistol. It was my psychological and physical reminder of command in its widest sense and of the need to maximise the potential contribution of all the assets ever available to me. Psychological and physical demands are magnified at the higher levels of leadership.

If you take the case of General Mattis at CENTCOM you would find someone who psychologically understands the consequences of his decisions at the highest level (theatre-strategic in his case), and with physical demands placed upon him that few senior officers in the British forces have to endure. He once answered 120 emails before seven in the morning and regularly dealt with 400 a day. (I make no judgment whether the equivalent of a chairman of the board should be doing this – but *he* did – and answered every one within 24 hours.) This, combined with a punishing 'Key Leader Engagement' strategy with princes and potentates in various time zones across the Middle East and beyond, often left him not knowing what day or time zone he was in.

General Mattis is a great leader, the closest I have seen to a military genius. My wife knew of my admiration for him, and wanted to get me something for Christmas that represented the man he was. She did not feel that the 'hoodie' she had found on eBay would be appropriate. First, because generals do not regularly wear hoodies, and secondly, because this one with the United State Marine Corps logo on it had the following General Mattis quotation (from when he commanded a Marine Division in the Second Gulf War in 2003 while engaging with tribal sheikhs): 'I come in peace: I didn't bring artillery. But I'm pleading with you with tears in my eyes: because if you fuck with me, I'll kill you all.'

The scale and responsibility for US Commanders is

incredible. General Mattis had a headquarters of 5,500, and 189,000 men and women deployed in his area of responsibility – more personnel than the entire British services put together. A command is built from the top down (this should be the same for industry too). There is nothing new in this. 'The personality of the general is indispensable,' said Napoleon. 'He is the head, he is the all, of an army.' The commander's thinking spreads out to include his behaviour throughout his command. The commander is so important to an organisation that it is not so much a question of whether or not he influences his organisation, but rather to what extent he can exert this influence with positive results. The relatively smaller scale of UK operations means that, in our case, you can change the opening lines of this chapter to read, 'UK three-star officers make shitty teammates.' You might also find that General Anachronism is out and about in Afghanistan, berating the British soldiers because their standards have slipped and their boots are not clean enough and their saluting is rubbish. Unfortunately, I'm not joking.

It is one thing for a senior leader (this also applies to leadership in industry) to know what should be done and another to get it done. Consider, for example, one commander who is successful in conducting informal staff conferences, in bringing opinions out into the open, and in obtaining full information for decision-making purposes. He is not, however, necessarily very effective in direct action. Consider, at the other end of the spectrum, a leader who is a driver of men; he may lack a sense of organisation but he is effective in anything he undertakes personally. Because of his hard-hitting, direct methods, he may not be inclined to carry others along with him and he is likely to ruffle the feathers of subordinates. Both commanders are restricted in their available repertoire of actions, so their potential for maximum effectiveness is impaired. The ability to shift behaviour according to the demands of the situation is a prerequisite for effective leadership. That was the genius of General Mattis, and of Rupert Smith.

Command at the theatre-strategic or operational level of warfare places different demands than those imposed on a tactical leader. A determination to outwit an opponent, to understand the political dimension and the media, moral courage, mastery of the profession of arms, and the robustness to withstand the shocks of war are all prerequisites. Command at the operational level – to sequence tactical engagements to affect an outcome in a sequenced campaign in support of strategic objectives – is about putting together a construct to change the situation to advantage. A 'way' must be found that suits the 'means', for that is the test of generalship. As General Rupert Smith put it, responsibility at this level is such that: 'Your head will know how heavy your arse is, when your neck is in a noose.'[17] The British military is now so small that the maxim that best suits us is: 'If you haven't got the "means" [and we have not], you have to alter your "ways", or join a coalition.' There is only one leader of that coalition today: it is the USA.

The Americans have a tendency to put their senior officers' heads in a noose more than the British. In America, a failure to convince, or an even a failure to be convincing to, the political leadership is enough for the butcher's knife to fall upon you. We saw this with General David McKiernan in Afghanistan in 2008, and again with General Stan McChrystal in 2011. The

Americans 'own' most of every modern campaign: they are a nation that needs strategists as well as warriors. We are a military that needs warriors but we may spend too much time on producing strategists (or at least the programmes at our staff colleges would lead you to believe it to be so).

As a junior but important partner for the Americans in all the campaigns fought in the 21st century, it is harder now for British generals to have the same burden of responsibility. There can be only one campaign plan, and if you have the greatest equities in financial muscle, deaths, troop numbers and global influence, there is one nation that has the most sway. We defer to what the Americans do first, for they will lead. We will largely conform to what the US does in both our going into operations and in our coming out of operations (and this includes the final withdrawal timeframe from Afghanistan in 2014). And we remain their most important ally. The relationship is based on a unique and enduring bond of mutual benefit to two countries with similar, but not identical, world views and outlooks.

I believe that President Zardari of Pakistan understands the relationship between economic power and the ability to campaign at the grand strategic level. Apparently, Presidents Obama and Zardari were talking at the 2012 Chicago summit, and in a demonstration of a new spirit of cooperation, Obama said to Zardari, 'I'd like to give you two of my generals for two of your generals.'

Zardari thinks about this and asks Obama, 'So who do you want?'

'Generals Kayani and Pasha,' replies Obama.

'OK,' says Zardari.

'And who do you want?' asks Obama.

Zardari immediately replies, 'General Electric and General Motors.'

Generals are either operational commanders, translating strategic concepts into concrete objectives or they are, at the highest level, strategists. Very few are now on the front line. It is not really their job to get killed: they had that opportunity as tacticians and as young platoon commanders, although I would acknowledge Field Marshal Slim's remark that, 'Nothing is so good for the morale of the troops as to occasionally see a dead general.' (Slim was known as Uncle Bill to his troops. I don't think the vilified Field Marshal Haig from the First World War was ever called Uncle Dougie).

You do not get to be a general unless you have some qualities. With the Iraq and Afghanistan campaigns of the last 10 years we rediscovered T E Lawrence (although he had never, nor should he have, gone away):

Do make it clear that generalship, at least in my case, came of understanding, of hard study and brain-work and concentration. Had it come so easy to me, I should not have done [command] so well. If your book could persuade some of our new soldiers to read and mark and learn things outside drill manuals and tactical diagrams, it would be a good work. I feel a fundamental crippling in curiousness about our officers. Too much body and too little head. The perfect general would know everything in heaven and earth.

So please, if you see me that way and agree with me, do use me as a text to preach for more study of books and history, a greater seriousness in military art. With two thousand years of example behind us, we have no excuse, when fighting, for not fighting well.[18]

The UK reached the zenith of its power in 1942. The invasion of North Africa in that year is the date from which we can trace the handing of the strategic baton of power from the UK to the US. From that moment on, we would be a subordinate in any campaign where allies fight together.

There have been occasions where the British army has campaigned alone. The obvious example was Northern Ireland, where the UK owned absolutely all the levers of power – the police, the judiciary and legal framework, the military and economic response and the social framework. But Northern Ireland was not a war, and it was an exception. It was 'military aid to the civil power', with the police in the lead for most of the campaign. It had no need to be underpinned by host nation consent or a United Nations Security Council Resolution to make it legal. The UK government never considered 'The Troubles' to be a war. The criminal law, with the minimum amendments necessary for a democratic society confronting terrorism, was applied by the State to all sides – including the army. Defeating terrorism is a law and order issue in the UK. We did not drop bombs from fast jets on terrorists in Northern Ireland because just as the police would not drop smart munitions to catch a burglar, no matter how dangerous that burglar may be, so the law struggles greatly with the notion of dropping smart munitions on a terrorist. I can't quite understand how we drop so many air-delivered munitions ('bombs' to the layman) in Afghanistan under the guise of protecting the population, when we would never contemplate doing so in Northern Ireland.

The size of the British forces means that we have had to cede the field to the Americans to construct campaigns. We may still bring influence and insight, but the US now owns the major levers of power. It is because of this that we do not get to sack any of our own generals any more: we are no longer important or big enough to make a real hash of things. When we operated on our own, at least at divisional level, we did get to sack our generals (or at least 'marginalise' them). We had effectively a small division in the field in both the Falklands campaign in 1982 and the first Gulf War in 1991. There were two manoeuvre brigades in each division. Those who are familiar with these conflicts can probably name the star performer of each brigade in the two conflicts, for they are both notable in commentating on military affairs – Julian Thompson from 3 Commando Brigade from the Falklands, and Patrick Cordingley from 7 Armoured Brigade from the First Gulf War. But I defy you to name the other brigade commanders whose wars were not so glorious.

The last brigade-level commander that we relieved was in Northern Ireland in the early 1990s. The army was in support of the RUC, and the RUC had lost faith in the particular individual, so there was no choice. We are not in support of the Americans but sometimes it is best not to ask them what they have really thought in the last 10 years: one of the traits that are so impressive about Americans is that they are very polite.

We can still remove senior officers, but often this means they go to another employment where they can do no damage. A senior officer named Admiral Hawkins was swiftly removed from the MoD when he fulfilled the role of the MoD's operations officer. He had trouble sorting out which country he was referring to when referencing essentially *land* formations in essentially *land* campaigns in Afghanistan and Iraq. Campaigns are generally now 'joint and inter-agency' affairs that emphasise the synergy of all parts of government including the Department of International Aid and the Foreign Office, along with the security agencies. Regardless of this, Afghanistan will remain, in my humble view, a land-locked country where the leverage of sea power does not play a major role. Sea power is important in many other campaigns and I do not decry the theorists of sea power such as Mahan or Corbett – or even Royal Marines who at least have to land on the shore to take part, very successfully, in the areas where men fight. The last time I looked, people continued to live on the land and not in the air or in the sea.

Admiral Hawkins cast around looking for HMS *Wheresthe...* and HMS *Navythati'm...* and HMS *Familiarwith* as he foundered on the rocks of his own inability to navigate two simultaneous campaigns. He was cast adrift until they managed to tie him to a safe sinecure where he could do no further harm. I felt a touch sorry for him, but it could have been worse. Samuel Pepys recorded in his diary for 13 October 1660 the following tale: 'I went to Charing Cross to see Major General Harrison hanged, drawn and quartered; which was done there, he looking as cheerful as any man could in that condition. He was presently cut down, and his head and heart shown to the people, at which there were great shouts of joy.' Two days later the authorities had obviously gone 'soft'. Pepys records that a Mr Carew was, 'Hanged and drawn; but his quarters, by a great favour, are not to be hanged up.'

Our admiral got off quite lightly. We politely clapped him out of the building. For the remainder of the Iraq and Afghanistan campaigns the army occupied the position of the MoD's operations officer. The air force may control the air, and the navy contributes to operations where there is sea by control of that environment, but you can only ever be decisive on land.

One of my favourite generals of the Second World War was Field Marshal Wavell. He was also a theatre strategic commander attempting to fight a series of linked campaigns with minimal resources. He understood Grand Strategy. At the darkest point in the war for Britain with the capitulation of France he wrote the following:

The Position – May 1940
1. Oil, shipping, air power, sea power are the keys to this war, and they are interdependent.
   Air power and sea power cannot function without oil.
   Oil, except in very limited quantities, cannot be brought to its destination without shipping.
   Shipping requires the protection of naval power and air power.
2. We have access to practically all the world's supplies of oil.
   We have most of the shipping.
   We have naval power.
   We have potentially the greatest air power – when fully developed.
   Therefore we are bound to win the war.
3. Germany is very short of oil and has access to only very limited quantities.
   Germany's shipping is practically confined to the Baltic.
   Germany's naval power is small.
   German air power is great but is a diminishing asset.
   Therefore Germany is bound to lose the war.

This is a profound example of the decision-making process that is called deductive logic (or analytical decision-making) and informs the 'estimate' process within the forces. Although Wavell was one of the cleverest and most intelligent officers of the 20th century, he was not renowned for his sociability. He was of a taciturn nature, and his staff endured long periods of his silences: he was not suited to the style of Churchill. Wavell urged that generals should be 'backed or sacked'. Churchill sacked him (or he was, at least, sent to a different theatre of war).

The opposite of analytical decision-making is the use of intuition. To use intuition you need a fair degree of experience to be able to recognise a problem from historical norms or by learned knowledge. Generals have a tendency to use big hands on a map, and their staff should then convert that intent in to some sort of reality. But to do that successfully one needs to know that it is within the art of the possible. The British army used to have a feel for the art of the possible because in the days of the Cold War we actually moved corp-sized formations of thousands of vehicles over real distances. The 1980 exercise Reforger was a clever use of language, for Reforger stood for 'Reinforcement of Germany'. If you made a wrong turning, so did thousands of other vehicles until you discovered your mistake. The most deadly thing in the world is an officer with a map.

The British army has been on operations almost continuously the last 10 years. It has been over-trained and under-exercised. It has trained for *the* war (be that Afghanistan or Iraq), and is in danger of losing its ability to train for *a* war. It is great at the tactical level of *the* war that each unit or formation is deployed to – and the soldiers and officers still perform magnificently. In the meantime, it has lost the art of understanding the yardsticks on mundane things, such as how much road space a formation of a certain size takes on a route, how much real estate you need, and how long it takes to load and unload ships. We are in danger of losing our 'seed corn' for the future. The parameters within the Staff Officer's Handbook used to be at the fingertips of every trained staff officer. We have slightly lost that ability in the noise of campaigning.

Let me illustrate. I was part of a Command Post Exercise (CPX) when I was commanding a brigade. This was a computer simulation of an invasion plan. The general commanding the division (I was a brigadier and a subordinate commander) waved his hand over the map; the staff converted the wave into some orders, and I received and analysed them. Here is part of my conversation: 'Let me get this straight. You want me to go further, faster than any brigade in history on only one route, with five obstacle crossings over rivers, three of which are likely to be opposed, and you want me to do all this in three days?'

'Yes.'

'You know that this is an impossible task, for time/space/distance calculations mean that there is no way I can achieve this unless every man has a jet pack, or three more roads are magically built in the next few hours. Did your staff not calculate any norms of movement and how far formations go in combat per day and how we would outstrip our logistics even if this were possible?'

'Not that I know of. Get on with it.'

And so I did. And we got bogged down (if you can get bogged down within a computer). We never did get very far. You can have as much dash and élan as you like as a commander, but one thing you cannot outwit are the laws of physics and motion. As in most things, events regress to a calculable norm.

There are differing styles of leadership. Wavell's intellectual but silent leadership was juxtaposed with what we would call the charismatic leadership of Churchill. I was fortunate to serve under many charismatic field commanders, such as Johnny Crosland in the Falklands campaign. There are limits to what a reclusive leader such as Wavell can achieve. My divisional commander in the 'big hand' scenario was also very charismatic, dynamic and someone I really admired, but the downside was that this could lead to 'group think' – no one wanted to tell him he was wrong. Alanbrooke spent most of his early days in high command visiting units and formations to find things out: he was a visible leader. Industry seems to have discovered this recently with the 'undercover boss' concept.

There is a huge difference between leadership and management. Management is process, protocols and procedure. Leadership is performance, pizzazz and passion. No one was ever managed up a hill towards an enemy – they were led there. On operations, it is an overt or covert manipulation of men to get them to do things that they would not rationally otherwise do. It really is a case of ordinary men often doing extraordinary things.

There is bad leadership and good leadership. I am fortunate that the worst leadership – complete lack of leadership – occurred during my exchange tour abroad with the Canadian Airborne Regiment (a fine bunch of soldiers, in this case with little guidance, thus giving credence to the 2,000-year old saying, 'Ten good men, wisely led, will beat a hundred without a head').

There was little cohesion between the various parts of the Canadian Airborne Regiment, which was made up of three individual fiefdoms, all exhibiting the characteristics that make up Canada. 1 Commando was made up from the Royal 22nd Regiment – the French Canadian 'Vandoos' (a misspelling of *vingt-deux*); 2 Commando were from the Princess Patricia's Canadian Light Infantry; and 3 Commando from the Royal Canadian Regiment – and in my time never the three would meet.

The Canadian Airborne Regiment lived in a lovely barracks in an obscure part of Ontario called Petawawa. There was a large parade ground, used as a car park for the soldiers when there were no ceremonial events, with barrack blocks on either side of the square that hosted the living accommodation of each commando. Tensions had been boiling, fuelled by the rivalry, partly racial and partly cultural, which existed within each of the parts of the regiment. 1 Commando was the Quebecois – and this was the time of the Canadian constitutional crisis that led to the Meech Lake Accord. 2 Commando could best be described as Albertan or Western rednecks; and 3 Commando were the homely boys from Ontario. Homely boys do not generally get themselves in trouble, and so it was in the following incident.

One weekend, the tyres of the French Canadians' cars were slashed on the parade square. The next weekend, the French Canadians of 1 Commando dragged a pristine new Jeep belonging to a young officer of the Albertan rednecks to the middle of the parade ground, gained access through the door and left a lit blowtorch in the back seat. It will not surprise the reader to learn that the pristine Jeep became a smouldering wreck.

The regimental commander now realised that he had a leadership challenge on his hands. He must have taken the words of the Baltimore sage, H L Mencken, as his guide in following his maxim that 'for every complex problem there is a solution that is simple, neat – and wrong.' His solution was to parade everyone together and trot off for a five-mile run. The problems were far more complex and deeper than this. I am unhappy to report that a new regimental commander arrived a few months later and realised the extent of the challenges he faced. He reported these to his superiors in Ottawa, as the regiment were about to deploy to Somalia. He believed he needed more time to address the underlying problems. He suggested that they were not ready to deploy. He was relieved of command, and all his fears came to pass with a series of incidents that led to the disbandment of what was, in reality, a fine regiment with poor leadership. Even sadder, his moral courage never led to his rehabilitation. He was forever tainted. Thus the Canadian Airborne Regiment became the first unit that I had served in during my career to be disbanded. Many others would follow with each successive UK defence review.

All leaders face challenges at one time or another. As a Company commander of three platoons I once had a bullying platoon. One individual was not part of the cohesive team. What was the problem? It was clear that we had corporals as leaders who were all cut from the same cloth. They were, to a man, very direct, forthright and controlling leaders. The Royal Marines would have classed them as the type who would look at a problem and attempt to go through it rather than around, under or over it – leaders of no subtlety, always utilising the direct approach. They had no foils – those who were nurturing and creative in their approach, who would try to go around a problem and look for the indirect approach. Once I had identified the problem, I broke up the leadership team and brought in some foils. This solved the problem, but in the eyes of the platoon, the young soldier who had not been, in their eyes, a team player was (like our Canadian CO) never fully rehabilitated. He was, sadly, a victim.

Teams need contrasts in their personalities. The styles and models of leadership vary. My bullying platoon was full of coercive leadership – nearly always negative in the long term. Our nurturing and creative leaders were of the more democratic and affiliative models. We have seen the charismatic leadership of John Crosland in the Falklands earlier and there are those who are coaching or pace-setting in their leadership. No model is right, but having a balance adds to the strength of an organisation. Those organisations that promote or recruit only in their own image will be prone to atrophy over time.

There is paradox in the army. Our best and most elite units generally attract the best leaders. The best and most elite units are generally those that cause most political difficulties when there are defence reviews. They are the most controversial to attempt to disband due to vested interests and hence are known as 'special needs units' in political terms. They include the Brigade of Guards, the Gurkhas, Scottish battalions (at least for the political period when we worry about the wider union of the United Kingdom), and (whisper it), the Parachute Regiment. There must always be at least one Irish Regiment outside the Foot Guards too – and a Welsh Regiment. That is why it is easier to disband the mythical Loamshires, even if they are well recruited, and why the Royal Regiment of Fusiliers can rightly be aggrieved at the outcome of the last review.

The most problematic units with the least-motivated soldiers are left with the also-ran leaders. In the order of things, the worst soldiers need the motivation of strong leaders. Strong and motivated soldiers need less overt leadership. Bad units can be statistically proven – they are the ones who have the most soldiers thrown out for using drugs (2 PARA was zero when I was commanding), where soldiers are Absent Without Leave (AWOL), where soldiers are sick at home, and where others are fat and unfit. There is probably a correlation with metrics in companies in civilian life there somewhere.

Commanders and leaders are supported by their staff. No one joins the army to be a staff officer. They join to command troops. The longer one stays in the army, the more inevitable it is that one will be 'on the staff'. To be on the staff (stand fast the MoD where you are a 'suit') is to be part of that organisation that will be despised by the subordinate units.

Happily, each formation has a higher headquarters that one can, in turn, despise. Brigades criticise divisions, divisions hate corps, and now that we have a small army we can no longer despise the large formation of armies and army groups of the Second World War, but can move straight to the MoD. When you get to the MoD there is no higher organisation to despise. Everyone despises the MoD: the press sees to that.

This has a certain timeless quality about it. As a young captain in the First World War (where we did have 'armies' and everyone despised 'chateau generals' and their staffs – think *Blackadder*), Field Marshal Wavell used an example from the time of trench warfare in 1915 when he was a brigade chief of staff. This was during the time when higher formations actually seemed to be assigning some mystical value to *individual trenches*. The ground itself in relation to the German opposition may have had absolutely no value as a tactical feature – but to higher commanders this did not seem to matter. It mattered to Wavell. One particular trench, K trench, was held by up to 30 men and was completely overlooked by the Germans. It had absolutely no value except that of producing 12 casualties a day – that number today would cause paroxysms in the House of Commons (and the military command chain, and with modern communications there would be great potential to have a video-conference to discuss it).

Wavell saw that K trench had no value, and decided to fill it in and dig one further back in a more tactically astute position. He made the error of telling the divisional staff what they were doing: not a yard of trench was to be given up, was the higher formation order. Wavell disregarded this but told the division that he had complied, and that casualties had reduced to less than a handful. 'There you are; I knew the trench could be held with a little grit and determination,' said the chateau general, for he was of the school who believed that with more leadership anything was possible.[19]

I never despised 'higher' as a commander. Often their presence was not known to the troops. The world of the soldier was the platoon, or company, or battalion. Things may be different at brigade level. Battalions can despise brigade headquarters and their staff (after all, it was not one of Slim's 'great commands'). This struck home to me when 2 PARA were in Northern Ireland on a two-year residential tour in 1994 – 1995. We were near the end of our tour and I was completing a series of lectures and exercises on airborne operations for our impending return to Aldershot and to 5 Airborne Brigade. All airborne soldiers know which brigade they are in, and they are proud of that fact. It is their closed ecosystem. I asked them, 'When we return to Aldershot, what Brigade are we in?' '5 Airborne Brigade,' they replied in unison. I then asked them what brigade they were in, in Northern Ireland. Not one of them even knew we were in a brigade. We were – it was 39 (Ulster) Brigade.

I commanded a brigade. It was transforming, as I took it over from a mechanised brigade with tanks and assorted armoured vehicles and capabilities, to a light brigade. I suppose, given my light infantry/Para background, that I had been placed there for that very task. I approached the conversion task with the normal intensity one brings to a problem. If the problem is everything, looking for a solution to the problem becomes the task. The collection of units in the brigade included the King's from the northwest of England, the Devon and Dorset Regiment from the southwest, the Prince of Wales' Own Regiment of Yorkshire and The Second Battalion, The Royal Green Jackets, along with the armour of the Queen's Royal Lancers, the heavy guns of 40 Regiment Royal Artillery with AS90, and the engineers of 38 Engineer Regiment.

If my belief in cohesion was to have substance, I had to look at the history of the brigade to identify if there was anything there that could bond the varied geographic and personalities of vastly different units together. Maybe that should have been a warning to me, for 19 Brigade had a pretty lacklustre history of being raised but subsequently disbanded. The first duty of the staff is to state the practical truth. With this in mind, perhaps my staff should have told me not to bother, for an inevitable future disbandment would follow.

And so it proved. Not one of the four infantry units from my tenure in 2004 – 2005 now exists in the army. They have been further amalgamated into the Duke of Lancaster's Regiment, the Rifles (which now has units encompassing both the Devon and Dorsets and the Green Jackets) and The Yorkshire Regiment. 19 Brigade was disbanded in December 2012.

The creation of 19 Light Brigade in 2004 followed the 2003 Defence White Paper. It was created to enhance our intervention capability and enable the army to better meet the demands of enduring peace support operations. It lasted barely long enough to make a splash. The phrases used within such august strategic documents are fit for all seasons and no seasons – and cleverly crafted to do just that (and generally followed by the get-out clause as happened in 2013 that, 'work is continuing to establish the precise nature of a sustainable and affordable future force structure to support the policy set out in the White Paper.' You could pin the following key phrases in any decade:

We need flexible armed forces that are structured and equipped to deploy globally and rapidly at small and medium scale.

and

The missions of the British armed forces formulated in the Defence White Paper remain largely unchanged:
1. Maintain the security of the UK.
2. Protect British territories overseas and carry out British treaty and other obligations.
3. Contribute to the defence of the free world and the prevention of war, in accordance with British alliances and arrangements with individual countries.

NOTES FROM A SMALL MILITARY

The first is from the 2003 White Paper, the second from the 1962 White Paper. When you don't have an enemy to deter, which the UK has not had since the 'stable uncertainties' of the Cold War, you might wish to ask what the role and task of the army/navy/air force should be (and that they should invest in good enabling capabilities, for shiny front-end weapon systems without such enablers are about as much use as a chocolate fireguard). It goes without saying that the forces were considerably larger in 1962.

Napoleon was once asked if he preferred courageous generals or brave generals. He said he preferred neither – he wanted *lucky* generals. My son did his 'A' Level history dissertation on the Falklands War (he had a primary source to consult) and was asked to answer the question, 'What role did luck play in the success of the British forces in the Falklands War?' I do not recall any campaign in history that was entered into on the basis that 'it will be OK; we might be lucky.' There is a distinction between a risk and a gamble: we tend to try to minimise risks and never to gamble. We are not bankers, as you will see in the final chapter.

There are lots of 'lucky' generals today. They are the ones who get to take their brigades 'on operations' as brigadiers. If they do not mess it up completely (a thing very hard to achieve when the Americans control the overall strategy) they will become generals: that is the currency. Those who do not take their brigades on operations will not be so fortunate. To take a brigade on operations requires a brigadier to be a Type A Commander. This is the equivalent of being an 'A' grade student, as you get to command an 'A' grade brigade. If you are not quite 'A' grade you might gain a Type B and or Type C command. These are regional brigades that will deal with infrastructure, budgets and the TA. They are as dull as dishwater. A brigadier will rarely get to be a general if he has commanded a Type B regional brigade. If he commands a Type C training brigade he really has no long-term future.

To get to the rank of brigadier is not to be considered a failure. It is a worthy rank to which not too many will get elevated in the future. We used to call brigadiers by the term that is still used in both the American and Canadian armies, which is 'brigadier-general'. In these countries all 'starred officers' (which range from a one-star brigadier to a four-star full general) are known by the collective term of GOFOs (for general officers and flag officers, as it includes naval and air force officers). We no longer use the same terms as our allies, because we did not think enough brigadier-generals had been killed in the First World War and stripped them of the 'general' title; in reality hundreds of brigadiers were killed. They were no mere chateau generals. The highest-ranking officers to be killed on operations in the last 40 years are lieutenant colonels: H Jones, Rupert Thorneloe of the Welsh Guards, and David Blair of the Queen's Own Highlanders, who was killed alongside 18 men of 2 PARA in the most devastating loss of life during the Northern Ireland 'Troubles' during the attack at Warrenpoint on 27 August 1979. I do not believe that lieutenant colonel is the senior rank of officers killed because our brigadiers have once more retreated to the Iraq or Afghan equivalent of the French chateau: they are exercising their 'command' wisely.

Careers are often guided by maxims. We all learnt the Principles of War by rote. They were easily memorable by applying the simple acronym (we love acronyms) of AM OF ACCESS: aim – selection and maintenance of, maintenance of morale, offensive action, flexibility, administration (now repackaged for the modern audience as 'sustainability'), coordination, concentration of force, economy of effort, security and surprise. Later, General Rupert Smith supplemented these by the 'functions in combat'. These were slightly trickier to remember. I did so, by the phrase, 'I'm forever caressing pretty chocolates' (although I deny ever having known any chocolates that were pretty). The six functions were: information, manoeuvre, command, firepower, protection, and combat service support (more prosaically 'logistics').

There was also a frivolous set of the great lies maxims in the real world:

'I'm from the Social Services. I'm here to help you.'

'The cheque's in the post.'

'Of course I love you.'

And, if the soldiers wanted to frag you or get you killed in combat because they hated you (as happened to the character Neidermeyer from the John Belushi film *Animal House*), 'Move now – I've got you covered.'

My own two guiding maxims throughout my later years were simple: 'Hold your nerve' and 'Don't chase the error'. This was because despite improvements in communications technology, it is still true (to paraphrase Field Marshal Wavell) that 60 per cent of the initial reports you will receive about an incident at war are likely to be wrong, misleading or inaccurate. There used to be a supplemental maxim in the Cold War, which was 'Don't march on Moscow.' Thankfully, we never attempted that. We may want to replace the Moscow maxim with a new one that would go something like: 'Avoid putting troops on the ground in Muslim countries in the 21st century.' Wavell's brilliant deductive approach cannot take cultural imponderables into account.

---

[17]General Sir Rupert Smith is one of the finest British generals of the last 40 years. For a book of greater depth than this one, see his *The Utility of Force*, Penguin, 2006.

[18]T E Lawrence to B H Liddell Hart, 1933 – perhaps not surprisingly referenced in the US military publication *The Joint Operating Environment*. I have always been fascinated by Lawrence and have visited Bovington and his house at Clouds Hill. In 2010 I was at a drinks party given by a wonderful 95-year-old lady called Joan, whose husband was an RAF pilot killed in the Second World War, when her son asked her, 'Didn't Daddy know Lawrence?' She replied: 'Yes, pompous little twat.' My bubble was burst. Lawrence died in 1935; Joan remains as bright as a button.

[19]From *Wavell – Soldier and Scholar*, pages 102–4, John Connell, Collins, 1964. This book is really full of military wisdom and should be on every officer's reading list.

CHAPTER 12

LA VIE MILITAIRE

Lieutenant Colonel David Chaundler parachuted into the South Atlantic Ocean to take command of 2 PARA following the death of Lt Col H Jones in the Falklands War. This operational parachute descent was a 'ballsy' act, as the sea state was high and it took a few minutes for a small craft to find him. It was a leap of faith. David Chaundler joined the forces in 1964 and retired in 1993. He frequently said that the best thing he did was to join the army, and the second best was that he knew when to *leave* the army (he retired as a brigadier). Leaving the forces comes to all who have served. David Chaundler's is a good maxim.

That is why there are books with titles like *We Were Soldiers Once – And Young* (Random House, 1992) written by Hal Moore and Joseph Galloway on the Battle of Ia Drang in the Vietnam War. The book is excellent. The Mel Gibson film much less so. We all grow old, and soldiering is for young men and women because of the qualities it requires from them. It is a tough profession and demands from those who serve on the front line – itself a grey area in insurgencies where there is no front line – that they are physically and mentally robust and fit. Everything an armed force does is focused on training for war or being prepared to conduct operations. That is why I used to use a section from the Moore and Galloway book in my directive to my troops as Commanding Officer of 2 PARA: because the consequences of not being as professional as possible in the profession of arms are profound:

> Only first place trophies will be displayed, accepted or presented in this battalion. Second place in our line of work is defeat of the unit on the battlefield, and death for the individual in combat. No fat troops or officers. Decision-making will be de-centralised: push the power down. It pays off in wartime.

We may not all get obese (you will note how I have now become politically correct rather than use the apparently upsetting 'F' word), but many soldiers do so when they leave the army. Their fitness regime is often not as extensive as it once was in their soldiering days – but their drinking habits generally are. Calorie intake in veterans often exceeds calorie burning. Their smoking habits, in most cases, remain the same. The black humour of the Toms extends even until death. The open casket of a notable hard-drinking, playing, smoking SNCO from the legendary mortar platoon of 2 PARA of the 1980s (known as 'Bulb' because his nose was gnarled, red and veiny) revealed him with his arms in a pose like the cross of St Andrew with a packet of cigarettes in one hand and a bottle of beer in the other. I don't believe they ever made it into the ground – that would have been a waste.

I have finally reached my level of incompetence. I cannot say that I have been an 'unlucky general', for I never contemplated getting beyond a 'buffoon (platoon) commander' as the Toms of the Paras might have said. Somewhere along the line I reached a position of conscious competence.

What do retired old soldiers, and officers, do? I'm not sure yet, but I know I nearly choked on my own blood as a wild American dentist of the rank of colonel drilled with relish around my gums while recounting his business proposition. I am still not convinced that his idea of selling second-hand Speedo swimming trunks from a beachfront in Florida is the sort of thing a well-qualified clinician should be considering – or even thinking about for that matter.

The constants of war will not change. It will always remain a clash of wills – both for those who fight, and for those who send the soldiers to do the fighting. It will remain an art, not a science. If everything in war was readily quantifiable at all times, it would be easy. It is not: it will remain a continuous interaction of opposites. There will remain the unpredictable reactions of the enemy. The realms of uncertainty and chance, suffering, confusion, exhaustion and fear – all these frictions are the environment of war. The causes of war and conflict will also refuse to be tamed – although we may now have rightly moved away from the time when going to war for 'honour' was a noble thing to do. Or maybe not: we started with Thucydides in chapter one. We acknowledged that my extended periods of sleep in the Churchill Hall at Sandhurst left me no time to study the profession of arms as a young officer. We have fought two wars (or variations on inter-state wars that then morphed into something else). In Thucydides' triumvirate of honour, interest and fear, we might conclude of Iraq and Afghanistan that one was the right war for the wrong reason, while the other was the wrong war for the right reason. I leave it to you to decide which was which.

Soldiering is at heart a simple enterprise. There are core skills that will never change: fitness, being able to shoot well to kill the enemy in the close battle or bringing firepower to bear to enable that at depth. (I prefer the latter approach. Fire and manoeuvre with small arms in the face of an enemy is not to be recommended.) Soldiers must communicate to enable them to be aware of what is going on around them, and they need high battlefield discipline. They must be able to help in saving the lives of those who may have been wounded next to them, and they will seek to do so because they are their mates. They must be able to read a map and understand it and the ground around them in relation to an opponent and the moves he might make (or to revert to it if their technology lets them down). They must know what other elements of combat power they can help to bring to bear and they must understand how they will need to be sustained. If they cannot be sustained, they will wither on the vine and be a hindrance.

The British army has been an active and engaged army in the last 20 years in a way that it was not for most of the 1970s and 1980s. Unless you were sent on a tour to Northern Ireland during those years you could live out your life in Cold War Germany without ever seeing a shot fired in anger, or experiencing the psychological and physical fear of the front line. There were those who went through a career in this era who received no medals. These are always the most strident in their calls for a retrospective medal.

They are the ex-soldiers who have a chest-full of purchased commemorative medals for (perhaps) two years' national service. You can now have a Cold War row of four medals, none of which are officially authorised, which include the National Service medal (£39.50), the British Army of the Rhine medal (£58.50), the British Forces Germany medal (£43.80) and the Cold War medal (£39.50). Medals should reward risk and rigour, not embarrassment at a clean chest. The risk and rigour that our soldiers have faced in the last few years means they deserve all the medals they are currently earning for gallantry as well as 'being there' in real combat.

No war in the last 30 years has been like the First or Second World War, but the risk and rigour element provides another constant between soldiers of all generations who engage in combat.[20] A tactical note from the 4th Army in May 1916 in France stated: 'There is a limit to human endurance in battle, and once that limit is reached the reaction is severe.' This was only a few short weeks before the Battle of the Somme: the battle that as every schoolboy knows provided the single most destructive day in the history of the British army, with 60,000 casualties. Or should that be 'as every schoolboy used to know?' A lot of folk seem not to know much today. I remember an advertisement on the London Underground in 2007 telling me that 80 per cent of people knew who Jordan the pneumatic glamour model is, but only 17 per cent knew where Jordan – the Middle Eastern country – was.

Commenting on German spies in Ireland spotting the shipping convoys going out across the Atlantic in the Second World War, Churchill declared: 'You can have too much war.' We have had that in the past 10 years. Sometimes we choose wars, and sometimes war chooses us. The military cannot solve all problems. We have learnt that too. Earlier, I quoted H L Mencken saying, 'For every complex problem, there is a solution that is simple, neat – and wrong.' It is apposite to repeat it. We thought we could solve problems by military means for the politicians as part of a 'comprehensive approach' with other government departments – and we were over-optimistic. And we know wars are expensive. The lesson the Chinese took from the Cold War was the need for economic strength. The West may have squandered that strength. It will be time to rebuild.

Although Eisenhower was a great coalition war commander (and often referred to by the Americans as 'the best British general they've got' due to his understanding of the requirements of coalition warfare), he was also prescient enough to know the costs of war. Twelve weeks after becoming President he gave this speech:

Every gun that is made, every warship launched, every rocket fired signifies in the final sense, a theft from those who hunger and are not fed, who are cold and are not clothed. The cost of one modern heavy bomber is this: a modern brick school in more than 30 cities. It is two electric power plants, each serving a town of a 60,000 population. It is two fine, fully equipped hospitals. It is some 50 miles of concrete pavement. We pay for a single fighter plane with a half million bushels of wheat. We pay for a single destroyer with new homes that could have housed more than 8,000 people.

Since the Second World War, there has been much theorising that geo-economic interdependence has made conflict less likely. This is a myth. Politicians do not calculate whether to initiate wars in mere economic and military terms. They calculate their chances of holding, expanding or retaining political power, or of being a reliable ally because it will help to consolidate their reputation and standing in the wider geo-strategic arena. That is what General Galtieri attempted to do with his invasion of the Falklands. The people now have a 'vote' too: the role of culture, religion and values all add to the complexity of the modern soup that conflict sips from. Kant's 'triangle of factors' for an enduring peace of open economies, democracy and engagement with the outside world have their place in peace theology, but do not give us a universal explanation of how to achieve that goal.

From 2014, the British army will still be willing to engage on NATO expeditionary operations, for well-defined military objectives and in a reasonably short time span, but we will probably be more reluctant to subscribe to more open-ended, enduring and expensive commitments. Just because a situation is awful (such as Rwanda for example in the early 1990s) does not mean there is a good way to fix it. We must resist the 'something must be done' school of strategy at all costs. This is also not a new concept. The Prime Minister for a young Queen Victoria, Lord Melbourne, tells us that 'the cry for something must be done, almost always leads to something foolish being done.'

We might have to ignore this 'something must be done' school of thought because our Army 2020 caveats us so much. A big stick gives you a big vote, and the British army will no longer have a big stick. Thucydides said of the Athenians that 'their hopes exceeded their power.' There is only so long that you can continue to punch above your weight until exhaustion takes over. Size gives influence and leverage that we may no longer command. We may merely be a couple of centuries behind the Spanish, Swedish, Portuguese, Danish and Dutch in finally relinquishing and competing in the power projection arena. Some have even suggested that the British style of generalship in the 20th century was a cult of unreadiness due to resource constraints. If we are to be part of a coalition with the Americans, we are either in or we are not – the US do not do 'air kissing' very well. Britain does not want to end up like a number of other European nations from the Iraq and Afghanistan experience who met the three tenets (as the Americans might see them) of a coalition operation: irritation, frustration and capitulation.

This book started with Ronald Reagan being elected to the White House in 1980. It is worth recalling, as we will still be committed in Afghanistan for some years even after combat operations cease in 2014, that Reagan is recorded as saying that 'the Mujahidin are the moral equivalent of the founding fathers of America.' The Afghan Mujahidin began to fight the Soviets following their invasion in 1979: you would get few takers of (or even believers in) Reagan's remark these days, as national security interests have changed. Reagan's Secretary of State was Cap Weinberger. He had six tests for the use of military force. I used to keep these in the back of my notebooks as a reminder. They were:

Vital interest
Clear intention of winning
Last resort

Reassessment and re-evaluation
National and alliance wide support
Clear political and military objectives

These may have fallen out of favour, in that they are clinical and take little account of moral, legal or ethical obligations – or of the so-called 'responsibility to protect' civilians which justified the interventions in Kosovo and the Balkans (particularly after the 1995 Srebrenica massacre) but which seemed so curiously absent in Syria. So let us give our politicians a clearer and easier set of obligations to be held to account to in the future. Before we campaign, it would be wise to ask whether an intervention is justified or worth it using the following questions, which I came across in the 19 March 2012 edition of the *New York Times*. (The answers are my own.) They were in relation to Iran, but the general principles hold:

1. **How is this our fight?** For the UK this might include a necessity – if that is what we believe it to be – of the absolute strategic desire to maintain a strong transatlantic relationship with America. We are only ever likely to be a junior, but important, partner to the US. It may include wider alliance obligations within NATO or wider treaty obligations. Is our interest a survival interest, a vital interest, a major interest, minor interest or merely a political and moral interest?

2. **At what cost?** This covers the totality of 'treasure' to be utilised – lives, economic opportunity costs lost in the manner articulated by Eisenhower, reputation and standing, or diplomatic leverage.

3. **Or what?** Policy makers always need alternatives. Policy states what is to be done as well as what is not to be done. It is different from strategy. Sun Tzu said, 'Tactics without strategy

is the noise before defeat.' There is a need for a clearly defined strategy that articulates how to conclude or 'get out' of an intervention, as well as the easy 'going in' decision. Mandates that are too precise can also be a plague – part of the reason that only *one* UN mission out of more than 60 since the Second World War has ever concluded.[21]

4. **And who else?** Coalitions give strength to the overall 'political treasure'. The only thing deemed to be harder than fighting in a coalition is not fighting in a coalition (to misquote Churchill).

5. **Then what?** The true strategist can see the second and third order effects that might arise, and that will need to be articulated. Every intervention must understand how it ends and visualise an outcome and an exit – or alternative outcomes and exits. Aims may change as an intervention progresses. Who, for example, really remembers why we went to war in 1914 or 1939 – or that the aims at the end were not the same as the when the wars began?

We are also not very good at prediction. In 2005, nine out of 10 assumptions that underpinned the British army's views on the relationship between Iraq and Afghanistan – and therefore where British forces would flow between the two countries and in what time frame between the two campaigns – turned out to be wrong. In my recent time at CENTCOM in America, more than 50 per cent of the assumptions that underpinned the Americans' theatre plans were also wrong. Even the sage author and scientist Arthur C Clarke, who was more right than most, cautioned us that, 'It is impossible to predict the future, and all attempts to do so in any detail appear ludicrous within a few years.' It is these uncertainties that lead us back to the dilemma of those who write the White Papers. If in doubt, refer back to the wisdom of Wavell: 'The increasing problem which faces the reformer of Armies in peace might be likened to that of an architect called on to later modernise an old fashioned house without increasing its size, with the whole family still living in it (often grumbling at the architects' improvements, since an extra bedroom can only be added at the expense of someone's dressing room) and under the strictest financial limitations.'

We have been involved in two messy insurgencies in Iraq and Afghanistan. These 'political' wars are those that should demand a focus on the population, not on the enemy. An insurgency is a war for the people. It is a competition in authority, not in popularity. This paraphrases Robert Thompson, the insurgency guru from the Malayan campaign from 1948 – 1960. There can be no decisive battle. While militaries have always sought a knock-out blow, insurgencies are like trying to win on points, but where this is the referee's decision, and not ours. It is not the money raised, the money spent or the number of troops deployed that is important. It is the proportion of the population that feels safe, that can access services, that enjoys social justice, and the rule of law. The notion of state building by outside intervention needs to be very carefully considered in the future. The core functions of a state are: legitimate monopoly on the means of violence, administrative competency and control, management of public finances, investment in human capital, delineation of the rights and duties of the population, provision of infrastructure services, formation of the market, the rule of law, to conduct international relations, and the management of state assets.

The world has become smaller, and the proliferation of 24-hour live news coverage means there is a likelihood of further political interference. Prime ministers can now talk directly to deployed commanders and their subordinates. We call this 'the unhelpful 3,000-mile-long screwdriver'. What the military desire – clear objectives, timely decisions, orderly preparations, adequate resources – differs from the set of criteria that the politician will consider – the political context, the presentation, Cabinet consensus, cost, parliament and legality.

There is some slightly cheering news for those soldiers who are to be deployed. Despite the additional names of those soldiers killed in action chiselled each year to the National Arboretum, it is becoming harder for soldiers to be killed in conflict. Force protection means that combat deaths have been in decline for some years. This is of no consequence to the suffering and grief that the families of the fallen have to face. The bad news is that three particular types of conflict now account for most deaths: civil wars, the killing of ethnic and political groups, and terrorist acts. We have seen all of these in Syria. These types of conflict landscapes will remain stubborn resistors to a peaceful world in the next 10 years.

I dealt with terrorism for much of the past 10 years. The Strategic Defence and Security Review (SDSR) may have missed a trick in not going far enough into the 'security domain'. Most people fear, to some degree, being blown up in a terrorist act. They do not fear being struck by lightning during a storm, which has a higher probability of causing death. There is debate about what the military should do in the future in both the UK and overseas arenas, and what the security agencies should do in the sphere of counter-terrorism and beyond. The security domain should be widely defined. People fear being insecure. Security is a better term than 'war' in many ways. Too many politicians have used warlike language for activities that cannot be concluded. In the last 10 to 15 years, various prime ministers have talked of 'wars' on crime, terrorism, drugs, and poverty. Both the police and security agencies are highly competent and professional. Public safety will always take precedence over the gathering of intelligence at all stages of an investigation.

The four horsemen of the apocalypse have traditionally been defined as war, pestilence, famine and death. There may be an additional one that we need to contemplate – complacency. There will remain a series of threats and drivers of those threats. Those drivers are poverty, energy requirements, climate change and ideology, which may lead to population shifts and resource conflicts. In the wider security realm, terrorism, nuclear proliferation, serious organised crime (including cybercrime and state cyber-attack) and major incidents such as the inevitable pandemic that will occur at some stage (with the H5N1 bird flu the most likely) will all challenge the traditional notion of what security is. Clusters of risks are emerging that include macro-economic imbalances, the illegal economy nexus that weakens the state, undermines the rule of law and reinforces poverty and instability, and the final water-food-energy nexus.

You can choose to 'securitise' any occurrence you wish if you give it enough momentum, such as the fact that an asteroid might hit the Earth and wipe out one-third of the population in the next 100 years. We have not chosen to 'securitise' that because it seems such an unlikely event that it is not worth investing resources to counter.

General K-O-T-A-B (Keeper-of-the-Army-Brain) asked three good questions that are worth pondering. (The answers from policy-makers help to inform the balance of investment decisions.) They are:

Are we living dangerously?

What does the nation expect?

Will history judge us harshly?

This debate is particularly relevant in answering, 'What does the nation expect in the UK?' The military are expensive, but the 'sunk costs' have already been accrued. The viewpoint might be taken that the military should therefore be used more in the UK and not just in armed situations – such as to clear Mrs McIntyre's driveway when snow arrives in Ayrshire. I am not in that camp. Civil recovery should be done by civil agencies (and using the military takes away business opportunities). The military is not quite the last resort, but my benchmarks have always been scale, simultaneity and an enduring challenge that requires a military response. ('Can you?' is a different question to answer than 'Should you?') The government response is based on 'when we tell you to' – for, as you know, the minister is always right. We should not kid ourselves that the use of the military at the 2012 Olympics had anything to do with a terrorist threat. It had everything to do with the commercial sector's failure – for the XXX Olympiad but less so for the XIV Paralympics – to generate capacity and capability in a timely manner.

You might also like to consider the three 'U's' of the Falklands War. For what 'uncertain', 'unexpected' and 'unimagined' future does the government and the taxpayer wish us to prepare?

The consequences of decision-making in the military and the security services are profound, because men get killed on operations. The motto of Sandhurst is 'Serve to Lead' – command is, in its simplest sense, something given to someone. It is authority *and* responsibility. We attempt to live up to that contract because of the consequences, in the way that those in financial institutions, for example, do not. They play with other people's money, not their own. We play with the reality of people's mortality: the military are given the greatest risk-management tasks in the world for absolutely no bonuses other than the honour of comradeship and a public service wage.

But these are things for the policy-maker and strategist, not the soldier. For the soldier in the field, conflict – from whatever cause – remains chaotic. It demands of him a war-fighting ethos, and the will to win. So, I will leave almost the final word to Private Thomas, for the death of each soldier is a human tragedy. On New Year's Eve 1980, Private Thomas of 2 PARA was part of a patrol that was ambushing an area in South Armagh while deployed to Northern Ireland. It was a dark night. For some unexplained reason, after the ambush was set, he was with the platoon commander who was checking on something. Suddenly, all hell broke loose with heavy firing. Thomas was mortally wounded.

'Did we get the enemy?' were Thomas's final words. He was a paratrooper. He was focused on what he thought was the enemy.

Thomas died shortly after. He did not know that confusion, uncertainty and the fog of war that will never be eliminated, meant he had been inadvertently killed by his own mates. He had been led through his own platoon ambush. At the moment of his death he was the exemplar of that gritty determination of the British soldier. To quote further words of wisdom from Wavell: 'The final deciding factor of all engagements, battles and wars is the morale of the opposing forces. Better weapons, better food, superiority in numbers will influence morale, but it is the sheer determination to win, by whomever or whatever inspired, that counts in the end.'

So, it is time to end with that final deciding factor: for that is the world of the soldier with his faults and flaws, but also his irrepressible character and immense 'can-do' attitude to all the tribulations that are thrown at him. I now bid farewell to the reader, the Parachute Regiment with its magnificent soldiers, and the great institution that is the British army, with the words of George Washington to his officers following the end of the American Revolutionary War at the Fraunces Tavern in New York:

'With a heart full of love and gratitude I now take leave of you. I most devoutly wish that your latter days may be as prosperous and happy as your former ones have been glorious and honourable.'

Utrinque Paratus

---

[20] As does the trauma that might continue to arise. On 25 January 2013 I went to the funeral of Hank Hood, a 2 PARA Falklands veteran who committed suicide. His is the face of victory at Goose Green in the film *The Iron Lady*.

[21] The UK has had a military peacekeeping force in Cyprus (UNFICYP) since 1974. The only divided capital city in the world is therefore in Europe. The UK does not generally contribute troops to UN peacekeeping missions.

CAREER CHRONOLOGY

This book has not been written in a chronological order. For those who like the 'what I did when' approach, the following is a timeline of my career and travels that took me to 49 countries, though not all are named:

1. Royal Military College Sandhurst (September 1980 – January 1981)
2. Pre-Parachute selection and jumps (January 1981 – May 1981)
3. Platoon Commander, 6 Platoon, B Company, 2 PARA (June 1981 – September 1982)
   (*Denmark, Kenya, Belize, the Falkland Islands*)
4. Medium Machine Platoon, Support Company, 2 PARA (September 1982 – May 1985)
   (*Belize, USA, Northern Ireland*)
5. Directing Staff, PCBC, Warminster (May 1985 – August 1987)

6. Adjutant, 2 PARA (August 1987 – March 1989) (*Belize*)
7. Exchange Officer, Canadian Airborne Regiment (March 1989 – November 1990)
   (*Canada*)
8. Army Staff College, Shrivenham and Camberley (January – December 1991)
   (*Germany, Holland, France, Belgium*)
9. Chief of Staff, 5 Airborne Brigade (January 1992 – December 1993)
   (*France, Holland, Russia, Spain*)
10. Officer Commanding, D Company, 2 PARA (January 1994 – July 1995)
    (*France, Northern Ireland*)
11. 2IC 1 Para
    (August 1995 – March 1996)
    (*USA*)
12. Directing Staff, Army Staff College* (March 1996 – July 1998)
    (*transitioned to Joint Services College)
    (*USA, France, Germany, Belgium, Japan*)
13. SO1 Operations, Headquarters Northern Ireland   (July 1998 – August 1999)
    (*Northern Ireland, France*)
14. Commanding Officer, 2 PARA (August 1999 – November 2001)
    (*Northern Ireland, Holland, France, Belize, Nepal, Macedonia, Kuwait, Germany, Falkland Islands*)
15. Colonel, Military Operations 2, MoD (December 2001 – December 2003)
    (*Israel [including the Occupied Territories], France, Holland, Germany, the Falkland Islands*)

16. Commander, 19 Light Brigade (December 2003 –
    December 2005)
    (*Greece, Norway, Belize, Bosnia*)
17. Chief of Staff, Headquarters, Northern Ireland (January
    2006 – June 2007)
    (*Northern Ireland*)
18. Head, Counter-Terrorism and UK Operations, MoD (July
    2007 – August 2010)
    (*Saudi Arabia, Pakistan, Bangladesh, Yemen, Burkina
    Faso, Northern Ireland, Bahrain, USA, Cyprus,
    Switzerland*)
19. October 2010 until retirement: Senior British Military
    Advisor, HQ United States Central Command, Tampa,
    USA
    (*USA, Qatar, Jamaica*)

GLOSSARY

2 PARA – The abbreviation used for The Second Battalion, The Parachute Regiment. I have used capital letters when describing 1 PARA, 2 PARA or 3 PARA throughout the book in accordance with army operational and staff writing. Capitals are not used when referring to the Paras or The Parachute Regiment.

Alpha Time – See Z Time.

AQ – Al Qaeda. The global terrorist organisation formerly headed by Osama Bin Laden from Afghanistan prior to 9/11. Al Qaeda 'Core' is headed at the time of writing by Al Zawahiri but he will be actively targeted by the USA.

AQAP – Al Qaeda in the Arabian Peninsula. A franchise of AQ Core, mainly active in Yemen but seeking to overthrow the Saudi Arabian regime.

AQIM – Al Qaeda in the Islamic Maghreb. A further

franchise of AQ Core. Active in the Maghreb and Sahel regions of Africa.

Battalion – A unit of the British army commanded by a lieutenant colonel. A parachute battalion consists of 687 personnel organised into six companies.

Bergen – Parachute Regiment term for a large backpack or rucksack.

BFT – The Basic Fitness Test in the army. It consisted of a one- to five-mile squad run followed by a 1.5-mile 'best effort' timed return. Now replaced by the Basic Personal Fitness Assessment.

Brigade – An army formation consisting of 'All Arms' of infantry battalions, engineer squadrons, artillery regiments, armoured regiments and logistic support. It numbers around 4,000 personnel.

CENTCOM – The United States Theatre-level Combatant Command, responsible for 20 countries in the Middle and Near East, including Iran, Iraq, Afghanistan, Pakistan, Yemen, the former Russian territories of the 'Stans' (such as Tajikistan) and the countries of the Gulf region. Its HQ is in Tampa, Florida. In 2012 it had 189,000 personnel deployed in the region.

CO – Commanding Officer. The senior officer in overall command of a British army unit. Commanded by a lieutenant colonel.

COBR – The Cabinet Office Briefing Room at 70 Whitehall, where central government crisis responses are formulated. It sits in Room 'A' and is therefore more widely known as COBRA.

Company – A sub-unit within a battalion. It has around 100 men in three platoons plus a headquarters and is commanded by a major.

C130 – The Lockheed Hercules transport aircraft. Also known as a Herc' or 'Fat Albert', responsible for air-drop of stores and personnel, as well as long-distance haulage and resupply.

CSM – Company Sergeant Major. The most senior Non-Commissioned Officer (NCO) in a company. The right-hand man of the Company Commander.

DMS – Directly Moulded Sole boots. Short ankle boots that were standard issue in the British army until the mid-1980s.

DS – Directing Staff. The term for those who instruct, teach or educate on military courses.

DZ – Drop Zone. The selected ground where paratroopers will land and gather to commence operations.

EOD – Explosive Ordnance Disposal, or more colloquially, the 'bomb squad' responsible for defusing bombs, ordnance, improvised bombs and dealing with ammunition accidents.

GPMG – General Purpose Machine Gun. A 7.62 calibre belt-fed MG, standard in the British army in 1982.

IED – Improvised Explosive Device. A home-made bomb.

KINGS and QUEENS – The KINGS were the King's Regiment and the QUEENS, the Queen's Regiment. Both have been amalgamated since 1980 to become part of the larger Duke of Lancaster's Regiment (King's Lancashire and Border) and The Princess of Wales's Royal Regiment

(Queen's and Royal Hampshires) respectively. There will be no room left for further amalgamations based on the current length of their full titles

MCTC – The Military Corrective Training Centre. Based in Colchester, it houses those who have been sentenced for military misdemeanours. It is, first and foremost, a rehabilitative centre.
MFA – Ministry of Foreign Affairs.
MoD – The Ministry of Defence.
MT – Military Task. A task that the MoD directs the army, navy or air force to be capable of completing and laid down in Defence Strategic Guidance (DSG).
MT – Motor Transport. The term still used for all vehicles in the forces.

NCO – Non-Commissioned Officer. Divided into Junior NCOs – lance corporals and corporals – and Senior NCOs – sergeants, colour sergeants, and warrant officers.

OC – Officer Commanding. The sub-unit commander of a company below the battalion level. Also known as Company Commanders.

P Company – See PPS.
PCBC – Platoon Commanders Battle Course. A 14-week course undertaken by all infantry officers on completion of Sandhurst to make them professionally fit for employment.
PCD – Platoon Commanders Division. Part of the School of Infantry Tactics branch that teaches the PCBC course.
PIRA – The designation for the Provisional Irish Republican Army.

Platoon – The level below a company. Commanded by a lieutenant. It comprises three sections plus a headquarters element. Around 28 – 30 men.

PPS – Pre-Parachute Selection. The course to qualify to wear a red beret. Also known as P Company.

PTSD – Post Traumatic Stress Disorder. Formerly known as shell-shock. PTSD is the mental trauma that can arise from participation in combat.

QUEENS – See KINGS and QUEENS

RSM – Regimental Sergeant Major. The most senior Non-Commissioned Officer in a unit. Works closely with the CO.

RTU – 'Return To Unit'. To fail or be removed from a course.

SA80 – The 5.56mm rifle introduced in the mid-1980s to replace the SLR. The SA80 A1 version was prone to stoppages. It was re-engineered by Heckler & Koch to produce the SA80 A2 version.

Section – An element of a platoon. Commanded by a corporal. Around eight to 10 men.

SLR – Self-Loading Rifle. The British 7.62mm semi-automatic version of the Belgian FN rifle. The Argentinians used automatic versions of the same rifle in 1982.

SO – Staff Officer. There are various levels: captains are SO3s, majors SO2s and lieutenant colonels SO1s.

TA – The Territorial Army. Under the government's Army 2020 reforms this will be renamed the Army Reserve.

TEWT – Tactical Exercise Without Troops. A TEWT occurs where a tactical problem is considered on the ground with imaginary forces.

MAJOR-GENERAL CHIP CHAPMAN

Tom – the term used for a private rank soldier in the Parachute Regiment.

UOTC – A University Officers Training Corps. I attended Liverpool University Officer Training Corps (LUOTC).

Z (or Zulu) Time – The NATO term for Greenwich Mean Time. All UK's wars are fought on GMT to conform to Whitehall timings. British Summer Time (BST) is A (or Alpha) Time.